Contents

Introduction

John Case and Rosemary C. R. Taylor

Not long ago we sat at the kitchen table of a big white-clap-board farmhouse nestled in a pretty valley in southern Vermont. Laura Wilson, the woman who was talking, is a thirty-four-year-old mother of two, Swarthmore-educated, an experienced teacher. In 1964 she took part in demonstrations aimed at integrating the city of Chester, Pennsylvania, and wound up spending a few days in jail. That started her brief career as a political activist, which took her into antiwar demonstrations, election campaigns, and Students for a Democratic Society's community-organizing projects. After getting a master's degree from Harvard and a job in a junior high school, she joined a group of teachers working on new ideas for radical education.

In 1972, she and her husband gave up city life and politics. The year before, they and half a dozen friends had bought a farm in Vermont not far from the Massachusetts border; some planned to use it only for vacations, others to live there full time. The Wilsons moved to the farm as soon as they could. Dick Wilson set up a woodworking shop and cabinetmaking business. Laura worked briefly as a social worker for the elderly.

In time, the group dissolved; the Wilsons bought out the remaining members (with the help of a small inheritance and a large mortgage) and took over the big white farmhouse themselves. Laura gave birth to their second child and gave up her job, which she hadn't liked much anyway. She and Dick planted, tended, and harvested a huge garden, cared for some young cattle that a neighboring farmer kept in their barn, helped out one neighbor with springtime sugaring and another with fall apple-picking. The first child, a boy, was soon old enough for nursery school. His parents found a cooperative school for young children that had been started not long before by people from backgrounds very much like their own.

Now, at the kitchen table, Laura was regaling a group of weekend visitors with stories about another co-op she and her husband were involved in: the local food co-op. Food cooperatives are ordinarily not very good storytelling material—you join the group, place your order, and every so often go to the central distribution point to help bag groceries or cut cheese—but this one was another matter.

The co-op's books, it seems, were a shambles. Some of the group's directors suspected that the bookkeeper had embezzled as much as $5,000. The bookkeeper was a local notable, disheveled and disorganized, with five children and a reputation for irresponsibility; she had got the job only because the co-op was her idea in the first place. Nevertheless, no one was quite sure she was a thief. The records were so badly kept they couldn't tell.

Two graduate students from a nearby business school were called in. They volunteered to go over all the records, put together a clean set of books, and check out the embezzlement suspicions. They carried off all the records—and were never heard from again. Repeated phone calls drew no response. Finally, a delegate from the co-op visited the university office of one of the students, only to find him gone and the group's books stashed—untouched—in one of his desk drawers. In desperation, she threw the books into a paper bag and left. It turned out later that the bookkeeper had not been embezzling at all; it was just that the board members found it hard to believe the co-op could be as deeply in debt as it was. The reason for the debt was simple enough: the co-op's markup was too low to cover its operating costs.

After Laura told this the story, others chipped in with similar experiences. An alternative school that couldn't pass building-code requirements. A commune that bought a house collectively, only to find that the title search had not been properly carried out. A new left research institute that nearly fell apart in angry recrimination over how much staff members were to be paid. Some patterns emerged quickly, for the problems of various co-ops, communes, and collectives turned out to be much the same. The encouraging part of the conversation was its indication that, despite their difficulties, "alternatives" like food co-ops and parent-run preschools continue to exist. The depressing part was the realization that, year after year, they make the same mistakes. Musing on that fact, Laura said, somewhat plaintively, "Where are our historians?"

Implicit in that question are two problems. One is what she means by "our": who are the people with whom she identifies? The other is, what are the events and the trends that she believes characterize the last decade?

The "we" implicit in Laura's question is partly a political generation, come of age in the turmoil of the 1960s and trained in the rhetoric of participatory democracy and a "counter" culture. But it is also everyone whose life has been touched by —or may yet be touched by—the beliefs, values, and ultimately the institutions created by that generation.

The relevant history is easy to misread. This introduction is being written in 1978. Ten years ago, Martin Luther King and Robert F. Kennedy, along with white students at Kent State in Ohio and black students at Jackson State in Mississippi, died of gunshot wounds. France faced a major political crisis. Tear gas and police billy clubs filled the streets of Chicago (and the nightly television news) as the Democrats nominated Hubert Humphrey for president of the United States. These are the events that are eulogized or condemned in the media on their tenth anniversary. And as the first general reflections appear on the decade called the sixties (roughly, 1963–1973), the symbols and themes are Vietnam, civil rights, hippies, Watergate. This kind of history is no different from the popular journalism of the time and that of the present. In 1968 we read about blacks rioting in Watts, the Yippies trying to levitate the Pentagon, the more flamboyant activities of the women's movement. Now, in the late 1970s, the hot topics are the rise of a black middle class, the new conservatism on the campuses, the successful integration of feminists and environmentalists into conventional politics. So the seventies are celebrated or deplored as the era of apathy and collective narcissism.

But fragments of the movement, traces of the genuinely creative impulses of the previous decade, remain, and not just for Americans now in their early thirties. To be sure, civil rights, the war in Vietnam, and everything else that is so widely written about had a profound impact on people like the Wilsons; all those events changed their ideas about politics and the nature of American society. But there was another side to the decade, which wrought enduring changes in their personal lives: the struggle to change the routines of everyday life through new forms of organization. These new forms—urban communes, free schools, law collectives, a whole range of "counterinstitutions"—came into existence with a variety of grand objectives. But the theme common to all was the members' hope that the new organizations prefigured a better way of living and working.

Just as the chroniclers of the last decade have largely ignored the birth of this part of the movement, so the chroniclers of the present ignore what remains and flourishes. Describing and analyzing these efforts to change life and work may thus help correct the dismal portrait of the late 1970s that we are ordinarily offered. It is important for another reason as well. The left in the United States suffers from a peculiar historical amnesia. Few free-school founders or food co-op enthusiasts in the sixties learned anything from their predecessors in previous decades, because they had never heard of them. The lessons of the recent past are just as obscure to the scattered activists of the present. New arrangements for living and working persist, but often in a vacuum. Without the support of a movement behind them, many soldier on in ignorance of the victories or mistakes of similar efforts in other parts of the country. A careful retrospective analysis of the last decade can help break that isolation.

Of course, the new left of the last decade was not limited to media events and massive demonstrations on the one hand and small-scale alternative organizations on the other. The history is more complex. It includes the consciousness-raising groups of the women's movement; it also covers the growth and in some cases the decay of political organizations such as Students for a Democratic Society and the New American Movement, to name only two. And it encompasses an immense variety of local organizing efforts, ranging from neighborhood action groups to tenant unions and welfare rights organizations. Like the alternatives, these too persist, and suffer from the same lack of attention and the same historical amnesia. And unlike the alternatives, these efforts have often had a noticeable impact on poor, minority-group, and working-class communities.

But we have chosen to focus on alternative organizations— co-ops, communes, and collectives—because the concerns that gave them birth typify the differences between the new left and its predecessors in America. Like most reformers and socialists in recent history, new leftists wanted to transform basic social institutions and reduce social inequalities. But unlike them, and especially unlike the Communist-led "old left" that flourished in the thirties, they also believed, in a catch phrase of the period, that "the personal is political." What this slogan meant for many people in the movement was that their deepest anxieties —about the choice or even the notion of a career, about the schism between life and work that they saw in their parents' lives, about the personal relationships inherent in traditional families—that these were not, or were not simply, the normal fears that accompany the transition to adult status but indicators of fundamental social and political problems. These problems could not be solved by individuals acting alone; they were, as the new leftists saw it, the common costs of life in capitalist America, and they therefore called for collective action. One fundamental concern of the movement, then, was to find new ways of living and working. Struggling to alter relationships in existing institutions was one way to accomplish this goal. Setting up experimental work situations, untainted by the practices of mainstream organizations, was the alternative.

The new left was more inclined to follow the latter course because of a second characteristic that distinguished it from the activists of previous decades and certainly from those of the more sober seventies. The literature of the time conveys the sense that new leftists felt they were part of a genuine historical moment, that after them things would never be the same again. They had a vision of unlimited possibilities, a conviction that they could overturn the habits and the institutions that had constrained their lives; they opposed the compromise of change in old organizations. Changes in the larger society made new alternatives seem both feasible and desirable, affluence itself made gradualism seem unnecessary, and the struggle to create alternatives seemed as significant as the struggle to end the war.

The movement for alternative organizations was particularly strong among professionals and other workers in the human services: education, medicine, social welfare, some branches of the law. That was partly because the new left was itself disproportionately middle class, and oriented by upbringing toward careers in these professions. It was also because the professions themselves seemed to hold out the promise of fulfilling work as well as economic security. As the decade progressed, however, the pretensions of the human services came to appear exaggerated at best, hypocritical at worst. In the eyes of the new left, lawyers and doctors practiced their arts for the benefit of those who could pay, and ignored the poor. Teachers were part of an educational system whose prime function was to track students into a class-divided society and to indoctrinate them with the prevailing ideology. Psychiatrists and social workers played the role of thought police, convincing people that their problems were personal rather than political. Government bureaucrats, from policy experts to welfare caseworkers, seemed oblivious to the fact that the programs they thought up or administered were ineffective or harmful.

For indeed, the liberal strategies of the sixties, which had promised to reform these professions by government fiat, were not working. Medicare and Medicaid, as it turned out, were not the opening wedge of a genuine reorganization of the health-care system. Federally financed legal services were inundated with unmanageable case loads and crippled by an inability to reach past the individual client. Universities expanded, particularly those supported by state governments, but education seemed no less bound to the needs of the corporate economy and the "war machine." The War on Poverty, begun by Lyndon Johnson in 1964, proved to be little more than a skirmish. The Office of Economic Opportunity, the strongest hope of those who looked to government for solutions to social problems, scarcely lasted the decade. In this context it was not surprising that the "long march through the institutions" seemed always to end in sellout, co-optation, or simple failure.

Alternative organizations embodied activists' desires to start afresh, to create workable institutions that could serve as models while they provided services unencumbered by old modes of action. Technology, bureaucracy, and "professionalism" would go by the board. Relationships in work would be personal and open. Members would participate directly in the affairs of the collectivity—one person, one vote. They would seek equality in other ways too, notably by rotating jobs and sharing the dirty work. The new organizations would provide goods and services cheaply, help stimulate political reforms, and restore feelings of community, purpose, and satisfaction in their members. Thus would the social services be restructured and nonhierarchical, humane organizations be created, all at once.

The articles in this book explain how this process has worked out, in the social services and in other areas as well. With objectives like those enumerated above, it is not surprising that many of the new institutions failed, or that those still in existence have been forced into compromises. Nor is it surprising that their problems should be similar: that what plagues a food co-op in Santa Barbara will also plague a free clinic in Chicago. The demands of democracy, for example, can conflict with getting the work done: you can't spend endless hours in meetings and still teach your students or get your newspaper out on time. Job sharing, job rotation, and egalitarian work relationships sometimes lead to ineffectiveness or inefficiency. Immediate practical goals—making the organization work, raising funds, and so forth—frequently conflict with the objectives of political reform. Most alternative organizations have found themselves caught in dilemmas like these every day, and have developed diverse strategies to cope with them.

In the first section of this book, six writers present case studies that compare those strategies. They provide concrete analyses of the achievements and dilemmas of alternatives in a variety of fields. One is the underground media, organized to counter the established press and radio. Another is new organizations in the basic social services—free schools, radical law collectives, free clinics. A third is communes and food co-ops, alternative ways of living. Four of the six authors worked in the alternative institutions they describe; the other two spent considerable time in firsthand research and observation. The articles convey something of the texture of life in the alternatives, and they address some common themes. They explore, for example, why alternatives were started in a particular field in the first place, how they were initially financed, what conflicts arose when the money began to run out. They look at the kind of people attracted to the alternatives, and the kind of clientele served. They examine the phenomenon of turnover, and members' struggles to promote worker participation and control. They describe the tensions between radicals who wanted to mobilize a community through grass-roots organization and clients who primarily wanted better services.

The writers' conclusions as to the achievements of alternative organizations reflect diverse assessments of the period. Most argue that the new organizations were successful neither in changing the larger society nor in building genuine "alternatives," entirely separate from and demonstrably more effective than the institutions they rejected. Allen Graubard points out that free-school innovations were easily absorbed by the public school system. Andrew Kopkind describes the gradual transformation of alternative media from their radical past to their commercial present. Daniel Zwerdling concludes that contemporary food cooperatives need to grow and work together if they are to be effective, but that they lack the common vision and political base that would allow them to do so. Rosemary Taylor finds that free clinics could not simultaneously provide adequate medical services and organize to change the American health-care system. Rosabeth Kanter views the seventies as the time when the urban commune "movement" became almost institutionalized, as a temporary living arrangement for those who were between families or who had not yet started them. And Anthony Sager tells how young lawyers abandoned law communes when the political movement the communes were supposed to support died out—and when it turned out that the legal work they were doing could be done as well by conventional lawyers or legal-services offices.

Yet none of the writers discards alternative organizations out of hand. Their importance, most conclude, lies less in the changes they made or failed to make in the larger society than in the experience and the training they gave their members. Through the new institutions, many people got their first experience of genuine collective work; they also got an opportunity to participate in their organization's management. Members trained each other in sensitivity and in skills—such as how to teach, how to buy good food wholesale, how to lay out a newspaper. Deprofessionalization—making skills less mysterious and more widely available—at times became a reality. So, too, did "community." Communes eased the pain of marital separation or the loneliness of youth, and most of the other counter-organizations provided satisfying work and companionship.

The second part of the book comprises five articles that reflect in more general fashion on the origins, the organization, and the legacy of the alternative movement as a whole. Larry Hirschhorn argues that conventional explanations for the growth of alternatives—the counterculture, the Vietnam War, the presence of large numbers of alienated youth born in the baby-boom years—are inadequate. He notes that the sixties witnessed a profound crisis in work and family life that left mainstream social-service institutions powerless and therefore deprived many professionals of a useful, credible role. Alternative organizations seemed therefore like a way to regain a meaningful professional identity. But since the crisis itself usually remained obscure, the new organizations did not always speak directly to its resolution.

One of the difficulties that beset most alternative organizations was that of creating a participatory, egalitarian democracy. Eliminating hierarchy was considered a goal on a par with giving better service to clients, but in practice, doing away with inequality was a constant struggle. Jane Mansbridge and Joyce Rothschild-Whitt analyze this struggle from very different perspectives. Rothschild-Whitt argues that most social scientists, steeped in the Weberian tradition, have concluded that the ideal of a nonhierarchical democratic organization is unattainable, that all democratic institutions succumb over time to bureaucratization, and that their utopian goals are thereby undermined. Her study of five different alternative organizations shows that the process is not as inevitable as some social theorists believe. Under certain conditions, which she specifies, organizations can retain both open structures and genuine membership participation. Mansbridge, looking at the issue from another angle, argues that equal power in the abstract is a misleading, unnecessary goal. Equality of power, she says, should be seen as a means rather than as an end. Only where an organization cannot claim identity of interests, equal opportunity for growth, and equal respect among its members should it attempt to reduce inequalities of power. Mansbridge illustrates her argument with a case history of a remarkably egalitarian crisis center that she studied for several months.

Since many of the alternative organizations endure and change, it is difficult to assess their overall impact. Hirschhorn contends that their abstract goals, lacking any reference to the mainstream social-service crisis, condemned them to marginal roles. He proposes that professionals learn more about how their clients plan and make decisions so they can design alternative organizations—"environments"—more conducive to learning and independence. Paul Starr argues that the hallmark of alternative organizations in the sixties was the longing for community, a response to the isolation felt by the middle-class youth who initiated them. But he divides them into two distinct categories: the "exemplary," whose members tried to embody their ideals in the very structure of the new organization; and the "adversary," which attempted to reform the larger society directly. Those that tried to fulfill both purposes simultaneously were short-lived; yet even those with a more modest approach met obstacles. Organizations that were most clearly exemplary in nature usually ended up meeting the needs of special groups rather than whole communities, and so were vulnerable to co-optation. Of the adversarial organizations that persist, Starr believes structural differences help to explain the success of some and the demise of others.

David Moberg's appraisal of both the sixties and the viability of a grass-roots strategy is quite different. He sees the distinction between the sixties and the seventies—and between the different types of alternative organizations that characterize these decades—as the difference between "reproduction" and "production." In the sixties the focus was on developing sensibility; now it is on the desire to change the workplace and the city. Neither effort, he notes, has yet created an alternative society: alternatives of all kinds cannot evade the influence of the dominant culture. Even in their heyday they failed to take into account the impact of class, and their appeal was therefore limited. Now they are no longer supported by the movement that gave them their creative force. Yet, like Hirschhorn's, Moberg's verdict on alternative organizations is optimistic. In his view, they channel the traditional American desire for self-determination toward more altruistic ends; they foster an enduring critique of daily life under capitalism; and they persistently raise the question of who controls society's wealth.

The contributions of alternative organizations cannot be assessed solely in terms of the current simplified distinction between the "active" sixties and the "passive," acquiescent seventies. The founders of alternatives in the sixties did not turn suddenly to introspection at the striking of the decade. Rather, the doubts that drove them to seek new ways of living and working probably persist. The distinguishing characteristic of that generation, as it grows older and as many of its members choose reluctantly to enter more conventional careers than they once hoped or imagined, may be a persistent malaise, an inability either to embrace wholeheartedly the putative rewards of success in America or to throw themselves without ambivalence into challenging them. Yet if that is a dubious personal victory, it is nonetheless a political accomplishment, for it symbolizes a permanent chink in the ideological armor of corporate America. The politics of the personal has also had a permanent impact. People who worked in alternative organizations are probably still working for more egalitarian relationships, particularly in the family, but also at work and in other collective endeavors.

For the generation ten years younger—those just out of college as the seventies draw to a close—the last decade looks different. The Vietnam War has receded into history, and the more tangible reality is a shrinking labor market. Yet even for them the alternatives have had an effect, partly because some still persist and partly because the "failure" of others wrought enduring changes in mainstream institutions. The public schools have incorporated many of the educational innovations of free schools, blunting the impact of the latter. The self-help movement fostered by free clinics has sustained a new concern for preventive medicine and home care, though it is still too early to predict whether this in turn will be co-opted by conservatives who believe that individuals are responsible for their sickness. Alternative organizations have contributed to significant reforms as they have lost their oppositional strength.

More positively, those who started co-ops, communes, and collectives, and those who came later to work with them, are still involved in politics. When someone at the Wilsons' local food co-op raised the issue of boycotting Nestlé for its callous marketing of baby formula to Third World mothers who have lost their own milk by the time they discover they cannot afford the product regularly, Laura organized the project. It was no good boycotting, she told the group, if they didn't publicize the action, and she volunteered to write two letters to local newspapers. When the letters appeared, she began to get phone calls —for an antinuclear demonstration, for a reform candidate for district attorney, for half a dozen other causes. And the local columnist, a right-winger, devoted two columns to attacking her stance.

Laura is not involved in any large-scale political movement. The alternatives have not coalesced, as their founders once hoped, into a solid base for a national organization; they have not developed a common political vision. But people have learned from the mistakes of the counterinstitutions. They are no longer inspired by the expectation that their efforts will have an immediate impact on political events or social ills, but many are working steadily at the more mundane task of building the groundwork for organization in the future. They are content with smaller victories at the local and state level. Alternatives have allowed them to experiment with one form of change and to test the limits of separate, uncoordinated attempts to lead better lives outside established institutions.

Part One
Cases

Free Medicine

by Rosemary C. R. Taylor

In the spring of 1969 a series of demonstrations shook the city of Gilford.[1] Gilford is a middle-sized city that houses a large state university, and the disturbances had been triggered by a student march against the university's administration. The pattern was familiar in those years. The university, acting overhastily, called up a huge police reserve to put down the demonstration. Citizens' groups joined students in protesting excessive police violence. The sporadic marching and rioting that followed became a focus for opposition to the Vietnam War and for grievances around a host of local issues.

One by-product of the violence, though, was that Gilford got a free medical clinic. During the riots a group of "street medics"—mostly nonprofessionals, but some with considerable training—took over a vacant school building and started dispensing first aid. The medics had acquired their skills in a variety of contexts: in the armed forces, in southern civil-rights work, or in training programs for antiwar demonstrations run by the Medical Committee for Human Rights. At the end of the week of disturbances, a curious coalition had formed behind them. Liberals in the community had been unsuccessfully pressing the city health department for years to provide an outpatient clinic for an area heavily populated by students and transients. Now they took the initiative. Ministers, nurses, shopkeepers, students, street people, and other citizens banded together and announced that the Gilford free clinic would stay open.

The medics began by offering routine primary care in the afternoons and emergency services on an ambitious twenty-four-hour, seven-day-a-week basis. In May 1969, the first month, a staff of about 25 saw 492 patients. By August the number of patients had risen to 890. When two doctors surveyed a sample of 85 patient charts that month, they found that 60 percent of the patients were male, their median age was twenty-one, and the most common illness was upper-respiratory infection. As the patient load increased, volunteers flocked to help. Donations poured in and the organization ran for six months on a wave of enthusiasm. But the coalition that had founded the clinic was not designed for permanence.

The first serious signs of trouble came roughly a year after the clinic opened, when its temporary quarters were slated for demolition. Medics approached owners of a nearby union hall and asked if they could rent the basement; the response was favorable. But the relocation proposal provoked an acrimonious controversy in the community. The new site was close to the campus but also perilously close, in the opinion of some local residents, to the street that had recently become the favorite hangout for an influx of "bikers," transients, students, and hippies.

Letters poured into the Board of Adjustments opposing the move. The reasons ranged from the anticipated decrease in surrounding property values to the problems of traffic congestion. An "owner of income property" was afraid that "such a facility could become a refuge for rioters during confrontations and a highly convenient headquarters for militant and anti-establishment activity." One hundred ninety-five signatories of a petition complained that the clinic was

patronized almost exclusively by so-called street people, a relatively small but extremely troublesome group of largely transient individuals, many of whom are identified with illegal drug sale and use, panhandling, petty thievery, pilferage, disturbance of the peace, malicious mischief, pollution of the environment, etc., as well as the more serious forms of law infraction all, of which require an abnormal amount of extra costly police coverage. These people are parasites for the most part and make no effort to contribute to the economy of the city. It would seem to be utter folly to provide any facility no matter how inadequate that would encourage this transient element to remain in the community for one unnecessary moment.

By and large, opposition to the relocation centered on political issues, not medical ones, and was not spearheaded by the medical profession. The few doctors who protested usually did so for the same reasons as others. "It is wrong to create a meeting place that close to the university for the liberal and immature minds who are attracted to Gilford in this era," wrote one prominent physician. Only occasionally did doctors raise the health-care issues involved. Another letter from an M.D. asserted, "Clinics for outpatient care can only be run successfully as a function of established recognized hospitals within the community, or under governmental auspices." The physicians' objections seldom focused on the possibility that an indigent population might be subjected to poor-quality care at the clinic. More frequently they expressed fears that medical authority was being undermined, orthodox procedures circumvented, and professional jurisdiction evaded.

Interestingly enough, nonmedical opponents later raised the problems of "health hazards" and the quality of care, but it turned out that they weren't thinking primarily about patients. The petitioners claimed:

> The Free Clinic services reportedly are directed principally to the treatment of social diseases, respiratory and gastro-intestinal disturbances as well as many other types of infections. These diseases represent a threat to the community and should be treated by the best physicians in the community and not by those who are unlicensed and have only rudimentary medical training.

Other interests in the city, meanwhile, saw the free clinic as a challenge to their authority over different groups. "A free clinic in this particular area," wrote a university researcher, "would serve as a haven for students and employees of the university community who wish to withhold medical information from their administrators and deans." As the opposition mounted, clinic workers realized that the "community," which they had so confidently evoked as a benign benefactor in their fund-raising letters, was an untrustworthy sponsor. Worse still, the Gilford free clinic, like other reform efforts of the time, counted "community control" among its most sacred principles. Was this, the members wondered, what they had wanted?

Clinics and the Community

Free clinics faced dilemmas of this sort more frequently than most of the alternative institutions set up in the late 1960s. The first clinic, the Haight-Ashbury, had been started in 1967 to tend to casualties among the flower children who had flocked to San Francisco. By 1972, according to estimates, more than 340 such facilities were operating in the United States.[2] Their founders sought to realize two potentially conflicting objectives. First, free clinics were a response to the escalating health crisis: medical costs had skyrocketed and insurance schemes provided total coverage for only a privileged few. The poor and the unorganized complained that routine primary care was unavailable, that hospitals were inaccessible, and that doctors were impersonal at best and inhuman butchers at worst. The concerned liberals and the political movements that started clinics saw them as one way to bring free medical care into the communities.

In this the clinics resembled free schools, food or housing co-ops, law collectives, and other enterprises designed to provide goods and services better and cheaper. If things go wrong in a free clinic, however, the consequences are both more visible and more serious than in a food co-op or a free school. Medicine's failures are conspicuous and often irreparable. If co-op food is sometimes less than perfect, or if children in free schools don't learn to read quickly, the reaction of outsiders will be less quick and less severe than if a clinic patient contracts hepatitis. The clinic's position in the community is also especially insecure. Most alternative organizations are exposed to pressures from the institutions they are trying to oppose or replace, but free clinics are particularly dependent on outside resources and therefore particularly vulnerable. They need drugs, equipment, and access to hospitals. They often deal with groups of people like drug addicts who are considered pariahs by the rest of society. And so they spend a large amount of time placating or avoiding funding agencies, organized medicine, police, and social workers.

The second inspiration behind free clinics wasn't always compatible with providing efficient service. Like other alternative organizations, they attempted to eliminate bureaucratic structures and boring, hierarchically organized work. Yet clinics faced particular difficulties in realizing this objective. For one thing, they are dependent on "experts" in a way that food cooperatives and free schools are not. Free schools may sometimes actively recruit people who have been "brainwashed" by training institutions that teach people how to teach, but they often prefer creative amateurs. Free clinics, although they may set up training programs for paraprofessionals and encourage peer treatment, are always dependent to a large extent on trained professionals.[3] A physician's license is necessary to get Medicaid funds, since provider numbers (which entitle the holder to receive reimbursement for Medicaid patients) are more often granted to individual doctors than to clinics. Physicians can also open informal channels to supplies and hospital beds, and clinic malpractice insurance is contingent on their presence. So, even when a free clinic makes minimal use of a doctor's technical skills, its legitimacy as a medical organization depends on doctors' participation and cooperation.

Then too, free clinics have a multilayered internal structure that complicates their ambitions to break down rigid hierarchical relationships. Food cooperatives and women's groups need only members, but free clinics house three distinct groups of people in one organization: professionals (doctors, dentists, nurses, and psychologists), lay workers, and patients.

The "free clinic movement," of course, covers a wide range of organizations. It is probably a misnomer, given that these clinics represent a movement only in the sense that people in a variety of situations chose the same response to inadequate medical care. Clinics like the Panthers' George Jackson in Oakland or the Young Patriots in Chicago—both of which were set up by identifiable political movements—have different priorities from those established from above by concerned professionals or from below by minority communities. Poor neighborhoods want services. Political movements want to build a social base and recruit members. So the various clinics established a wide range of relationships with the communities around them.

Despite their differences, however, most free clinics agreed on a platform of community control. It was, after all, the hallmark of reform strategies in the late sixties. But community control has always been an ambiguous idea for policy-makers, political activists, and free-clinic organizers. Control by whom and over what? In the field of medicine it has meant, variously, control by patients, control by health workers (skilled and unskilled), and finally control by the potential consumer and the wider, amorphous "community." Free-clinic people frequently agitated for collective decision-making over every conceivable issue: from the technical and medical (who can diagnose and treat, and how) to the administrative and personal (where the clinic should look for funds, whom it should treat, where it should be located, and whom it should pay).

The relocation battle was the first serious test of how far the Gilford clinic could rely on its community, and it made clinic workers wonder whether they really wanted to give the neighborhood any influence in their affairs. The flurry of enthusiasm that had greeted the opening of their experiment seemed to have worn thin quickly. Fortunately for them, Gilford is a city with a well-established tradition of supporting leftist causes. A large liberal constituency remained dormant for long periods but could always be rallied in emergencies to oppose almost anything that was presented as a threat to basic democratic rights. In response to clinic appeals, they turned out in force at the Board of Adjustment hearings and eventually succeeded in getting the board to reverse its decision denying the clinic a use permit for the union hall. But the incident had several unpleasant implications.

First, it was clear that community control meant little in a community as politically diverse as this one. The various interests and coalitions in the neighborhood obviously had different stakes in the clinic's survival or demise. The clinic needed an organized, enthusiastic clientele to counterbalance local power brokers. Since they couldn't count on their largely transient patients, clinic workers realized they would have to convert Gilford's free-floating liberal sentiment into a more solid political base in the community. Second, the permit incident demonstrated that the ways in which medical services are delivered and illnesses defined can be used by an apprehensive lay public as ideological weapons to control politically threatening groups. And finally, it clarified the kind of threat that the clinic posed to the local medical establishment. It wasn't quite a "thorn in the flesh of organized medicine," as clinic workers sometimes liked to claim, but it had challenged one of the central tenets of the medical profession's ideology: treatment is the prerogative of the licensed, who practice in accredited medical institutions.

Was there a reasonable way of letting the neighborhood have some voice? A community board seemed an obvious solution, but the Gilford clinic's board wasn't exactly representative of the neighborhood. Like other free-clinic organizers, Gilford's had learned from the experience of the poverty programs in the mid-sixties that a citizens' advisory committee or board had a lot of disadvantages and didn't necessarily guarantee "maximum feasible participation." As an administrator of the People's Medical Center in Redwood City put it:

I think we had essentially a correct political justification for it [admitting only workers to the board], which was that the notion of community control in an institution depends upon an institution existing according to some overall principles, and that clearly isn't true of any community I know of in this country. To say that the clinic is going to be run by representatives of different community groups means that you're opening up control of your organization to people who are your political enemies. You know, a good example of that is some of the OEO programs which have community boards, and they find that some people sitting on the boards are representatives from the parole department, representatives from the churches, representatives from the city council. It became clear that we couldn't operate that way.

Gilford clinic workers didn't formulate their apprehensions with such a coherent political analysis. But as their clinic grew to incorporate a new range of service sections and developed nightly shifts or cohesive work groups, they found it hard enough just to coordinate the various arms of the organization. Their board—one minister, a representative from the union hall, a couple of doctors, and a motley assortment of interested supporters—more or less rubber-stamped the decisions of clinic staff.

Spare Change

If the community wasn't to be trusted with internal clinic affairs, perhaps it could at least be tapped for money. When the clinic started to pay rent for the union-hall basement—and when the union hall insisted that the clinic take out insurance —workers were suddenly faced with an extra $9,000 a year in expenses. Occasional patient donations were never going to meet the deficit, so the clinic decided to intensify one of its more unusual strategies for raising money: panhandling.

Panhandling had started soon after the clinic was founded. Watching the hippies who "sparechanged" passers-by for a quarter, clinic workers who were often short of money themselves decided to capitalize on their success. Volunteers and medics spent some part of each day soliciting funds on the street with a box marked "Free Clinic." Thirty percent of the day's take went to the box-holders and the rest to the clinic. For the first six months the clinic made about $800 a month this way. The early panhandlers also served an important public-relations function. Scattered around the neighborhood with leaflets describing the clinic, they were eager to provide help and information.

But with the expansion of the clinic and the new push to find a more secure financial base, the nature of panhandling changed. As one worker put it:

> As they [the paraprofessionals] got more involved in providing
> the services, people would come into the clinic and say, "Gee,
> I want to help but I don't know how to do this and I don't know
> if I could take the medic's course and I don't know if I'm going
> to be in town that long," and they'd say, "Well, why don't you
> go out and panhandle for us." And then it gradually got to be
> a livelihood for people.

It had seemed like such a good idea—involve enthusiastic
volunteers and take the financial pressure off the clinic at the
same time—but in expanding panhandling, the clinic succeeded
in creating a scruffy bunch of professional money-raisers who
didn't necessarily share the workers' enthusiasm for their organization. As panhandling became a livelihood, the panhandlers
became strangers, detached from the tight little clinic collective.

After two years, panhandling was no longer seen as "real"
clinic work. One worker recalled how it made him feel like an
outsider: "That was one of the first things I did for the clinic,
but I didn't consider myself a clinic worker when I did that
because panhandlers really weren't that much." Worse still, the
take from panhandling didn't increase significantly. Clinic
workers began to suspect that more than 30 percent was going
from box to pocket. Someone was appointed to "oversee" the
panhandlers, but nothing much changed. Opinion had it that
the supervisor "was into this really heavy patriarchal trip, and
that's the way he did panhandling, and a lot of times he would
slip people a higher percentage than they really should have
gotten." How to control the panhandlers became a favorite
subject for clinic meetings. The treasurer complained about
irregular records; others complained that disreputable-looking
panhandlers were hurting the clinic's reputation. The panhandlers, for their part, began to complain that they were treated
like dirt, that they didn't have a say in anything. They were
invited to meetings, but few came.

The problem of regulating the panhandlers' cut eventually
resolved itself as a self-policing system emerged naturally on the
street. "There are two types of panhandlers," one told me de-
fiantly, "responsible and irresponsible"—and the responsible
ones took it upon themselves to monitor the size of the illegiti-

mate cuts. Anyone who took more than the agreed-upon fair share was promptly beaten up. "Among the panhandlers there's a definite pecking order and a spoils system," said one clinic worker with relief. "They're kept in line by a number of bouncer types. It's important for some people to keep their reputation for being able to beat up other people." Ironically, the laissez-faire model that clinic workers were determined to eradicate inside the organization was working for them on the street, and they had helped to legitimize panhandling for anyone else who wanted to hang out in Gilford—a group that was to cause the clinic a lot of trouble in the future.

The ideal of community control began to pall as workers found the more urgent problem to be how to stave off unwanted community intrusions. Money almost always provided the entering wedge. Had the clinic restricted the scope of its operations to routine primary care, it is possible that patient donations and the panhandlers, with their "honor among thieves" code, could have kept the place running. And a small, tightly run organization would have stood a better chance of regulating outside participation in a sensible way. But the clinic instead chose to expand, and expansion required additional funding that seldom came without strings attached.

Real pressures from the neighborhood fueled the push for expansion. Amphetamines were replacing marijuana on the street, and increasingly there was a chance that they might be cut with something more lethal. One flourishing dealer had been found selling tablets of pure strychnine. A minister in the area remarked wistfully, "A lot of the dealers in psychedelics, who were very conscientious dealers in good psychedelics only, were also volunteers on LSD rescue. It was kind of a thing where they were doing their social responsibility thing. . . . That kind of purist psychedelic dealer, you just don't see it any more. . . ." With the change in drug traffic, the clinic needed not only more workers but more highly skilled ones; empathy and stamina would do to talk someone down from a bad acid trip, but to recognize and cope with a case of strychnine poisoning required training.

Drug cases weren't the only new arrivals in the waiting room. When the city hospital closed its outpatient psychiatric service, the only options left for seriously disturbed patients were the county hospital—an expensive taxi ride away with only a couple of beds available for Gilford patients—and the clinic. Clinic workers hadn't had much experience with "*really* crazy" patients, but their fledgling counseling service coped well under the strain and promised to become one of the clinic's real successes. However, psychiatric cases started to turn up at night because the clinic had a twenty-four-hour service, and when the police augmented the load by dropping off "weird" cases that they couldn't classify, the burden became too much.[4] Up to this point the night shifts, or "graveyards," had been manned by a skeleton staff who counted on being able to sleep through most of it unless they got an emergency call. Now inexperienced workers were faced with a series of frightening experiences: suicide attempts, break-ins, and threatening behavior that they couldn't handle. The graveyard shift obviously had to be trained and paid.

Clinic workers were also pushing for more funds to implement other ambitious programs. A dental section, a switchboard, a transportation scheme, and psychiatric and referral services, they felt, were the minimum they needed if they were going to offer anything approaching comprehensive care. So they began the time-consuming business of finding more money —despite the uneasy suspicion that they were inviting more outside interference.

The city government seemed the logical place to start. It was accessible; informal contacts had already been built up with several city-council members. Workers decided that the best strategy would be to capitalize on one of the city's insoluble sociomedical problems—venereal disease. Because the free clinic spared patients a moral lecture and the indignity of appearing in a place that cared exclusively for venereal disease, it had been much more successful in attracting VD patients than the city clinics (which were open only for limited periods during working hours three days a week).

The exact proportion of the city's venereal disease cases that the clinic treated wasn't known: clinic estimates ranged as high as 70 percent, and the city public-health department put the figure at 40 percent. Either one was certainly high enough for clinic workers to demand adequate reimbursement from the city for their services. They marched down to the health department, dumped a load of gonorrhea culture plates on the director's desk, and held a press conference. The publicity had its effect. The city had just received a federal grant to help fight the venereal disease "epidemic," and it allocated some of that money to several free clinics in the area.

Predictably, the funds weren't enough, and clinic workers felt that maybe the strategy hadn't been such a good one. They had got their money, but they were still taking a lot of dirty work off the city's hands and supplying it with a cheap labor pool. The city public-health director said as much: "Another thing free clinics do well is attract volunteers. There's loads, loads of people happy to volunteer their time. Here's a county hospital, also typically serving people who are down and out, who lack resources, who are sick and desperate and underserved, and you don't see a volunteer in a carload. Maybe a few candy-stripers and that's about all." By dumping the treatment of VD on the free clinic, the city didn't have to train more workers, improve its facilities, or risk antagonizing Gilford citizens who didn't approve, in one elderly woman's words, "of that kind of behavior."

So the city was happy enough to leave the free clinic alone, except for one issue: following up the sexual contacts of venereal-disease patients. Clinic workers were genuinely concerned about preventive medicine, and they were in a good position to get names of contacts from patients who ordinarily felt assured of sympathy and confidentiality. But clinic workers "were so paranoid about anything that smacked of fascism," as one medic put it, "that they didn't want to press anyone for that kind of information." At the city's insistence they did set up thorough contact interviews for syphilis cases, but even then they resisted reporting their findings to the city. "We made it clear that we would do VD follow-up in our own way," a clinic administrator told me. "We would control how we were going to do it, and we made it clear we would report to the city such things as we wanted to report and not report other things."

Ironically, this was the same system of selective reporting—the bane of infectious-disease control agencies—used by private doctors in the United States.[5] Caught in the battle between public-health officials and physicians, and torn between an obligation to the health of the community and an obligation to the feelings of their patients, the clinic followed conventional practice. Without the kind of revolution in social values through which China claims to have eradicated venereal disease, they had few other palatable options. But the pressures that made them reproduce the same old inadequate approach to stigmatized infectious diseases were exacerbated by the ambiguous attitude of paraprofessional workers to their jobs and to their patients. Since they wanted to be comradely, they didn't have the distance from their jobs that might have protected them against the personal embarrassment caused by frank and friendly questions about their patients' sexual activities. The line between protecting privacy and copping out is a fine one. The whole issue raised the larger dilemma of how much responsibility and initiative medical reformers are entitled to demand from their patients within the outmoded framework of American capitalist medicine.

Politics and Prevention

The tensions with the city over VD led clinic workers to look for money that wasn't earmarked for the treatment of one specific disease. When they heard that their county had been allocated some revenue-sharing money designated specifically for local programs, clinic workers figured they were entitled to a share. But they hadn't bargained on the huge amounts of time subsequently spent on writing proposals, lobbying, and negotiating.

Money, it appeared, never came without strings attached. In this case, accepting a grant meant developing a fee schedule and sending bills to all the patients who came to the clinic (even if they didn't intend to collect). Patients would be required to sign a sworn statement divulging their real income, and the county would have the right to track them down, through a system known as auditrails, to verify whether they had actually visited the clinic and told the truth about their finances.

These regulations were clearly unacceptable to the clinic. Through a well-organized media campaign, and with the help of a lawyer, the clinic negotiated a compromise. Their proposal was rewritten to fund the clinic for indirect services ("education and outreach") rather than direct medical ones, and statistical summaries of patients treated were substituted for auditrails.

Buoyed by their victory, clinic workers didn't realize for some time that accepting the money had nevertheless wrought a profound change in the clinic. One of the oldest members complained that it wasn't just the extra bookkeeping work that worried her: "The other thing . . . which I feel is even more damaging is that people now refer to our services in terms of direct or indirect. And people are really adopting language that the county set up for our program . . . and people are keeping track of percentage of time [worked]. It feels really funny." Although people at the clinic were still working for the same reasons—that they enjoyed it, that they could maintain flexible hours—the county grant requirements had imposed some of the trappings of a "straight job" on their work.

Months later, when the clinic was being evaluated for refunding, workers realized that the county was trying to impose even more fundamental changes. The new group of county negotiators did not appear to be fully aware that the clinic had applied for "indirect" services. "They hadn't read our proposal and they didn't know what they were evaluating," complained a frustrated medic. "They kept asking questions about direct medical services of the drug program. . . . I had to first explain that the proposal [wasn't] for direct services, and they didn't understand why. They said, 'Well gee, if there's such a VD epidemic, don't you want funding so you can take care of it?' " These questions were the result of misinformation, but it is likely that they reflected the county's opinion of what a free clinic *should* be doing, namely, taking care of drug abusers and venereal disease.

As a result of the evaluation, the new outreach-and-education proposal was rejected. It was only then that clinic workers began to suspect that the county's reason for funding them in the first place was not their innovative approach to health care. One clinic administrator hazarded a guess that they had received money "not because we're us and that we fulfill some need of theirs with the services that we provide, but more that we're a lot lower risk than some of these other programs. Like we've been in existence for five years and that's just about the longest that any community agency has been around."

Furthermore, once the evaluators realized that the clinic was receiving money from other sources for what they perceived as the more useful direct services, they did not seem impressed by the clinic's indirect service work. "They don't understand what outreach and education is," said one clinic member bitterly.

> They don't understand that what we do is teach people how to prevent themselves from getting venereal disease or cavities. They don't really hear the preventive-medicine aspect. And one of the reasons why is the majority of the committee is middle-class housewives who have husbands that pay for medical insurance and they don't have to worry about preventive medicine. They're healthy, they have nutritious meals; preventive medicine's just part of their life style.

The evaluators' apparent lack of interest in prevention also probably stemmed from the crisis orientation of conventional medicine, which has traditionally neglected preventive measures.

Organized medicine's monopoly of training and licensing may also have contributed to the negative judgments in the county report. One of the evaluating committee members was a doctor who, according to another member of the committee, had "heard that people can come in [to the clinic] for services and four weeks later, with a little bit of training, are the people that are giving out the treatments for venereal disease." Clinic workers finally realized that medics who weren't part of an approved medical training program were considered a liability rather than an asset to their service. The very aspects of their program that they regarded as innovative, challenging, and productive—their emphasis on prevention and their use of lay workers—were the elements that would stand in the way of refunding.

Worker Control

Keeping the larger community from controlling the clinic took up such an inordinate amount of energy that clinic members stopped looking for more ways to welcome it in. But they were still serious about their plans for building a participatory structure that would allow a say to all those who worked at the clinic. It was no easy task to break down both traditional medicine's barrier of "clinical autonomy" and a rigid division of labor supported by traditional sex roles. However, the doctors, the skilled paraprofessionals, and the lay workers all worked out a fairly comfortable modus vivendi. Several factors contributed to this accomplishment.

For one thing, the traditional nurse's role had been virtually eliminated in the clinic. Most of the medics were men, and some were former army corpsmen. The few nurses who stayed for any length of time often went through the medics' training program, which undermined much of the traditional basis for their deference toward doctors. Then too, the medicine practiced by the clinic eliminated the intermediary of baffling technology or pharmacology. Few illnesses treated were life-threatening, and many remedies appeared to be matters of simple common sense.

Despite narrow legal restrictions on the autonomy of paraprofessionals, most clinic doctors were prepared to grant the medics a fair degree of freedom: "[Unlicensed] people are diagnosing sore throats and they shouldn't be. But I mean you don't have to be a mental giant to diagnose a sore throat or a lot of other things here." This kind of attitude went a long way toward breaking down the myth of the physician as omnipotent healer. Of course, the select group of doctors who volunteered their time to work in an atmosphere charged with antagonism toward the medical mystique had to start off in sympathy with the clinic's egalitarian objectives. Otherwise, as one doctor put it, "Why bother to go there and take abuse?"

Some doctors, to be sure, were often exasperated by their inability to elicit complete cooperation from lay workers. Yet even they stuck it out, partly because the clinic offered them both valuable experience and a number of alternative career options. One doctor admitted that he had gained practice in diagnosis and treatment that his internship hadn't given him:

> In the early months that I was at the clinic, a number of medics were more experienced with the management of venereal disease than I was. Frankly, they see an awful lot of it, and I hadn't in my practice before coming on. I think in the time that I've been there it's been a valuable learning experience for me, and you know in that sense the medics have been my teachers as well.

Another physician had been able to move from the specialist job he disliked to a community-medicine program, and he attributed this opportunity in large part to his years of volunteer work at the clinic: "A lot of medical schools now are trying to develop themselves into kinds of community medicine, family practice kinds of things, and a place like the free clinic is a good training for that. . . . The free clinic prepared me for that job. I immediately have a calling card where I can sit down with them and say, 'Well, we speak the same language.' "

Yet most doctors, even those who were prepared to forgo the money and the prestige of a "straight" job to work full time in the clinic for a while, were careful to limit their commitment. "My life wouldn't fall apart without the free clinic," said one such individual. "It's important not to have too much investment in it because then you are threatened if the free clinic is threatened. If the free clinic fell apart I could find other places to do what I want."

This tenuous connection strengthened the hand of the paramedics and gave them control over many medical decisions. Few medics were afraid of "too much investment" in the clinic. On the contrary, the involvement for many of them was crucial to their sense of self and their daily existence. "I think that I'm typical in a lot of ways in coming to the clinic," one long-term worker told me.

I'm typical in the sense that I was in college at the height of the Vietnam antiwar movement, which at that point also included a realization that it was more than Vietnam. And a whole lot of us kind of dedicated our lives to political work and then everything sort of faded away, and we were left with a feeling of dedication without a sense of where to plug in. What I did was go back to school and try to make myself, try to force myself to make a career decision when I couldn't make one. Every time I tried to make a decision, the only thing that seemed relevant to me was working at the clinic.

The commitment that sustained many of the lay workers made them look forward to the medical section's interminable Sunday meetings—occasions that most doctors avoided. But in trying to prevent the clinic from encroaching on their precious free time, physicians jeopardized their prerogative to adjudicate medical matters. In one meeting, the issue came up of whether the clinic should carry Valium and codeine. Some workers argued that they were often necessary for treatment; others feared that keeping them would open the clinic to "rip-offs" by both patients and workers who had nonmedicinal uses for such drugs. When the vote was called near the end of the meeting, a medic protested: "You know, doctors should carry more weight in this decision." "Yeah, but they're not here," was the reply, and so the decision to stock both drugs was taken without the input of the clinic's medical "experts."

Paramedics' enthusiasm, however, didn't always lead to intelligent medical judgments, and was even counterproductive in some neighborhoods. "My feeling is that they're misdirected in their enthusiasm," a nursing student in a midwestern clinic told me.

They thought they would go block by block and bring women in to screen them for pap smears. But the greatest problem in that community is undernourishment. People are fat, they're anemic, and they're hypertensive. And so I said, "If you want to do something, you should go out and talk about nutrition." Well, talking about nutrition, that's not very exciting. They were very much into: it's really nifty to do a pap smear, or it's nifty to check for anemia, but it's not so nifty to be passing on information on balanced diets.

Similar conflicts arose over medical issues in the Gilford clinic—many more than in some of the minority clinics I observed, where attacking doctors for their elitism was considered a foolish and self-destructive luxury. Doctors often had to improvise to reassert control and stop the untrained from making dangerous mistakes.[6] But by and large the quarrels that really threatened to tear people and unity apart were not over medicine. They centered on the perennial problem of how to build an organization that promoted equal participation, rewards, and responsibility.

The Ideal of Voluntarism

Enthusiasm can carry people a long way, but it doesn't pay the rent. Clinic workers had been ambivalent about lobbying for grant money to pay for equipment and supplies, but this was nothing compared to their quandary over whether they themselves should be paid. Initially, salaries were out of the question. When the issue came up the first year, one of the clinic organizers summarized the prevailing mood: "If everybody can't be paid, nobody will be paid. If you start paying people it means you start getting into money hassles, haggling about money, who's going to get paid, and then people are going to lose their dedication. They'll be working for money and not for ideals."

The "concerned citizens" who had thrown their weight behind the project at the beginning were definitely of the opinion that money corrupts: "I remember arguments time after time against anyone making their living by working in the clinic," one old-timer told me, "because it was a philanthropic organization, it was where people volunteered and gave their time to help. They were helpers, not workers. They were supposed to earn their living somewhere else and then volunteer some extra time at the clinic. It's a very liberal view."

But it was a view shared by most of the early volunteers. A medic, reminiscing about the old days, recalled with pleasure that "there was like this whole principle of working there for free and feeling proud about that and doing it because I wanted to . . . working for forty hours a week for nothing and knowing everybody else is doing it."

That kind of self-sacrifice couldn't last, however. Eventually the clinic found that many categories of funding could be tapped only by applying for money for workers' salaries. More important, an unwieldy and often unreliable group of volunteers made for a lack of continuity and accountability. But if paid positions were to be created, what criteria should determine who would fill them?

The meetings to work out salary guidelines caused enormous tension. Technical expertise was ruled out immediately as grounds for a salary. "That's part of the whole elitism trip," said one worker. "Why should somebody get paid who's been here only six months merely because they have a skill while other people put in a whole lot more work?" A simple seniority rule was also rejected.

Who then should be paid? Elsewhere, the clinics I saw that had ruled out the criteria of skill or experience had no ready answer. One, for example, followed the lead provided by the political movement that had started it: "When [the movement's] line was based on Third World leadership, what happened in the organization was people would be recruited not based on political understanding but on whether they were Third World or not, and the same thing happened at the clinic. There were people hired to work simply because they were black and brown and for no other reason." This strategy soon brought complaints from white volunteers that they knew more or had worked there longer, and it was finally abandoned on the grounds that it heightened racial tension.

The Gilford clinic eventually drew up a set of ill-defined guidelines emphasizing two criteria: personal characteristics like honesty, reliability, and administrative capacity, and the elusive requirement of "need." This meant that candidates for positions had to undergo a rigorous personal interrogation and pass an informal means test. The system was cumbersome and caused great resentment. The criteria were vague, and people often ranked differently on the two scales. If someone had proved to be reliable in the past, but was obviously not as needy as a rival, who should get the job? Candidates started to conceal their incomes and were ritualistically exposed: Phil was receiving a monthly allowance from his father; Mary's boyfriend was earning enough to support both of them, and so on.

A split between "workers" and "volunteers" also emerged from the new system. Many volunteers were opposed to setting up any paid positions, because they saw more structure as a threat to their own autonomy and even to their participation. The clinic had had few formal jobs with clearly defined duties, and so volunteers had been able to commit as much or as little time as they wanted and to carve out areas where their special talents, like fund-raising, were recognized. Paid positions might well limit their initiative. A worker who was struggling to get a salary said ironically that the volunteers saw the clinic as "a sort of strange flora and fauna where people live, breathe, eat, and shit without economic necessities. . . . It means that if a worker asks for a salary the volunteer doesn't know why." On the contrary, however, the volunteers did know why, and they had a sizable stake in keeping the clinic's structure fluid.

This position had unfortunate consequences for the volunteers as well as for the clinic. The most immediate cost to the organization was that unless someone volunteered to do something it didn't get done. The costs to the volunteers were frustration and confusion. They protested that the work in their chosen area of competence was overwhelming, that no one would help them out consistently, and that they would find themselves having to stay up all night alone to file charts or to write proposals.

They also suffered from constant feelings of inadequacy. There was no way of knowing whether they were doing a good job because the job appeared to have no boundaries. Many who left said they were "burnt out"—they couldn't cope any more with a situation where they felt they were always doing too much work but never enough to finish the job. The demand for "limits" became a dominant theme in organizational meetings. The issue couldn't be resolved satisfactorily because the limits were defined as a matter of collective support ("I need this group to help me define my limits") rather than the product of a clear job structure, which remained a "bureaucratic" anathema. ("I don't want any sort of accountability here. That's what happens in bureaucracies.")

Volunteer frustration periodically reached crisis levels, and sporadic attempts were made to introduce some sort of coherence. One strategy involved imposing a requirement that trainees had to commit themselves to working in the clinic for at least six months after taking a clinic training course. In addition, salaried positions imposed on the clinic by grant requirements were to be administrative positions: people could be paid for coordination, but not for providing direct services to patients.

A few months after these rules were implemented, volunteer participation had dropped dramatically. The clinic's organization had tightened up and it ran more smoothly, but the range of people who worked there under the new restrictions was severely limited. The training requirement had driven away many people who had hung around the clinic waiting for the excitement of a crisis situation like a drug overdose case. These were the people who had in fact become particularly good at dealing with emergencies and acted as informal bouncers. Because the medics who dealt directly with patients couldn't pick up an occasional stipend for their work any more, some of them couldn't devote so much time to the clinic, and people who no longer had the option of dropping back into town to work several months after completing a training cycle stopped coming. "Who are the people who can *afford* to volunteer long hours at the clinic now?" asked one worker indignantly.

A lot of them are part-time workers, or people who have a family and are working part time, or people going to school and getting credit, or people who have time. We're losing a lot of workers because they just can't afford to work those hours here. They have to be white, middle-class, childless, young, and hip to work at the clinic. Minorities won't touch the place as far as I can see, because they're not into starving.

Yet the clinic's very existence depended on the flow of energetic volunteers, and so the training rules were gradually relaxed. The paradox from which the clinic never escaped was that it needed a stable crew of workers, but the people who passed through it saw their work there as an experiment—in participatory democracy as much as in alternative medical care—and for each person the experiment was short-lived. In the long run the Gilford clinic could afford the luxury of a continuous turnover because the university community around it was an attractive place to live and guaranteed a steady stream of student volunteers, as well as ex-students and political activists who didn't want to leave the area.

Turnover also provided a constant infusion of enthusiasm and new ideas; it meant that old quarrels didn't linger to block creative innovations. But the clinic lost the benefit of the training it had given, and the costs were high in terms of discipline and continuity. Clinics in the boondocks or unattractive ghettos that couldn't count on an unlimited supply of volunteers often elected to spend their limited financial resources on the incentive of small salaries to everyone. The price they paid was that the poorer ones had that much less to spend on equipment and services, and inevitably restricted membership to those workers who could afford to survive on subsistence salaries.

The Gilford clinic never really solved the problem of worker control because it could never quite decide who should be counted among the workers and what they should be controlling.

Most general policy decisions were made by huge all-clinic meetings that could also be attended by outsiders, and clinic workers were proud of the fact that in their organization the "community" was the ultimate court of appeal—everybody could voice an opinion. But open forums lent themselves to the deliberate tactic of stacked meetings. The introduction of a "women's night" (which would exclude male workers and treat only women patients) was a notable example. A worker who had opposed the innovation told me how it had come about:

> The women marshaled and they came to present their case. It was a terrific meeting. There were about twenty workers plus all the hangers-on. A lot of them were black males who had a lot of prejudice against the women and the kind of attitudes the women hated the most. And the women were most of them outsiders who had come to defend this kind of thing, all screaming back and forth at each other. Of course the men in the clinic were scared to death and it won by an overwhelming majority.

The community had exercised its will and the majority had got its way, but this meeting left many with the uneasy feeling that somehow the whole process hadn't been exactly democratic.

The question of an appropriate voting unit became even more complicated when the clinic decided to allocate jobs by election in open meetings. On the night of the first election. Fred, the medical director, was getting married. He and his supporters (mostly from the medical section) returned the next day to find that the community meeting had voted to replace him and two other people with three representatives from the psychiatric section. An uproar ensued over whether the people who had voted were the "real" community. The election was finally declared invalid, and the next one reinstated Fred and his friends.

Though worker and community control were reiterated on every possible occasion as one of the raisons d'être of the clinic, it was now obvious that there was no consensus over who was to be counted among the real community. "New people would drift into a meeting just because they were there that night," complained a medic. "And then there would be an issue, and they didn't know what the hell was happening, so they didn't even know when to raise their hands. We just asked that people be responsible. We didn't count, you know, keep track of it, but we asked that people be responsible in the voting, and that they not vote unless they'd been there a couple of times or something." The appeal to "responsibility" was the same one that had been raised over the issue of limiting job responsibilities, and there was the same reluctance to set up definite rules or criteria. When decisions had to be made, some people were found to be more equal than others. But workers refused to make explicit the de facto distinctions by clearly defining the electoral unit. As a result, community support in its most visible form—the community meeting—failed to confer legitimacy on most collective decisions.

Patients' Rights

The exhausting struggle to build a participatory democracy, which really differentiated the free-clinic strategy from previous efforts at medical reform, often obscured the business of delivering medical care and strengthening patients' rights. Furthermore, even those clinic workers who were sustained by a dedication to help the needy were slow to recognize that needy patients constitute a large and heterogeneous category. The kinds of patients they served had a profound effect on the kinds of reform they could achieve.

Groups like the Black Panthers in Oakland or the Young Lords in Chicago wanted to build political organizations in their neighborhoods, and delivering medical care was one way of creating support. But because these movements held themselves accountable to a clearly defined community, they often had to curtail the range of their medical programs. Clinica de la Raza in Oakland, set up to serve Chicano patients, did occasionally treat the adolescents who showed up on the doorstep suffering from the effects of drug use. But they didn't encourage such patients and they never developed a drug program. "One of the main reasons for not going after certain money is its derailing effect," explained David Hayes-Bautista, the administrator of Clinica. "A lot of clinics went after drug money. . . . What we realized is that it's very easy to get locked into doing things for money and then never get out of it . . . so then you would start to get a lot of different sorts [of patients] who in turn would start to drive the other patients out because they would say 'that's a hippie clinic, not my clinic.' " Clinica also turned down Oakland's offer of funding to help them take care of VD patients. The community tended to see VD exclusively as a moral problem, and by accepting VD money clinic workers knew that they would get a bad name. Encouraging patients to come in for treatment of a simple medical problem—venereal disease—was tantamount to sanctioning promiscuity in that neighborhood.

Similarly, mothers who brought their kids in for treatment were suspicious of doctors who grew beards and didn't wear white coats. Nor did they take kindly to doctors who urged them in a friendly way, "Call me Dave." They hadn't come in to be "practiced on" by hippies. They wanted *real* doctors and professional treatment. In return they provided a great deal of moral support for Clinica workers, who built up a stable clientele and began to establish strong relationships with an identifiable community. But the price paid for this support by Clinica and the workers in many other minority clinics was that they had to practice pretty "straight" medicine, and eliminate care for two of the community's growing health problems—drug effects and venereal disease.

The Gilford clinic and many white street clinics like it started out to serve a really down-and-out clientele. The street people were young, scruffy, transient, and often had few places to turn if they got hurt. It wasn't very safe to call a hospital if you overdosed on drugs, because the police would probably arrive with the ambulance. Gilford clinic workers were able to make substantial improvements on the type of emergency-room care these patients were used to receiving. The free clinic offered them a relaxed atmosphere, minimal form-filling, and lay workers who had the time to talk extensively about problems that weren't just medical. Doctors were hard to distinguish from paraprofessionals because they didn't appear draped in uniforms, stethoscopes, and an impersonal manner.

But the problems of dealing with a poor, disenfranchised clientele are notorious. Middle-class doctors often can't interpret or don't spend the time to listen to their vague descriptions of symptoms. The patients will often wait until a chronic complaint has become a dangerous illness. They won't return for follow-ups, and they don't always keep appointments. The Gilford clinic was constantly revising its appointments system to accommodate everyone who needed help. "If we had made appointments in advance, people wouldn't have kept them," said one harassed medic, "because of the nature of the people . . . you know, drifting around, not having a clear sense of what they would be doing when, so that it would be unrealistic for them to have a little appointment book and write down when their appointment was a week from now."

Patients like this also thwarted the clinic's best efforts to implement prevention and political-education programs. "When you have some poor person who doesn't want to know about their disease—not intellectually minded," said one doctor, "well, that's very frustrating to my kind of thinking, because I know that all treatments are fallible. I would rather have them working with me." But many patients didn't want to work with doctors, and even less did they want to listen to a political analysis of how capitalist medicine was profit-oriented and dangerous. They just wanted to get better.

Clinic workers who had chosen to serve this kind of clientele enjoyed a supportive atmosphere for practicing peer treatment, and they were able to discard the forbidding symbols of clinical authority and build more egalitarian relationships among workers and patients. But they couldn't create a solid organizational base from transient, disorganized patients, let alone reach out to other community programs or pressure the medical institutions around them. And the one-shot medicine they were forced to practice was demoralizing.

A hard-headed weeding out of the patients they should or shouldn't serve was almost impossible for clinics bent on correcting the selective procedures of hospitals and private practitioners. The Gilford clinic complicated things even further because its workers conceived the roots of their patients' problems as primarily social rather than medical. So they were prepared to take in almost everyone: transients who needed somewhere to spend the night, adults who needed a physical examination for a job application, people who wanted to find out if the street drugs they had bought were pure. After a while their case load became too large to handle. But clinic workers could think of few palatable ways to pare it down. One of the most damaging consequences of their reluctance to cut some people off was that most of their frustration was vented on their patients. "Free clinics just promote the class system," said one overworked medic in a meeting. "Poor people who come here don't have to face realities; they could get on Medicaid. We're not a free clinic. Someone has to pay for it. We have to make people responsible for their own care. I'm burnt out with all these demands. We're abused."

Medics who had been stabbed or roughly handled by patients had a hard time remembering the clinic code that unemployment and injustice were the root causes of most of their clientele's problems. But their disillusionment was only partly fostered by the nature of their clientele. Workers' unhappiness also stemmed from their own precarious position. All the work they had put in and all the training they had gone through in the clinic didn't equip them to compete in the medical job market. The State Medical Practices Act in California, for example, doesn't recognize "common practice" or experience in the practice of medicine. Only a license is a valid measure of skill under the law. So competent medics who knew that the free clinic couldn't be their life's work were unqualified to apply for any but the most menial and unskilled jobs in the health-care field.

In the Gilford clinic, this produced a situation where the medics' sense of achievement came to depend largely on the successes of the clinic's reforms and on the perceived importance of their own position in the clinic. They became extremely hostile toward any attempt to trivialize their work. "The clinic isn't a playroom," exploded one medic in a meeting. "People expect to come in here and be *treated*. Some people seem to think that they can act like 'and now it's time to play free clinic.' There's been a tightening up in the medical [section]. We flunked a quarter of the people in the last [training] class." Patients who suffered from chronic, intractable problems that were beyond the resources of the medics to solve were obviously a real drain on their energies and a serious threat to their feelings of personal efficacy. So it was not surprising that they became less sympathetic and more brusque towards their clientele.

Patient control seemed as hard to implement as community control. The few mechanisms of grievance resolution that modern medicine provides aren't available to free-clinic patients. Most of them weren't even aware of the American Hospital Association's patient bill of rights, although it has proved so ineffective in the larger medical system that their ignorance was probably an irrelevant point.[7] Transient hippies would rarely think of resorting to a lawyer to press a malpractice suit, and couldn't afford it if they did.

Admittedly, patients who come to free clinics are unlikely to suffer the kind of serious iatrogenic injury that they might undergo in a hospital, because the clinics by and large stick to routine primary care. But clinic workers worried that they seemed to have done little better than the institutions they attacked in giving patients a means to voice their complaints and to secure a remedy. The open relationship between clinic doctors and their patients helped; the option for patients to join the clinic as workers provided a resolution for those few who could afford that choice. And free-clinic patient advocates who accompanied the sick to hospitals and guided them through bureaucratic obstacles to care were a boon to poor patients who needed extensive treatment. But within the Gilford clinic, workers found that patient control was an elusive phenomenon. Sick people don't want to come to clinic meetings, and the harassed medics were more prone to attack troublesome patients than the laws and the institutions that victimized them both.

A Diagnosis

What have free clinics achieved? Are they the right way to go about medical reform? Can they really provide an "alternative" in any meaningful sense, or do they simply replicate the flaws of American health-care delivery?

The Gilford clinic survived where many others did not largely because it was located in a liberal community and could draw on a huge supply of volunteers. But its history points to the necessity for free-clinic organizers to make some hard political choices if they are to do more than stagger along on borrowed time. Do you stay small and uncompromised, or take money from the feds—which carries the charge of "selling out" and is distributed in accordance with the moral and medical priorities of HEW? Do you choose to serve the most desperate clientele you can find—who seem to need help most but may give nothing in return—or do you move into a community that is already organized around other issues and will provide you with a satisfying, stable patient population of families? How do you create incentives to persuade patients to help sustain their clinic? How do you build loyal community support and build structures that will give community, workers, and patients a say in their own health care without tearing the clinic apart? Do you keep the clinic alive with paid staff, who may get ground down by the pressure, or with a steady stream of enthusiastic volunteers who will diffuse bad blood?

Most of the "alternatives" of the sixties had to face some variant of these dilemmas, but medical reformers faced a tougher task than most. Sick people aren't the easiest to organize, and lobbying for preventive medicine isn't the most exciting task in the world for the healthy. The structural barriers posed by organized medicine are overwhelming: the licensing restrictions on paraprofessionals, professional opposition to regulation, the insistence that Medicare and Medicaid have taken care of old and poor patients (which stops the money flowing to innovations in care for those populations).

In light of the compromises free clinics had to make to adjust to those pressures, it would be easy to dismiss them as victims of "co-optation." Indeed the Gilford clinic workers came close to doing so in their more discouraged moments. "Sometimes doing what we're doing seems really important," a medic told me, "like it's having an effect on people's lives, and even though

it feels like we're not getting anywhere, we have to keep plugging away. And sometimes it feels like, oh, we're just putting
on Band-Aids, we're just bailing out the Public Health Department."

The clinic did take care of a large part of the city's VD
problems, it provided a source of cheap labor, it gave medical
students experience in treating cases they would never see in
their internships, it taught the city fire department how to take
care of drug-overdose cases, and it probably took the pressure
of "difficult" patients off private practitioners and emergency
rooms. It acted as a medical safety valve. Its aspirations to band
together with other free clinics in a broad coalition to pressure
the medical establishment foundered after the first accusation
from a black clinic administrator that the white organizers were
trying to rip his clinic off. Similar schisms in the National Free
Clinic Conference—and the fragmentation of the Rainbow Coalition of Free Clinics in Chicago—indicate that the tensions
among the political groups that sponsored many clinics can't be
resolved easily.

But the bankruptcy of the free-clinic movement as an organizing strategy for wholesale medical reform shouldn't blind us
to its real achievements. The money that free clinics squeezed
out of city councils and states financed primary care for patients
who had nowhere else to turn. It also provided many people
with the first jobs they had ever enjoyed. The struggle to build
an alternative organization was an achievement in itself. It gave
clinic workers an intimate knowledge of the real obstacles to
medical reform. Many of them began to recognize that the old
liberal ideology of consumer control, decentralization, and
more access to medical care wasn't enough. American medicine
just didn't work. Free-clinic work gave some of them a sense
of what was involved in building a worker-controlled organization: participatory democracy was messy, time-consuming, and
complicated but worth it in the end—"because it serves that
function of allowing people to grow up—grow is really a bad
word—to mature," said one medic who had previously worked
in a drugstore selling expensive tranquilizers to old people. "So
I came in as a basically powerless, helpless woman who was no

good for anything except the service job I had, and now if I were even a service representative again, they would know about it, right? Ten minutes after I had walked in I would be organizing at the least."

The lesson of the free-clinic movement seems to be that you can't both provide a better service and mobilize effectively to bring organized medicine to its knees. Its most enduring achievement was probably to prepare people for the next round. If free clinics were to become "successful" in conventional terms they might only succeed in further institutionalizing a two-tiered system of medical care.

Notes

1. Because the clinic members who are the subject of this article wanted to preserve their anonymity, all names of people and places have been changed.
2. Reliable estimates of the number of free clinics in existence at any one time are hard to come by. This figure is cited in David E. Smith, Donald R. Wesson, and Rod Ciceri, "National Free Clinic Movement: Historical Prospectus," *Adit; Approaches to Drug Abuse and Youth* 2 (Oct. 1973): 1, 2, 12–16.
3. "Peer treatment" generally meant treatment by lay workers with very little training who were of the same age, sex, etc., as the patients they saw.
4. Egon Bittner has found that one of the most important criteria used by police in deciding that individuals engaging in bizarre behavior are mentally ill, and then taking action on the basis of that judgment, was whether they knew in advance that they would have somewhere to take these people. See Egon Bittner, "Police Discretion in the Emergency Apprehension of Mentally Ill Persons," *Social Problems* 14 (Winter 1967): 278–92.
5. See Roy L. Cleere et al., "Physicians' Attitudes Toward Venereal Disease Reporting: A Survey by the National Opinion Research Center," *Journal of the American Medical Association* 202 (Dec. 4, 1967): 117–22.
6. The nature of these struggles is described in detail in Rosemary C. R. Taylor, "The Proving Ground" (Ph.D. dissertation., University of California, Santa Barbara, 1975), pp. 327–76.
7. The bill was passed in 1972. One observer has attributed its ineffectiveness to the fact that there were no public hearings on the issue, and no local health boards have been set up to review decisions. Amitai Etzioni, "Health Care and Self-Care: The Genetic Fix," *Society* 10 (Sept.–Oct. 1973): 31.

From Free Schools
to "Educational Alternatives"

by Allen Graubard

Like previous rounds of educational reform, the last decade's movement for "free schools" appears to have evaporated. For both public and private schools, the financial squeeze is on, and the watchword in the media is "back to basics."

In this bleak educational atmosphere, it is hard to remember the heady days of the early 1970s. Then, one of the "free-university" movement's leading theorists, Berkeley's Michael Rossman, could predict that 1975 would see between 25,000 and 30,000 free schools in existence, with some 2 million students attending them. The only possible limits to such growth, said Rossman, were political repression, economic depression, or radical reform of the public schools.[1]

Evidently, neither the first nor the last of these conditions has come to pass. Though an economic recession has intervened, it alone can hardly explain why the free-school movement has *shrunk* since Rossman's prediction. By the same token, however, the diligent reporters who are now describing the back-to-basics movement are mistaken as well. Contrary to what they write, the recent wave of radical school reform has not simply died out. It has just taken a somewhat different form from what Rossman and many others in the movement expected.

"Free school" meant a school that encouraged student participation in governance, parent and community involvement, work in the outside world, student choice in curriculum, more social and personal "relevance" in subjects and projects, and opposition to conventional attitudes about authority and discipline in schools. To realize these objectives meant pulling out of the public schools and starting one's own small, independent, utopian institution. Hundreds of groups did exactly this; and, following the common practice of those days, the participants christened the "free-school movement." But the rosy glow of the first couple of years was a false dawn. That mushrooming movement of free schools, which people like Rossman thought would include millions, leveled off and began declining a couple of years after its invention. As we know, movements move fast in contemporary society.[2]

Nevertheless, the number of people involved in educational reforms that incorporate the sort of free-school perspectives noted above is much larger now than during the heyday of the free-school movement.

The solution to this apparent paradox is that the reform impetus moved *inside* the public system. The key concept was "alternatives"—alternative schools rather than free schools, and not so much of a "movement." Instead of starting their own schools, parents, teachers, and students who shared the educational and cultural ideas of the small band of free-schoolers worked to establish the idea of parent and student choice in the kind of education provided by the public system. Some administrators, educational "experts," government policymakers, and foundation officials supported this approach; in fact, official acceptance of the "alternatives" idea (and even a good deal of the critique of traditional school doctrine) is astonishingly extensive. There have been several major studies of secondary education over the past ten years sponsored by groups with impeccable Establishment credentials: the Office of Education, the Kettering Foundation, Nixon's Scientific Advisory Commission, and others. Without exception they advocate a strategy of alternative schools as offering the best hope for improving a sadly deficient high-school system.[3]

As far as alternative schools themselves are concerned, however, the usual story was parents, students, and teachers doing some hard work (though occasionally the initiative came from a principal or superintendent). Different communities have different stories, but the shape of the development can be discerned fairly easily.

In Cambridge, Massachusetts, for example, a group of parents of small children gathered together in the fall of 1971. Like many other such groups meeting in many living rooms throughout the country, they were committed to the spirit of educational reform articulated in the writings of people like Paul Goodman, John Holt, and George Dennison. They were graduate students, junior faculty, single mothers; most had participated in the antiwar movement. The organizers of the group had been part of two parent-controlled, integrated preschools, both infused with a spirit of informal, nonauthoritarian pedagogy and parent participation in all aspects of school life. Now that their children were reaching school age, they faced the prospect of sending them to traditional public schools. (Cambridge, despite its reputation as the home of Harvard and MIT, is a fair-sized industrial city with a large, mostly Catholic, blue-collar population; the schools at this point were as traditional as could be found anywhere. And Harvard-type parents seldom sent their children to public schools anyway.)

The group considered starting an independent free school for their children. But even at this time, when predictions like Rossman's were in the air, the difficulties of founding and nurturing a new free school were becoming all too apparent. Tuition would have to be charged. Teacher salaries were bound to be low, and job security for teachers would be virtually nonexistent. Buildings that met city codes for schools were hard to find and hard to maintain. In the absence of foundation funding —which went only to black, working-class, or other "apt" schools, and even so dried up quite quickly—the idea of funding through the public school system looked remarkably attractive. Public funding would have another benefit too. Without it, a school would have a hard time appealing to poor and minority-group parents. With it, the integration that these reform-minded middle-class people believed in might become a reality.

So the Cambridge parents launched a campaign for an alternative public school, calling for open education, effective parent control, and serious attention to issues like racism and sexism. Calling themselves the Committee for an Alternative Public

School (CAPS), they recruited more parents, printed brochures, organized petition campaigns, lobbied school-committee candidates, gave talks and slide shows, and entered into frustrating negotiations with a generally unsympathetic school bureaucracy. After two years, however, their work paid off. The school committee voted 5 to 2 in favor, and an alternative public school—kindergarten through second grade, scheduled to grow a grade a year—came into being.

The first years were difficult, as was often the case in such experiments. Participants felt dissatisfied, confused, argumentative; there were serious staff and director problems. Unsympathetic school-department administrators, including the superintendent who had vehemently opposed the idea of this parent-controlled alternative school, made survival even more problematic. But the school survived, grew, stabilized, and found a new building. The parents chose as principal a man who had started something called the Teacher Drop-Out Center at the University of Massachusetts Graduate School of Education. This was a free-school job-finding service for teachers who wanted to get out of public schools into the new wave of free schools; now he was the principal of an alternative public school, a personal path that wonderfully reflects the course of the educational reform movement.

By 1975 the school had become a complete elementary school, through the eighth grade, with a racially and economically mixed student body of over two hundred. The school has special bilingual and vocational programs, and its racial mix makes it eligible for various sorts of federal and state "magnet school" grants, including state aid in the construction of its own building. (For the past few years, it has been using a former Catholic elementary school.) The policy of parent participation and power has been maintained, and there are more applicants than the school can accept.[4]

In the late spring of 1975, some Cambridge parents who did not get their children through the school's complicated admissions process (race, class, and neighborhood are all used as criteria, to ensure various balances) launched a mini-campaign for another alternative school. With the alternatives idea already established, only a few months were required this time; in fall 1975, the Open School began operations, using classrooms in one of the regular public schools (a situation that made for considerable tension).[5]

At the high-school level, the push for public alternatives was also effective. Although the first of the alternative high schools in Cambridge had to withstand intense pressure from conservative school-board members who wanted to close it down after its first year, by now the idea is generally accepted. School-department publications take evident pride in the range of choices offered to high-school students, and the most recent new program was billed as the eighth alternative program. (In fact, five are real alternative schools; the others are more like part-time programs for some of the students in the regular high school.)

The oldest of these schools, the Pilot School, was founded in 1969 by graduate students and faculty from Harvard's Graduate School of Education and financed by some of the federal programs for educational reform that were so important in the founding, and sometimes the demise, of many public alternative programs. (Dubious local school officials can often be mollified by alternative-school supporters if the latter can show that all the money required will come in from outside the district.) Over the next few years, two other programs similar to the Pilot School were started. All three emphasize participatory democracy, student choice, and community involvement.

The most interesting of the alternative high-school programs listed by the school department is in fact not a public school. Called the Group School, the unusual experiment is now in its seventh year. It is an independent school for working-class youth. Students are a majority on all governing committees, including policy and teacher-hiring committees. All must come from working-class backgrounds. There is no tuition; funding comes from a variety of public and educational agencies, and from foundations concerned with social-welfare programs and new curricula. The staff shares income, with the typical salary well below that in the regular public-school system. The curriculum combines work on basic skills and job preparation with consciousness-raising study of working-class history, women's history, and the like. Some of the teachers have received funding through the school district to give workshops to public-school teachers on the working-class studies that the Group School has developed over the years. Their women's-studies curriculum has been published by the Feminist Press.

The public alternative schools throughout the country appear quite diverse, especially in comparison with the standardized institution most adults experienced. But there are really only a few basic kinds of alternative schools. Consider some examples. Brookline, Massachusetts, and Scarsdale, New York, are predominantly wealthy, highly educated suburbs. Their regular public high schools are very highly regarded. But both cities have significant numbers of students and teachers who want an alternative high school. Brookline's is called "school-within-a-school," sometimes shortened to "SWS." Housed in a section of the regular high-school building, the school typically has between fifty and a hundred students. The Scarsdale Alternative School has about seventy-five students, and utilizes an old Boy Scout building within sight of the regular high school. Both schools serve the predominantly white, middle-class, often intellectual constituency that has always supported the alternative-school idea.

Living according to the progressive ideals of the alternatives doctrine—maximum freedom, participatory decision-making, self-motivation, concern with the emotional and personal, and so on—while still meeting the expectations of parents and the students for academic success is a constant tension. The Scarsdale school has effectively countered its detractors and doubters by printing up a list of all of the colleges from which each student had received an acceptance, with Ivy League names like Brown prominently displayed. Able students from progressive middle-class homes who go to the alternative high school have typically gone on to college, just as they would have done if there had been no alternative school. These students are not "failures" or "educationally disadvantaged."

At the other end of the social and educational spectrum is the second major reservoir of alternative-school population, especially at the high-school level. In the Williamsburg section of Brooklyn, for example, there is a public alternative school that boasts progressive and committed teachers, students who work individually and in small groups, and much student participation in governance—just as in Scarsdale and Brookline. But High School Redirection, when I visited, was 100 percent black and Puerto Rican. Although an "open-style" space—the seventh floor of an old factory building—the setting was depressing, as was the neighborhood. Almost all of the students in the school were "failures," as is most of the general school population they are part of. Some are especially bad "failures," having been unable to make it in the very bad traditional high schools of the New York ghettos; they already have a history of school suspension, academic difficulties, and trouble with the law. Reasonably regular attendance, some progress in basic skills, and some inklings of self-motivation and initiative would be considered great success for most of the three hundred or so students of this inner-city alternative high school. Large cities with substantial minority populations frequently support one or more of this sort of alternative program. In fact, often the local "continuation high school," where the delinquents are sent, is the only school that runs according to alternative, progressive pedagogical style; these continuation schools would be included in classifications of alternatives. For parents, whose own educational views are seldom progressive, and even for conservative school officials, the attitude is often "why not try this? Nothing else has worked."

Some of the urban alternative high schools combine elements of both diverse constituencies. Metro High School in Chicago, a "school-without-walls" that has proved to be more successful than its more famous progenitor, the Parkway Program in Philadelphia, draws students from all over the city. Students range from poor black adolescents for whom Metro seemed the least bad of a set of bad possibilities, to hip, white, middle-class students who wanted very much to participate in an institution like Metro. This situation is especially characteristic of cities with a single alternative high school. Besides the general political imperative of integration, the federal education money that helped start many of the alternative high-school programs mandated integration of race and socio-economic status.

As might be expected, the variety of alternative elementary schools is much more limited. There are a very few K–12 experiments, a model more common among free schools. (Summerhill, the world's most famous free school, took in all ages.) The St. Paul Open School is one of the oldest and best-known of the public alternative schools, and it has 500 students of all school ages in a converted old warehouse. But much more typically, the alternative elementary schools are of the sort represented by the Cambridge Alternative Public School (CAPS). In Stockton, California (the "Fat City" of the novel by Leonard Gardner and the film by John Huston), the Open Alternative School has about 110 students, K–8. It is housed on one floor and the basement of an old elementary school building formally earthquake-condemned. It was started by a small group of parents and teachers, and had to fight hard to maintain its existence; it draws students from the whole district and is well integrated by class and race.

Stockton began a court-ordered busing plan in 1977. (The original court suit had been brought by a teacher in the district who became the head teacher of the alternative school.) The Open School, along with the 3Rs alternative school, were written into the court order; and the two opposites in school philosophy are treated as a single alternative school for the purpose of receiving extra "magnet school" funding from the federal government (which wants to encourage "voluntary desegregation"). Whether a single open-classroom mini-alternative or the complete K–6 or K–8 elementary school with its own building and principal, alternative open elementary schools are quite uniform in style and philosophy, though the range of success and failure is large.

Alternative schools, especially the private free schools, are thought of generally as being very short-lived. Although even free schools lasted on the average longer than the eighteen months that was frequently quoted (without any supporting evidence), many alternative schools opened and closed within three or four years. But some, for example most of those mentioned above, are in their sixth, seventh, eighth, or even ninth year of existence. They are accepted parts of their local school systems. They have developed their own traditions, their own methods of governance, and their own ways of evaluating students, staff, and program. They continue to attract a solid core of active and committed teachers, parents, and students. The strong opposition that often characterized the early years has generally died down.

But the exuberant excitement and commitment that once accompanied the sense of embarking on a great educational experiment has also declined. In the early, high-visibility days, when the media had "discovered" a burgeoning alternative-schools movement, laudatory articles about a program such as Philadelphia's Parkway project pointed out that Parkway got several thousand applications for its few hundred places. People involved with alternative schools believed that students, teachers, and parents everywhere would react like that; the waiting lists would be long. The only obstacles, it appeared, were reluctant administrations.

But that isn't what happened. Today's alternative schools have a constituency, and it is considerably larger than the number actually in alternative programs. (Many people still have no chance to choose.) But they aren't breaking the doors down. To get a sense of the size of the support, it is worth looking at the numbers carefully. The well-established and effective alternative high school at Cubberly High in Palo Alto enrolls about 130; the population of the Scarsdale Alternative School was recently between 70 and 80. But there were no waiting lists. Even in schools where there are, the lists aren't overwhelmingly long.

The most serious attempt to list, describe, and study the public alternative schools was undertaken by the National Alternative Schools Program at the School of Education of the University of Massachusetts. In itself, the program reflected the early heady days of alternative public schools. Supported by federal money, it trained teachers and administrators specifically for work in progressive alternative public schools. In a 1974 survey, program staff concluded that there were more than 600 alternative public schools (this did not include the recent wave of 3Rs schools, which the Alternative Schools Program would in no way have supported). The average size was between 160 and 170 students, which led to an estimate of approximately 100,000 students involved nationally. Since the past four years have not been times of active progress for the alternative-school idea, this figure is unlikely to have grown significantly.

The University of Massachusetts estimate amounts to around 0.25 percent of school-age youth. The extreme outer limit suggested by other estimates amounts to just a little less than 2 percent. Private free schools, at the height of the movement, had less than 15,000 students. These are very small numbers. In exceptional cases, like Cambridge or Minneapolis, the number of those in alternative schools might get up to 5 or even 10 percent. But the normal figure in a community with an alternative school is much lower, even when parents and students are free to choose.[6]

Why did the movement level off so quickly? Part of the explanation, of course, is the general waning of reform energies. But circumstances particular to the educational system itself are important also. There has been a widespread spirit of liberal reform in recent years, of which the bona fide alternative schools are only the most complete expression. (Conservative critics exaggerate the depth and scope of this trend, but it is real). Classrooms that are not truly open are nonetheless often looser and less rigid than they used to be.

Strict discipline, punishment for whispering in class, desks bolted down in perfect rows, and hands neatly folded on the edges of those desks—all have begun to go the way of the one-room schoolhouse. Many conventional high schools, particularly those in middle-class communities, offer students some choice in curriculum and considerable freedom during school hours. So the motivation for change—and the attraction of a "real" alternative—are both somewhat blunted.

Another reason for the decline of energy and enthusiasm is

that the alternative schools' real accomplishments could never live up to their advance billing. The rhetoric of radical reform in any area of human life tends to underestimate the difficulty of change, and to turn worthy hopes into promised results. Alternative-school theory was no exception. Expectations and goals presented in popular writings and funding proposals were rosy. But for many students, the troubles and difficulties of school did not vanish with their new surroundings. Alternative schools couldn't find any way around the rock-bottom fact of educational reform: most educational problems that are worth worrying about have deep roots in a society's culture and politics, and pedagogical change alone will soon run up against conditions it is unable to transform. When the alternative schools discovered this, the optimism that generated them began to wane.

Perhaps the most important drag on the spirit of educational reform is the economic situation. The recession, the increase in unemployment, the sense of heightened competition for good jobs (particularly in the professions) have all led parents and students to emphasize winning the educational races that the schools offer. That translates into a concern with learning basic skills early. It forces young people to work hard for grades— and for the credentials demanded by colleges, professional schools, and the job market. In other words, no nonsense, and taking part in an alternative school smacks of frivolity to many students and parents. Just as college students now prefer grades to the pass-fail option (because an "A" looks better than a "pass" to a medical-school admissions officer), so do high school students seem to accept traditional pedagogical methods —"for their own good."

Schools are financially strapped too. Long-term demographic trends are reducing the number of school children, and funds for experimental educational programs have become much scarcer. The job market for teachers is very tight, meaning both that fewer young, innovative teachers are being hired and that those who already have jobs are discouraged from trying new, risky ideas. When there are four hundred qualified people ready to jump into your job, you tend to be less bold and less defiant than when school systems were desperately recruiting uncredentialed liberal-arts graduates to join their staffs (the situation a decade ago).

The alternative-school situation is unlikely to change in the foreseeable future. A Gallup Poll taken in 1975 asked people about the "back-to-basics 3Rs" elementary schools that had already appeared in some school districts. Many parents expressed conventionally conservative attitudes. A majority (56 percent of public-school parents and 70 percent of parochial-school parents) wanted their children to go to a school with strict discipline, testing and grading, a traditional curriculum emphasizing basic skills, and even corporal punishment. Only 36 percent of public-school and 22 percent of parochial-school parents said they would *not* send their children to such a school. When these figures are broken down by age, however, an interesting trend appears. An overwhelming majority of older parents favored the back-to-basics approach. But a *majority* of younger parents, aged eighteen to twenty-nine, said they would not send their children to a "3Rs" school, and only 43 percent said they favored such schools.

Similar results could be obtained for high schools. There is, evidently, a solid constituency for alternative schools, and they will continue to gain at least some rhetorical support from government agencies and commissions, foundations, respected educational leaders, and teacher-training institutions. Some districts will take official pride in the choices their school system offers and others will tolerate a small alternative open school. Ironically, a recent "alternative" high school opened by the Cambridge system is a highly structured "fundamentals" school with a traditional curriculum and strict discipline.

A confident judgment on the political effects of the decade-long development of alternative schools is hard to make. If we look at the American educational system as a whole, the effects of the movement seem quite marginal. The most pressing issues in education today are busing, vocational training, school finance, teacher layoffs, competency standards, and minority achievement. Alternative schools do not touch these concerns. The small but significant minority of parents that want alternatives will continue to support them, and they will get some support from outside institutions. But the system as a whole won't show much change.

Is that because the original impetus toward alternative schools was somehow "co-opted"? A lot of the people involved with free schools in the early days of the movement worried that accepting money from "the system" would somehow destroy a school's radical potential. According to this view, clever administrators and educational planners would support the idea of alternatives as a way of occupying the energies of dissident students, teachers, and parents—and diverting them from more disruptive confrontations with the school system. At the same time, alternative schools would be used as a place to dump problem students from conventional schools, thereby relieving another potential source of discontent.

A more subtle view of co-optation is put forward in the widely discussed book *Schooling in Capitalist America,* by Samuel Bowles and Herbert Gintis.[7] Bowles and Gintis see the nonauthoritarian, open pedagogy of progressive education as occupationally functional for children destined for middle-class jobs.

In an assessment which puts the very small free-school phenomenon (even assuming the authors would include all public alternative schools, which is not clear) into an unjustifiably grandiose historical role, Bowles and Gintis write:

> There is a considerable potential for the assimilation of the free school movement into a program for streamlining and rationalization of the advanced capitalist order. The new corporate organization itself requires a shift in the social relationships of education. Direct discipline and emphasis on external rewards, characteristic of the assembly line and the factory system, have given way for a major segment of the work force to motivation by internalized norms characteristic of the service and office worker. . . . Entrepreneurial capitalism, which brought us the chairs-nailed-to-the-floor classroom, has given way to corporate capitalism. It may belatedly usher in the era of the open classroom, minimization of grading, and internalized behavior

norms contemplated for at least a century by so many educational reformers.[8]

The only way this co-optation can be avoided, say Bowles and Gintis, is for the free-school movement to acquire and transmit a socialist consciousness, to espouse a policy of a "participatory and egalitarian workers' democracy," to turn free schools into "seedbeds for revolutionaries."

In my view, both these perspectives obscure more than they illuminate. Co-optation is always a real problem for any reform movement, but it is not the key to understanding what happened to alternative schools. Many of the people active in alternative schools were not co-opted because they didn't need to be: they were less interested in radical politics (indeed, may not have been radical at all) than in a certain kind of education for their children. They wanted choice, participation, open pedagogy—not schools for socialists. Reading the brochures of hundreds of schools and talking to the participants across the country leaves no doubt about this. Most administrators and teachers who support alternative schools see them from this perspective. Their long-term objective might be a better, more successful school system producing people who are happier, less alienated, more competent cognitively and emotionally, and better able to function in a changing world.[9]

In general, apparently progressive ideas and actions (like starting an alternative school) are always utilized by people and individuals not interested in the radical transformation of society. The will to "reform"—to change things a little without altering the basic social system—is widespread in American society. In May 1977, for example, the *New York Times* reported that Consolidated Edison was using Brazilian educator Paolo Freire's techniques of teaching adult literacy to prospective employees. The techniques of Freire, who is perhaps the best-known "educator for revolutionary consciousness," include various ways of raising the student's political consciousness—for example, dialogues based on the learner's experience of racial prejudice. Using these techniques, a large capitalist firm taught reading and writing to poor illiterates and then gave them jobs, for which they reportedly felt quite grateful.

Whatever one's sense of the systemic co-optation built into such a reform development, on the grass-roots level many thousands of students, parents, and teachers have taken part in the experience of taking some control, often by serious political struggle, of an important institution. The school experience for many of these people has been more engaging politically, more stimulating intellectually, more involving emotionally, and more *educational* in the broadest sense than it would have been otherwise. There were people who were deeply affected, however small the number in comparison with the tens of millions who are directly involved with schools. In individual cases (notably working-class dropout alternatives), it could even be said that alternative schools have literally saved lives.

Paul Goodman's writings were very influential in the early years of free-school activity. In the first of his 1960s books, *Growing Up Absurd,* which appeared a couple of years before the earliest radical educational reform tremors, Goodman looked back in sorrow at the progressive-education movement of the early decades of the century. For Goodman, it was one of the "missed revolutions" that were the tragedies of our national past. The values of equality, freedom, and a cooperative participatory society which were central to the progressive-education visions of reformers like John Dewey, Bertrand Russell, and A. S. Neill were not carried out by the movement which waved the banner of progressive education. The dominant institutions resisted, co-opted, blunted, and absorbed any radical potential.

The people involved in the recent progressive wave of alternative schools didn't have much sense of the history Goodman was lamenting. They wanted something for themselves and their children that they didn't get in traditional schools, and they cared enough to work hard to realize their goals. Some hoped for larger effects and would doubtless like to make the connections between education and radical politics more explicit, but the absence of an organized political left in the United States makes such a job nearly impossible. Free schools reached the public consciousness during a period of intense political activity, when the idea of alternatives was closely connected to the general spirit of radical cultural and political protest in the late 1960s and early 1970s. But alternative-school activity has spread slowly since then, without the same exuberant spirit of reform. Whatever ideological or political threat alternatives may once have seemed to present, the public-school system has absorbed them quite easily. School alternatives, perhaps more than any other institutional alternatives, have taken root, and have a solid base of support. But the "missed revolution" is still missing.

Notes

1. For details and for a general sense of the extravagant expectations for radical educational change as the sixties became the seventies, see Michael Rossman, *Learning and Social Change* (New York: Vintage Books, 1972).

2. For a detailed description of the theory and practice of free schools, see Allen Graubard, *Free the Children: Radical Reform and the Free School Movement* (New York: Pantheon Books, 1973).

3. See, for example, James Coleman's report *Youth: Transition to Adulthood* (New York: McGraw-Hill, 1974). For the most widely read Establishment-educator support of alternative schools, see Charles Silberman, *Crisis in the Classroom* (New York: Random House, 1970).

4. For an excellent case study of CAPS—detailing the history of the development of an exceptionally successful public alternative school—see Fred Sperounis's doctoral dissertation, "The Cambridge Alternative Public School: A Case Study of School Reform" (Department of Sociology, Brandeis University, 1978).

5. It is worth noting that beyond the alternative schools, there are several "open classrooms" in the various elementary schools. This situation is common. Many districts that don't have an alternative school have some representation of the open-classroom idea, which came over from England and was growing in popularity along with the free-school notions around a decade ago. These classrooms—and the teachers and parents who choose to participate—represent the most widespread and attenuated expression of the educational-reform movement.

6. For a survey of free-school growth and development, see Allen Graubard, "The Free School Movement," *Harvard Educational Review* 42 (Aug. 1972): 351–73; reprinted in Mario Fantini, ed., *Alternative Education* (New York: Doubleday and Co., Anchor Books, 1976).

7. Samuel Bowles and Herbert Gintis, *Schooling in Capitalist America: Educational Reform and the Contradictions of Economic Life* (New York: Basic Books, 1976).

8. Ibid., p. 254.
9. Some of the most popular books of the radical school-reform movement expressed this perspective explicitly. See especially Neil Postman and Charles Weingartner, *Teaching As a Subversive Activity* (New York: Delacorte Press, 1969), and George Leonard, *Education and Ecstasy* (New York: Delacorte Press, 1968).

"Sea-Level" Media:
Up from Underground

by Andrew Kopkind

The revolution will not be televised
You will not be able to stay home, brother
You will not be able to plug in, turn on and cop out. . . .
The revolution will not be televised.
The revolution will be live.

—Gil Scott-Heron

On a good day in the early seventies, a hundred thousand young Bostonians were plugging into and turning onto one, two, or all of three media products that had created—and cornered—a vast local countercultural market. The three were FM radio station WBCN and two weekly newspapers, the *Boston Phoenix* and the *Real Paper.* When the going was good, they had exclusivity as well as dominance in their field. That heyday has waned with the years; but taken together (which many people do), they still inform, entertain, or intrude on the lives and minds of the most politically active and commercially expansive fraction of the population. Each of them has its success story to tell, and the history of all three expresses in some measure the progress and prospects of the Great White Bourgeois Cultural Revolution of the last ten years.

The Boston hip media complex has long been an attractive subject for analysis and opinionating, not only because of the profitability of its three leading ventures and the magnitude of their audience, but also because the youth, student, and studentlike community retains more of its old coherence and early characteristics than can be found anywhere else. Elsewhere, students have evidently lapsed into well-publicized apathy, and ex-student radicals have grown older, gotten jobs, and above all left town. In Boston and Berkeley and a few other localities around the country, enough people who remember the ethos of an earlier decade have stayed on—and so have been able to infuse the footloose campus generation with something that still resembles the spirit of a movement. To be sure, Boston's special demographics are not immune to the forces that have distorted or dissipated the integrity of the market around the country. To some extent, age has withered and custom staled the variety of the media offerings. But there are institutional preservatives which have kept some of the old spirits strong, and they are rooted in the history of the weeklies and the radio station.

WBCN grew from an overlookable classical and "MOR" (Middle-of-the-Road) outlet—the call letters denote Boston Concert Network—to one of the most popular radio stations of any kind, AM or FM, in New England. The two weeklies developed into journalistic and advertising competitors for television and the big Boston dailies. Only a few years ago, the *Boston Phoenix* was a throwaway entertainment sheet called *Boston After Dark,* and the *Real Paper* (then in its incarnation as the Cambridge *Phoenix*) was an unsuccessful alternative to the radical underground press. Now the "sea-level" weeklies (midway between underground and top-notch) reach more or less 200,000 readers, depending on the weather (which affects hawkers' and newsstand sales) and the academic calendar (which determines the size of the youth population of the Boston area). During prime time, WBCN may be locked into 50,-000 local FM tuners.

How much counterculture all those readers and listeners get is open to argument. WBCN offers twenty-four-hour-a-day "progressive rock" music, broken frequently by commercials and occasionally by news and public-affairs audio-documentaries perched far out on the left wing. The weeklies do as much investigative reporting and hard news analysis as talent and energy permit, but much of their space is now filled with advertising, entertainment listings, and what used to be called "feature articles" in the big-time press.

Swelling audiences are attended by swollen advertising revenues. So much so, in fact, that WBCN's annual income far exceeds $1 million—quadruple its pre-progressive figure. Its management has considered offers to sell the station for more than $3 million. The resale value of the weeklies is said to range from $750,000 to $1.5 million on the used-newspaper market; advertising income has doubled in the last three years at the *Real Paper,* and executives there report it is a "multimillion-dollar business," while the exact balance is a secret.

Only a few years ago, the publisher of *Boston After Dark* could put out his slim sheet for $500 a week. Now a single issue may contain four sections and more than a hundred pages. All the usual trappings of new wealth can be seen at the three institutions. WBCN moved out of a loft in back of the bus station to the observation deck of Boston's second-highest sky-scraper—the one without the blow-out windows. The *Real Paper* moved up from basement digs in Cambridge's seedy Central Square, through a tasteful College Gothic duplex, into a modular-plan suite in a new apartment high-rise. Editors and staffers were simply amused, but not moved, by the ironic history of that site: in the hot years of protest in Harvard Square long ago, the building's developers had to evict militants in the Ecology Action office that stood on the land. As for the *Boston Phoenix,* it is rising across the Charles River in spacious quarters on the edge of Back Bay.

But despite the Establishment success styles, an assumption remains current in Boston that the three media operations are still connected to the radical political and cultural movements of the 1960s. A radical sensibility, however attenuated, is not the only vestige that has survived in these repositories of move-ment messages from that earlier time. All the contradictions and ambiguities of the counterculture have been handed down as well: the tension between "cadre organizing" and a mass audience, between ideological authenticity and commercial suc-cess, between collective work and the efficiency of command. The assumption of a radical context for these media is reason-able; the connection with the counterculture holds. But it is no easier than it ever was to reconcile the skyscraping and the street-hawking, the ads and the ideals, the movements and the music. The weeklies and the station are events in the political and cultural history of a generation, but they are also events in its commercial development. It remains to be seen which historical version makes the most sense.

Conveniently for the chroniclers of this Boston media complex, its genesis resides in the ambition of one man alone, a youngish Missouri lawyer named Ray Riepen. In the late sixties, Riepen ruled a small hip media empire. He ran the local rock-and-roll emporium, called the Boston Tea Party. He managed WBCN. He put out the old Cambridge *Phoenix.* He put on the biggest and best Boston pop concerts.

Riepen's thoroughly midwestern fantasy in the classy East was to create a sophisticated media network out of the top drawer of the new culture of the times. He told people he wanted to rival the *New York Review of Books,* in print and on the air. He brought a Reuters news wire into WBCN because he had heard it was the best available.

The flowering of "underground" media in those days lent a certain logic to Riepen's dreams of conglomeration. He had not been able to do much with staid old middle-of-the-road WBCN, where he was manager. But chance gave him the opportunity to make drastic changes. The station's owner and founder, a former electronics engineer and inventor named T. Mitchell Hastings, became seriously ill and gave Riepen absolute control at WBCN. Not long ago, Hastings said:

> It was in the hands of a higher power. I was in the hospital having an operation for a brain tumor. Riepen decided to begin broadcasting rock music from the Boston Tea Party from 11 P.M. to 5 A.M. Then he went to full-time rock. I know it was the hand of a higher power because I never would have had the guts.

Fortunately, the higher power did not object to Riepen's cancellation of WBCN's religious programming, which brought in $150,000 yearly (half the station's income in the mid-sixties). Faith and hard sell did, however, let him replace that tithe with a like amount from newly affluent advertisers in the boutique business and the music industry. With the financial transition effected smoothly, Riepen had no trouble convincing the board of directors to approve the rock format; the station was a million dollars in debt, with no other prospects of solvency. And so in May 1968, WBCN declared that henceforth it would play only the new music from the vanguard culture, and proclaimed itself—literally—"The American Revolution."

Musical Politics

White rock culture and the white radical movement came to some sort of climax in 1969 and 1970, between the Woodstock and Altamont music "festivals," on the one hand, and the Chicago Days of Rage and the Kent/Cambodia political actions on the other. The old Cambridge *Phoenix* had started in the autumn of 1969, in conscious imitation of New York's *Village Voice,* and as a peace-love alternative to the power-struggle politics of the radical underground *Old Mole.* In six months, the *Phoenix*'s founder had blown his $50,000 investment, and Ray Riepen began sniffing at the wreckage.

"Ray understood that rock music was the underpinning of the whole thing," Harper Barnes, a sometime editor of the Cambridge *Phoenix,* recalled. Riepen quickly organized the ambition and fortune of a Harvard Business School graduate, Richard Missner (father: Chicago commodities; in-laws: Weyerhaeuser paper) and bought the paper for a paltry $15,-000. Missner was ultimately to sink $700,000 into the venture. Riepen sank the energy and imagination.

"He was an archetypal figure, a classic American entrepreneur," Barnes said. And in classic entrepreneurial style, Riepen knew how to create new demand, manipulate a cheap labor supply, and mix media enterprises in one handy package.

Although radicalism and rock were both themes of Riepen's various outlets, it was under the rock that all the money lay. There wasn't much profit to be made from street fighting or teaching-in. The music industry—records, audio hardware, live performances—was already supporting the "underground" press with advertising; more professional publications with smooth sales staffs and stable schedules could garner even bigger slices of the industry's ad budget. But changes would have to be made.

"Ray knew that the hippie ethic and 'quality' didn't necessarily coincide," editor Barnes continued. So Riepen set about to hire "professional" editors—Barnes himself had worked for a St. Louis daily—and a competent string of writers from the enormous pool of Boston/Cambridge overeducated, superfluously literate collegians. At that time, many of them seemed unable to bring themselves to work for more traditional institutions. "They'd get thirty-five dollars [from the *Phoenix*] for an article that would take three or four days to report and write," Barnes said. "But where else could they go?"

The string of leather shops, beads-and-bells boutiques, brown-rice-based restaurants and groceries, and rerun cinemas survived in Cambridge and the "freak" neighborhoods of Boston largely because of the plentiful cheap labor supply. But when a job in a "head shop" no longer seemed to be the idealistic, Aquarian act it once seemed, the subsistence wage scale suddenly became unattractive. Employers were faced with either economic demands from workers or a lack of talented employees. For this reason and others, many $35-an-article writers on the early Cambridge *Phoenix* ultimately drifted away to the mastheads of more established journals, or into other occupations, hip and straight. In that particular heyday, however, radical cultural consciousness seemed to restrict the employment options to the underground and sea-level press.

Old Mole had not been able to leap from its political burrow to address a mass audience. It was unambiguously an event in the Boston radical community's political history, and it was almost entirely unencumbered by commercial considerations. *Mole* provided a distinct service: it created a niche for radical intellectuals who could find no other comfortable place in the movement. They were talented and energetic, but they were tortured by their sense of isolation from action. And they inflicted all the expressions of their guilt on the collective operation of the paper. As one of the older Moles reminisced some time ago,

> People saw the paper as a political project or an expression of their lives—but certainly not as a journalistic job. We'd have endless debates about whether we should *ever* use established journalism's third-person form; first-person stories were supposed to be so much more real and revolutionary. I believe now that that discussion is the first symptom of terminal illness leading to the death of a radical publication.
>
> It was "The Year"—1969/1970—and all the problems of the student movement came to an excruciating head: extreme factionalism, ardent feminism, increasing militancy. The more dogmatic political people quit the paper, but the more introspective, self-involved people stayed. It was a real "living-room left." They stayed inside all the time and only got out for demonstrations. Then they'd come back in and talk to themselves.

Working for low pay in high tension made some sense while there was a political and social context to furnish support-by-other-means. Looking back on my own experience in movement media, I can remember how the existence of a real and pressing historical struggle in the sixties (or so it seemed) allowed me to believe that I was not crazy for dropping out of an established professional career in the high-reward, low-purpose conventional press. When the political context disintegrated (again: so it seemed), the feeling of support vanished apace, and it was harder for me to believe that I wasn't loony out there on the cold fringe. Steady salaries and some security were tempting again too, in the absence of loftier ideals for comfort. It saddens me a little, but hardly surprises, that the white radical movement was unable to develop institutions to house and employ its troops after the movement's own forward drive had been halted or diffused. Those who believed that the media would replace the movement, or at least form its vanguard, never understood that the role of radical media is to reflect, resonate, and relay the ideas—Correct and Incorrect— of the radical community. Without a moving, self-conscious community, the underground press had no reason for existence; and in due course it began falling of its own weight.

I gather my experience is generalized and recapitulated in the lives of many other professionals and intellectuals in the new left radical culture. As movement projects, organizations, and journals disbanded, the "activists" slid into more or less traditional slots in sea-level operations. Safely up from the underground, we found a newer (or younger) generation of colleagues who had not been in or out of the movement, just around it. Teddy Gross, who was editor of *Boston After Dark* and the *Boston Phoenix,* put it this way:

> We weren't political activists, really. By the time we were politicized we were alienated from the movement. We were very different from the *Old Mole* people. Our paper was supposed to be "radical," of course. But it was going to reach out to the community (wherever and whatever that was), deal with local problems, deconceptualize the rhetoric that was killing the movement and the *Old Mole.* So we were allowed to flatter ourselves and believe we were doing something radical and at the same time feel superior to it. It was simply radical voyeurism.
>
> We started out feeling we were a secondary line of the struggle, a supporting line for the front ranks of the movement. But then there was no front line. Everyone in the front ranks was moving back. I remember when Eric Mann, who was a heavy Weatherperson, got out of jail, he wanted to write for us. I thought that was a great idea, and then I realized that all of a sudden he was a journalist, not a revolutionary. Eventually, we all became very cynical, or career-oriented. The whole aspect of the paper tended to stress professionalism and legitimacy, and that inexorably led us away from a movement—if it still existed.

"Vanguard Capitalism"

To say that the newer sea-level institutions were more stable and "professional" than the old underground ones is not to endow them with much more than a smattering of the traditional styles of work. At WBCN and the weeklies, the ideological and interpersonal struggles may not have been as desperate as they were in the old radical institutions, but they were no less disruptive. The difference, of course, was that the struggles at sea level were being waged in a context of commercialism, around and against real bosses who played the game with hard cash. The power of money and employment to sour relations among workers is hardly unreported, but it is instructive to see how that power was felt in places where it was widely believed to be weak.

The old Cambridge *Phoenix* and its successor, the *Real Paper,* underwent a series of collective and corporate disruptions that repeated and even elaborated the radical experience of underground newspapers. By one count, there have been nine discrete incarnations of the original *Phoenix:*

1. origins: half a year under the founder;
2. first collective: the Falloon (the name derived from a Kurt Vonnegut concept), lasting six weeks;
3. take-off: the era of Ray Riepen and Richard Missner;
4. consolidation: Riepen leaves Boston, leaving Missner in complete control;
5. strike: employees unionize and are refused recognition;
6. union: Missner capitulates;
7. collective II: Missner sells the paper to *Boston After Dark,* but the old *Phoenix* staff continues to publish, collectively, under the name *Real Paper;*
8. stratification: the management "commune" begins a transformation to more traditional hierarchical and bureaucratic arrangements;
9. regression (or rationalization): the collective members sell out, or cash in, to a syndicate of financiers and lawyers, who inject new capital, energy, and respectability into the operation and manage the paper successfully along fairly conventional lines, administratively and journalistically. They agree with hardly a whimper, much less a bang, to the unionization of employees.

Conditions at WBCN were never quite so frantic. The nature of the radio business is such that technology, public "responsibility," governmental oversight, and professional status dampen the hottest hassles. But that is not to say that the contradictions were much different at WBCN than at the weeklies, or that they were unexpressed. The problems began from the very start, as Ray Riepen developed his fantasy of a new national Concert Network (WBCN had originally been one of four stations in the old Concert Network), with WBCN as the flagship. The great rock fleet would stretch from coast to coast, surrounded by Phoenician newspapers and never-ending Tea Parties.

The audience then was assumed to be the new communities of college-age and collegiate freaks, the Aquarian vanguard of a new-age culture. Eventually, Riepen and other "vanguard capitalists" believed, the tastes and values of the young would spread to older, more stable elements of the population. If WBCN could appeal to—and sell to—freaks in Cambridge in 1968, it could do the same in suburban Needham in 1978. Boston's half-million school-time students and student-age young people were considered America's most promising base for a test of that theory.

No one thought very much about the class aspects of that plan, needless to say. It was taken for granted that the audience of WBCN (and the weeklies) was and always would be more or less middle-class, educated, white, and somehow consumptively aspiring—despite the anti-consumption fads and rhetoric. There was no anxiety then that the "youth culture" would migrate to a younger, working-class base, and that it would be difficult to appeal to—and, again, to sell to—audiences of both classes at the same time.

To tighten up his flagship, Riepen brought in an old top-forty AM-radio hand named Arnie Ginsberg as WBCN vice president. Ginsberg had made a name for himself as the most hysterical and popular disc jockey in Boston during the fifties. The name he had made was "Woo-Woo," an eponym for a strange caterwauling sound he made at intervals during his disc-jockeying. Not long after Ginsberg's arrival, Riepen stumbled on all the obstacles he had foreseen at his mixed media operations, and cleared out of Boston.

"Ray saw exactly what was going to happen, right from the start," Harper Barnes told me. "He knew all these things were potentially huge successes, but that it was impossible to deal with the political feelings of the staffs and the wishes of management. Everyone had axes to grind."

Chopped off in due course, Riepen retired to a mountaintop in the High Sierra, where he remains to this day. But back in Boston, Ginsberg was tightening up WBCN. With no understanding of how valuable "looseness" was to WBCN's image, the smoothness of its internal workings, and its sales pitch, Ginsberg rushed in to "rationalize" the business. First, he discarded the nightly lost-and-found "Cat and Dog Show," a favorite in the youth community for its sound as well as its service. It was one of the things that made WBCN a friendly voice in an identifiable community; Ginsberg couldn't believe that very many people needed or wanted to find out who had lost or found a pet.

In a somewhat more sinister vein, Ginsberg began toying with national "spot" advertising possibilities. He saw that an economic foundation of waterbeds and record albums, however appealing to trendy listeners, was ultimately unstable. Flu remedies, jingles, beer ads, and shampoo spots seemed to promise a valuable addition to the economic base. No matter that the staff recoiled at the prospect, that even venturesome Ray Riepen had called national spots "garbage."

The level of paranoia among the staff rose dangerously. "No one knew what his plans were," an announcer recalled. "People sensed that he would ruin the station and abolish their jobs. The two ideas that WBCN was built on—that it was a big family with no hierarchy and a lot of self-management, and that it really served a new youth community—he almost totally disregarded."

The culminating conflict came when Woo-Woo summarily fired the station's leading announcer and guiding spirit, Charles Laquidara. Ginsberg made no specific charges and would not explain his action when questioned by other employees. At once, the staff began thinking about a counterattack, and discussions rapidly led to plans to unionize. Danny Schechter, the one-man news department, had been active in radical politics all through the sixties and had some academic and practical background in labor organizing. He made inquiries of the

United Electrical Workers, a left-wing industrial union expelled from the old CIO in the cold-war era. The UE was undergoing a renaissance of a kind, and while it had no experience with young "professional" workers in the counterculture, the union took on the WBCN organizing project. Management at first refused to take it all seriously, then panicked and threatened a lockout. But without much of a fight, the staff voted for the union, and the disc jockey on the air at the time broke into the song "Joe Hill."

Labor Pains

In the fullness of time, similar scenarios were played out at the two weeklies, with widely different consequences. The trouble began at the old Cambridge *Phoenix* when owner Richard Missner fired the editor, Harper Barnes—again, for generally unspecified high crimes and misdemeanors. What really seemed to be going on was that Missner, like Ginsberg, had become convinced of the evanescence of the hippie culture and the hippie economy. He wanted to explore different "demographics," decrease reliance on entertainment advertising, and reach out into a straighter, richer, older audience. The Barnes editorship was too strongly identified with a "loose," freaky, struggly image and operation.

As at WBCN with Laquidara's sacking, the old *Phoenix*'s staff organized in protest of Barnes's firing and voted to form a union. There was staff sentiment against a national union of the kind WBCN had adopted: the available models (the Newspaper Guild, the American Federation of Television and Radio Artists) were thought to be old-fashioned, bureaucratic, professionalistic, elitist. The sea-level workers of the counterculture were on to "new" issues: collective decision-making and self-management, antisexism, multi-issue politics, communitarianism, good vibes, good food, and good taste. The Cambridge *Phoenix* staff decided not to affiliate nationally.

Schechter at WBCN had seen nonaffiliated radio-station unions collapse after a few huffs and puffs from management. In fact, WBCN's bosses were following the tactics developed by the management of San Francisco's KMPX during a strike by a nonaffiliated staff "collective" there. An article by the KMPX management on collective-busting was duplicated and distributed to members of the WBCN board of directors. Schechter argued that a nonaffiliated local could never consolidate any success it might win with the energy of initial protest.

The nonaffiliated local at the Cambridge *Phoenix* "won" its strike, but the staff never got the leverage on the paper's management that they needed for control. Two months after Missner recognized the union he sold his paper to Stephen Mindich of *Boston After Dark.* There, too, the factors that led to unionization at WBCN and the old *Phoenix* were piling up. A few days after Mindich had bought the Phoenix "name" from Missner (for $320,000), he decided he had had enough of the radical/freak audience.

"My objective . . . has been to create an urban weekly newspaper that would reach out to a broad young adult consumer," he said in an interview at the time he consolidated *Boston After Dark* into the *Boston Phoenix* (the summer of 1972). "Well, damn it, we're not an underground newspaper." Mindich insisted that he was aiming at a new out-of-college audience, in which "suddenly you're faced with earning a living, you're probably getting married, having a household. We seem to be moving more and more toward this group . . . the adult McGovern supporter—people who are not ready to chuck the country and run away, or say 'down with America' . . . and we're looking for people who are consumers. Our readers have bank accounts . . . they have investment portfolios."

Mindich saw the *Boston Phoenix*'s competition as the daily *Boston Globe,* the radio stations, and the monthly magazine *Boston,* a slick journal of the "city magazine" genre. To reach their audiences and their advertisers, he wanted "more representation," he said, of center and right-wing opinion. Costs had risen from the $500 it took to put out *Boston After Dark* in 1966 to $18,000 or more for the weekly *Boston Phoenix.* "You can't put out 90, 100, or 120 pages on waterbed advertising," he noted sagely.

Pressures to "reach out" for consumers and advertisers in new audiences were expressed as strictures against radical politics, as rules for full work days, as a need for entertaining or sensational articles, as a rejection of the less salable aspects of the countercultural ethic. The staff began to feel the restraints, and reacted. As editor Teddy Gross explained,

> For a while, we very successfully blocked Stephen and his motives out of our minds and assumed that this was some kind of convenient marriage of Heaven and Hell. Our justification was that these capitalists want to reach the same people as we do: their market is our constituency, their consumer is our activist. Cohn-Bendit said that if he had come to a publisher with a manuscript before May 1968, they would have thrown him out; after May they were begging at his feet. We thought that if these publishers are fool enough to let us do what we want, so much the better.
>
> What happened? We simply got sucked in.

The external conditions of commerce and respectability on which a successful weekly was predicated were internalized by the writers and editors as surely as they were by the salesmen and managers. Gross and the other editors did not have to be told what the new order was, what restrictions on tone and politics should be maintained, what compromises should be made. When some staff members complained—about sexist advertising, for instance—other staff members argued that advertising policy was "not our department," and that what was good for the paper's business was ultimately good for the employees. If writers wanted, they could write anti-sexist articles —so the argument went.

Somewhat tardily, the less co-opted writers and clerical workers on the *Boston Phoenix* staff followed the steps to unionization taken earlier by WBCN and former Cambridge *Phoenix* workers. By early 1973, an employees' association had been formed. It affiliated with the United Electrical Workers, which by that time was buzzing around several workplaces of the counterculture.

But despite a favorable ruling by the National Labor Relations Board and help from friends in related "shops," the employees at the *Boston Phoenix* were not yet recognized as 1974 began. Publisher Mindich was strongly opposed to unionization; he has often threatened to close the paper rather than submit. He was charged by employees with squeezing out those who were active in union organizing and insisting that anti-union applicants be hired for new jobs. The NLRB cited him for more than twenty unfair labor practices, and some fired employees won back pay. But the struggle drained too much energy. Half the employees on the roster in mid-1973 were gone six months later, and the organizing drive finally slowed to a stop.

Given the history of disruption caused by union organizing at WBCN and the *Boston Phoenix,* it was logical for the savvy new owners of the *Real Paper* to recognize an in-house "employees association" without much of a fight. (Only minority-stockholder David Rockefeller, Jr., among the *Real Paper*'s new owners, argued against recognition.) Unlike ego-involved Mindich at the *Boston Phoenix* and conservative-minded Hastings at WBCN, the cool corporate types at the *Real Paper* figured that what was good for General Motors or CBS was fine for them, too; there was no reason that a union could not be made to fit very well into their corporate plan for the paper.

Tightening Up

The arrival of the weeklies and WBCN at the threshold of financial success, status, and stability produced almost identical results in the relationships within the various staffs and in the attitudes the writers and announcers brought to their work.

Self-censorship

At WBCN, the announcers and the news and public-affairs producers had stretched industry mores and federal regulations about as far as any commercial broadcaster in the country. The daily news programs and the public-affairs documentaries (which I worked on from the summer of 1972 to 1977) were as radical, in the post–New Left sense, as our imaginations could make them. But increasingly, the staff's eagerness to be culturally and politically radical was circumscribed by internalized values of commercialism. Punches were pulled, and although it was hard to determine whether the restraints were imposed by the need to organize a mass audience or the need to soothe it, the bite to WBCN diminished. How it came about was not always easy to see. There's no need to hatchet radical opinions or analyses; it is smoother to jumble them in a welter of music and sound effects, to lay on a veneer of professionalism or "objectivity," or to avoid tricky issues in favor of entertaining "features." The line between selling out and cashing in is hard to draw, and more often than not the effect deemed to be the most "commercial" is merely the one you can get away with.

"Free-form" radio survives in only a handful of American cities, at only one or two popular and financially successful FM stations. WBCN was probably the last and most prominent example. What's free about free form is that announcers' taste and discretion determine the music programs. There is no "play list" of prescribed records, as at almost every AM station (and most of the commercial FM ones). "Sets" of songs may be connected musically, lyrically, emotionally—or in any way that makes sense to the announcer. Talk and music shows are integrated as much as possible. An announcer may play a version of Bob Dylan's song "Stealin' " after a news commentary on the ripoff aspects of a Dylan concert tour. The disc jockeys refer to their four-hour stints on the air each day as their "shows," and they take some pride in their creative manipulation of music and other sound elements to produce an artistic entity, like an improvised dance or an ad-lib monologue.

But commercial considerations limit the freedom of the announcers' free forms. Unrecognizable jazz, unfashionable folk, and minority-oriented music are heard less and less as audience and advertising increase. An early sign of such limitation came at WBCN in 1973, when the program director (a disc jockey not much different in style or attitudes from the others) decreed that only a few rhythm-and-blues songs could be played during each announcer's show. Listeners were thought to prefer white rock. (As it turned out, R&B exploded into a new level of popularity a few months after the rule was imposed, and it was never seriously followed; but the theory behind the rule remains in force in each announcer's mind. Free form now means catering to popular taste *most of the time.*) Several times a year, during the weeks when survey agencies are "rating" the various Boston stations by polling listeners, programming is carefully monitored to appeal to current fashions of the majority audience.

An egregious example of commercial pressures affecting announcers' freedom came in the summer of 1973, when one of two women announcers was laid off. The step was taken officially for economic reasons (the move to high-rent offices and a bad first quarter were squeezing profits) but actually because her show and her temperament were thought to be too stridently feminist. Out of guilt and a sense of union obligation, the staff supported the woman in a brief battle to get her rehired. In the end a "compromise" was reached whereby she would supervise an hour-a-week Women's Show, with no other responsibilities. But in private, most announcers, of whatever political persuasion, agreed that her show had only a limited appeal, and that it was not conducive to reaching the biggest audience possible.

The deterioration of WBCN's free form accelerated as other stations stepped up their struggle for high ratings in the same demographics that WBCN courted. The upstarts' competitive advantage lay in their lower standard of freedom in the progressive format. They hyped up the "mellow" FM style WBCN announcers practiced, they limited the allowable play list, and they curtailed political and public-affairs air time—all in the attempt to reach a bigger, less discriminating audience.

And they were successful. WBCN's ratings dipped and the management panicked. The long-time station manager was fired and a new man with no connections to the counterculture was imported. What had been the most stable staff of any such FM rock station in the country suddenly broke apart: in the space of several months the program director, the star disc jockey, several popular announcers, the leading news and public-affairs staffers, and several other employees jumped ship. Every case was unique, of course; but there is no question that the passing of the order of eight years' duration was occasioned by the pressures on WBCN to respond to the new level of competition by becoming similar to it.

Hierarchy and Bureaucracy

The palmy days of communal management at the *Real Paper* (successor to the Cambridge *Phoenix*) faded shortly after the spirit of collective ownership encountered the same "demographics" that informed the WBCN and *Boston Phoenix* managerial outlook. The two weeklies are read by roughly the same number of people, according to every survey. The *Boston Phoenix,* however, has convinced advertisers that it appeals to a less freaky, more professional, less Cambridgey, more suburban readership. (There is no way to measure the truth of this claim.) Consequently, the *Boston Phoenix* gets big ads from local department stores, automobile dealers, and appliance retailers that elude the *Real Paper*'s salespeople.

To survive in this competitive atmosphere, the *Real Paper* tightened up, straightened up, and lightened up—its management, its image, and its editorial content, respectively. The collective's decision to sell the paper in 1975 must also be seen as a response to commercial competition. The old editors and writers in the collective were tired and dispirited—"burnt out" in the familiar phrase—but their alienation was not only of their own making. They had been forced, without much thinking about it, to imitate the more rigid, hierarchical managerial styles of the *Boston Phoenix* and the noncollective world outside the *Real Paper*'s door. It was a natural, if not inevitable, response to the demands of keeping a weighty financial operation in motion. But it ceased to be fun. The new owners have no illusions of collectivity, and will be slower to burn.

Both professional and clerical workers at the three workplaces entertain fantasies, from time to time, of real self-management, or participation to some degree in the operational and policy decisions affecting their media product, their work styles, their relationships within the institution. Only during the *Real Paper*'s brief communal phases was true participation and self-management achieved. At WBCN, the union (which excludes the program director, the chief engineer, the bookkeeper, and some ad salespeople) has won moderate economic benefits. At the time of the layoff of the "feminist" woman announcer, it won a very small victory in the compromise that resulted in the addition of the Women's Show to the weekly programming. But other programming policy is laid down by "management" and adjusted—if there are grievances—by informal negotiations with the most personally powerful announcers. A "Special Committee" of union and management representatives, set up under the current contract to provide more day-to-day operational liaison, did not prove effective. Staff resentment at the tone and political content of ads (some are blatantly sexist, others promote products of colonialist countries, etc.) cannot be translated into successful action. "I used to get upset at Costa do Sol ads [Portuguese wine]," one announcer said, "but after four years of getting upset, it's not worth it anymore."

Isolation

WBCN's retreat to the stratosphere atop the Prudential skyscraper is nicely symbolic of its isolation from the lives of its listeners. But location is not the only isolating factor. Professionalism, careerism, and financial comfort—all attributes of success—keep the media and the media stars and starlets from the world beyond the microphone or the press.

At the same time, the media cease to be receptive to the culture and politics that gave them their genius. Listeners say that WBCN "isn't what it used to be." There is a tendency for staffers there to answer, "nothing is": the music isn't what it used to be because the counterculture isn't what it used to be . . . and so forth. But WBCN is certainly more remote. The announcers are in touch with a media world rather than a broader community of people. Their taste reflects what their colleagues say is good and what the record industry is pushing this month. Every one of those sources says that "the people" are demanding this or that style; but what happens more surely is that audiences are accepting the convenience-packages of the industry as sold by announcers, artists, and critics. "Glitter rock," for instance, was invented by the record industry to exploit some of the gaudier sensations of sexual liberation. Disc jockeys and performers went "into" it because they believed the audience wanted it. But who's the chicken and who's the egg?

Culture and Media

"The people who started these organizations didn't anticipate their exploitative nature," a WBCN staff member mused over lunch one day at the Orson Welles Complex restaurant (another pillar of the Boston area hip-capitalist infrastructure). "No one foresaw how banal and how inevitable exploitation would be." There has not been much heavy-handed repression, outright censorship, or callous manipulation at the three media institutions. Rather, the exploitative aspects of work there and their effect in the community follow subtle attitudinal and structural responses to plain old business competition and expansion.

Together, these media have been responsible both for some positive developments of consciousness and for an advantageous creation of workplaces in the communities they reach. Not only the short "generation of the sixties," the agitated political radicals of the civil-rights and antiwar movements, find comfort and succor in countercultural capitalism. Succeeding waves of young, white, middle-class collegians (and college dropouts) find sea-level businesses and middle-ground professions much more *possible* than the high-up, Establishment institutions of the straight culture. Places like the Boston weeklies and WBCN meet a very real need for the post-sixties class of young people who have assimilated the styles and tastes and some of the values of the counterculture and demand places to live and work within those loosely bounded lines.

My own experience with all three of these Boston media operations is that despite unpleasant and at times ominous backslides into straight business practices, they still provide more communitarian, unintimidating, nonauthoritarian, and service-directed opportunities than their traditional counterparts. Similar countercultural institutions in other fields—clothing stores, restaurants, groceries, cinemas, health services—appear to be equally "comfortable" vis-à-vis conventional outfits. Of course, all the contradictions and ambiguities seen in the media enterprises surely hold true elsewhere in the alternative business infrastructure. But as long as the demand for them continues—from workers perhaps more importantly than from customers—they are not likely to "sell out" completely to old styles and consuming values.

That demand is felt in the Boston-Cambridge area more strongly than in most other parts of the country. Its half-million students and student-age young people are the region's most striking demographic feature. That accounts for much of the success of the media and other hip businesses. WBCN's little-sister station WHCN in Hartford, Connecticut, was sold in 1974 because Hastings and the Concert Network board of directors despaired of finding enough countercultural listeners to make "progressive rock" programming attractive to advertisers. Hartford has a *potential* youth culture audience of about 25,000.

Boston's exceptionalism also explains the survival of two financially viable weekly newspapers when few can be made to show a profit in other cities that have tried them. That is not to say that the alternative press, as the sea-level media are commonly known, is limited to the enclaves of Boston and Berkeley: at a Seattle conference in 1977, for example, representatives of some thirty weeklies much like the two Boston papers met to discuss the problems of their trade. But the *Real Paper* and the *Phoenix* are in some ways both prototypical and archetypal. The alternatives around the country are survivors, either literally or figuratively, of what was once a burgeoning underground press. To assure that survival, papers elsewhere had to follow similar historical paths: tighten up the business, lay back on the politics, follow the demographics of the eighteen-to-thirty-five "upscale" market.[1]

In a sense, of course, the *Phoenix* and the *Real Paper* are simply two incarnations of one phenomenon. Despite differences in internal organization and certain stylistic disparities, the two have always been indistinguishable to most readers; no one I've ever met can remember in which paper he or she has seen a particular story or advertisement. *Boston Phoenix* publisher Stephen Mindich once said that he saw no "need in terms of both the advertising community and the readership community for two publications doing very much the same thing. There aren't enough dollars to go around." Although Mindich's perceptions are no doubt colored by his interest in monopoly, that argument is fairly widely heard—and yet the two weeklies progress, side by side. And both are quite profitable to this day.

What effect they've had, and WBCN too, on the climate of Boston is of course a subjective judgment. But it is fairly clear that the tolerant and to some extent radical "breathing space" identifiable in this region is reinforced and partly organized by the day-to-day operations of these three outlets. Some attribute Massachusetts's majority for McGovern in 1972 to the influence of the counterculture and, by implication, to its media. Atmospheres and climates, of course, are hard enough to measure, and harder still to analyze in terms of origins and causes. One obvious effect that can be traced, however, is the pressure generated by the weeklies on the daily press, particularly the *Boston Globe,* to investigate the murky depths of local politics and payoffs. *Boston After Dark*'s penetrating investigations of a downtown real-estate development scheme and, on another occasion, of the shady practices of a city politician got the paper wide publicity and to some extent shamed the *Globe* into undertaking similar muckraking projects.

In time, however, the *Globe*'s commanding position in finances and logistical resources let it overtake the weeklies in the muckraking game. That, and the feeling on the part of many of the weeklies' writers that muckraking was "going nowhere"

—except, as *Boston Phoenix* editor Teddy Gross said, "to strengthen the system by pointing out its weak points. Unless you stumble on a great scandal, it doesn't do much."

Without a political purpose such as investigative journalism, the weeklies have nothing striking to offer except "entertainment," fine writing, and some analysis. Editors of both papers are always looking for a new formula to replace the original plans. And if the papers do not advance journalistically, they will be unable to keep the best and the brightest of the young countercultural writers and reporters. Publisher Mindich is convinced that the *Boston Phoenix* can be only a way station for good journalists on the way to bigger and better careers, either as freelances and independents, or in national counterculture media such as *Rolling Stone,* films, or book publishing.

The future of the sea-levels, in the end, depends not so much on this or that journalistic formula, or the details of management and structure, but rather on the ability of a viable political culture to sustain its own media. The media reflect the social context as well as transmit it. The myth of media-as-politics dies hard; it is only reinforced by the sensations of Watergate and the relationship of the press and television to exposure and shock. The media didn't make the radical movements of the sixties, despite the claims of columnists and commentators. If anything, the myth of the media dragged the movements down. A real radical culture will not be televised, taped, and rerun. It will be live, and the media it spawns will organize and inform the culture, not supplant it.

Note

1. For a report on the Seattle conference and some reflections on the late-seventies state of the alternative press, see Calvin Trillin, "U.S. Journal: Seattle, Wash.," *The New Yorker,* Apr. 10, 1978.

The Uncertain Revival
of Food Cooperatives

by Daniel Zwerdling

A winter's Saturday morning at the Bethesda Community Food Store co-op, in a suburb of Washington, D.C. But it could have been any one of hundreds of co-op storefronts sprinkled across the nation. I find the store, the size of an old-time mom-and-pop grocery, squeezed among an auto-supply outlet, a Jeep showroom, and a greasy-spoon luncheonette in a car-jammed shopping district. Inside, I discover that the first aisle is reserved not for food but for neighborhood communiqués. A large bulletin board is two layers thick with file cards advertising for yoga students or a "sensitive woman to join communal house"; offering recipes for sesame-seed buns and soybean casserole; and condemning ITT's meddling in the Third World.

I take a worn, wrinkled shopping bag from the recycled-bag bin, pass "Breast Milk Is Best" and "Kick the Junk Food Habit" posters, and stop at the pasta stand—nine varieties of whole-wheat noodles sold in bulk from the cardboard cartons they were shipped in. Shoppers crowd around the bulk-liquids stand, a rack of five-gallon jugs sticky with six different kinds of oil and three varieties of honey.

A co-op volunteer, an economics professor at a local university, is unloading baskets of tomatoes, leeks, yuca root, and nectarines into the well-stocked produce bins; other volunteers are slicing hunks of cheese from a large wheel and piling them in a cooler stocked with forty different domestic and imported brands. I take a carton of milk from the small dairy cooler— "We feel that food is a basic right and that it shouldn't be sold for profit," a sign proclaims. "Milk, being a staple necessary to most diets, is being sold for only a few pennies above our costs so that those in need can afford it."

Then I come to the Bethesda co-op's tour de force. In the middle of the store are sixty plastic barrels, altar to the noble grains, legumes, beans, seeds, flours, dried fruits, and nuts that the supermarkets have shunted aside. There are barrels of rye flour and soy flour, bulgur wheat, millet and rye berries, wheat flakes and turtle beans, pinto beans, mung beans, sunflower seeds, soy grits, cashew nuts, macadamia nuts, dried peaches, and dried pineapple.

I squeeze past the community craft stand—home made pottery, jewelry, and T-shirts for sale—and join the long checkout line, waiting for the lone, and painfully slow, volunteer cashier. Most of the shoppers clutch a few sacks of flour and beans, a couple of vegetables, perhaps a jar of wildflower honey and some dried fruits. Average purchase: about six dollars.

The Bethesda Community Food Store, with its sticky honey tins, whole-wheat lasagna, slow checkout line, and all, has joined the most important surge of food co-ops since Franklin D. Roosevelt's New Deal promoted co-ops as a path out of the Depression. Some observers call the contemporary renaissance of food co-ops the "new wave": between five and ten thousand have blossomed like wildflowers during the last decade, according to the Cooperative League of the U.S.A. (CLUSA), and rough estimates indicate that perhaps several thousand still exist.[1] These new-wave co-ops—scattered from Louisville to New York City, from Chicago to rural Maine, from Austin to the Puget Sound—are selling more than half a billion dollars' worth of food each year.

The new-wave co-ops come in different shapes and sizes. Many, perhaps most, resemble the buying club that transforms a New York City hallway each Saturday into the neighborhood produce market. There, according to researcher William Ronco, members chip in $5 a week; a volunteer plunges into the massive Hunts Point wholesale market and buys a grab-bag of whatever produce looks best; then the members, back in their Manhattan hallway, divvy up the riches.[2]

But some co-ops, such as the Bethesda Community Food

Store, have revived the disappearing neighborhood grocery. In Phoenix, Arizona, for instance, the members of thirty-six labor unions have transformed a fast-fried chicken outlet into a co-op storefront that sells hamburger 40 percent cheaper than the local supermarket. And perhaps a dozen of the new-wave co-ops, in cities such as Boston and New Haven, Minneapolis and Denver, have blossomed into full-scale supermarkets. Denver's Common Market co-op sprouted in 1972 as a weekly buying club, funded by the University of Denver student government. Today the co-op sells almost $1.5 million worth of food each year from a former Safeway in downtown Denver.

New-wave co-ops—sometimes called "food conspiracies" in the early days—first began to appear around 1970 on college campuses, as radical activists shifted their focus from confrontation politics to the quiet, methodical task of building alternative neighborhood economic institutions. But when food prices exploded—increasing almost 50 percent between 1972 and 1976—the co-op idea began spreading into working-class and even upper-class neighborhoods as well. So while the workers at one food co-op in Washington, D.C., proclaim they are working toward the "overthrow of capitalism," the family of Vice-President Walter Mondale contributes its $5 every week to a co-op food-buying club in an upper-crust neighborhood not far away.

Despite their dramatic differences, the members of most co-ops and collective alternative food stores share a certain spirit: something has gone wrong at the conventional supermarket, they believe, and by joining together in co-ops with their friends and neighbors, everyday citizens can create their own food-supply system and do the job right. In an era when supermarket chains are hiking food prices to increase their profits (Safeway more than doubled its profits between 1970 and 1975, according to *Business Week*) food co-ops can cut food prices because they are nonprofit—or "antiprofit," as the more radical ones put it. In an era when most resources are controlled by private corporations, food co-ops return a measure of control to the average folks on the block, who can elect the store's board of directors and even vote directly on major co-op policies. And in an era when most food stores promote highly processed and hazardous foods, food co-ops can promote the old-fashioned, wholesome staples. This common chemistry gives most co-ops a similar look. At Safeway and A&P the diet comes plastic-wrapped, artificially flavored and freeze-dried in a pouch, and often priced by a laser beam. At most co-ops, the food comes in big barrels or pour-your-own tins—and is rung up by a volunteer who still can't find the $10 key on the cash register.

"Today's giant corporations, with their monopolistic prices, are like the royalty the colonists overthrew," declares the Washington-based Exploratory Project for Economic Alternatives. "Co-ops are a practical, self-reliant alternative—they are a declaration of independence from the corporation."[3] In their efforts to declare such independence, the new-wave co-ops have come to symbolize the present era's struggle to create new, democratic political and economic institutions.

It would be a mistake, however, to picture the nation's new food co-ops as a *movement,* united in their purpose and striving for common goals. For while most co-ops agree on what they are declaring their independence *from*—the oligopolistic supermarket industry—they sharply disagree on precisely what kind of food system they want to establish and what kinds of goals they want to pursue instead. Some co-ops seek mainly economic benefits—purchasing fresh and wholesome foods at a low price. Others seek the camaraderie of joining in a useful activity with their neighbors. Still other food co-ops see their business as a pretext for organizing members of the community in a struggle for radical political and economic change. Seldom has a single economic form, the food co-op, served such dramatically different interests.

Whatever their objectives, food co-ops have taken on an immense task: like David challenging a thousand Goliaths, the co-ops have plunged into battle with one of the nation's most powerful and seemingly unstoppable forces, the $200 billion food industry. How they fare in the battles—how some co-ops grow and why some co-ops collapse, what goals they achieve and what goals they feel forced to abandon—offers valuable insights into the potentials and problems of any movement to restructure the American economy from the ground up.

The seeds of the Bethesda Community Food, like those of most new-wave co-ops, were planted more than a hundred years ago. Twenty-eight weavers and artisans in Rochdale, England lost a work strike in 1844; to maximize their meager and dwindling resources the strikers pooled $140 in savings and formed a cooperative nonprofit store, stocked with basic items such as sugar, candles, and flour. The members of the co-op jointly controlled store policies on the basis of one member, one vote, and at the end of each year they divided equally whatever surplus they had earned. These strikers became known as the Rochdale Pioneers. By the 1860s, more than four hundred consumer co-ops like theirs had spread across England.

Immigrants brought the idea to the United States, and by the end of the century, food co-ops and other co-op stores were sprouting across the Northeast and Midwest. Many of them were formed by labor organizations such as the Knights of Labor and others whose ranks were filled with immigrants. Co-ops were weapons for economic self-defense: "Like the frontiersmen who banded together for protection against the Indians," writes co-op historian Joseph Knapp, "these newcomers banded together to set up cooperative stores to protect themselves from economic exploitation."[4]

With these early co-ops came grandiose visions of what they might accomplish. In the late 1800s Edward Bellamy (author of *Looking Backward*) proclaimed the coming of a "cooperative commonwealth." In 1915 a rich visionary named Nelson Olson launched a network of cooperative stores and food factories in Louisiana that he said would transform the impoverished countryside into a land of prosperity; he actually had established more than sixty retail stores, plus a bakery, milk plant, and farm before he filed for bankruptcy. Around the same time the Cooperative League of America (forerunner of the present CLUSA) was formed, backed by liberal luminaries such as Walter Lippmann, Paul Douglas, and Jane Addams. The League painted visions of consumer and manufacturing co-ops growing up across the nation, creating vast networks that would transform the entire society.

But these visions, and the co-ops that were part of them, were doomed to a fleeting existence. Big business was on the march, and the finance industry was scarcely in the mood to bankroll democratic people's co-ops. Banks ignored them, some state legislatures tried to outlaw them, and (according to some historical accounts) hostile business interests even tried to burn them down. In this climate, few co-ops were able to survive more than a few years.

During the New Deal, however, co-ops fared better. Hundreds were begun, with government funding, under the aegis of the Federal Emergency Relief Administration's Division of Self-Help Cooperatives—food stores, bakeries, farms, manufacturing plants. Utopian visions again: one of Roosevelt's top aides proclaimed the coming of a "new village life" in America founded on "closer relationships and cooperative enterprises." But financial support for the co-ops died with the end of the New Deal, and most of the co-ops died with it. Not all: at least two have survived until today, the Consumers Cooperative of Berkeley and Greenbelt Consumer Services, near Washington, D.C.

One kind of co-op did take root and prosper—farm marketing co-ops. What made them work was not so much any intrinsic differences between them and the consumer co-ops, but the fact that the government assured them a long-term source of capital from the Farm Credit System of farm co-op lending banks. Today farm co-ops have become big business, thanks in part to the $26 billion that these banks lend to them *each year.* Sunkist, the nation's largest citrus marketer, is a co-op; so is Farmland Industries, an oil, fertilizer and feed empire with annual sales approaching $1 billion.

A bill introduced in Congress in 1936 would have created the same kind of banking system for food co-ops and other consumer stores, but it never emerged from committee. And so with few exceptions, consumer co-ops in America were doomed to an ephemeral, if inspired, existence: individual co-ops would constantly appear and disappear, but co-ops as an economic institution would never take root, never build a secure economic foundation from which future co-ops could grow.

This is the dowry that U.S. history left to the "new wave": inspiration and vision, but no economic support. The new-wave co-ops were born in the same feisty spirit as those of the early immigrants: "Co-op food stores are a self-defense measure," said one Washington, D.C., activist who helped organize co-op food stores. "People are getting ripped off by the supermarkets, and they need to do something about it right now. It's an emergency measure, a matter of survival." And, like the co-ops a century before them, the new-wave co-ops were launched not with capital but with volunteer labor and sweat. When Safeway opens a new supermarket—and it opens 125 in an average year, according to the corporate annual reports—it sinks more than $1.2 million just to build and stock it. When student organizers of the New Haven Food Co-op decided to expand their association of basement and backyard buying clubs into a tiny store, they struggled to raise $2,000 from friends and neighborhood residents plus $900 from a benefit dance. To launch the food co-op in Bethesda, organizers knocked on hundreds of doors in the community until they sold $8,000 worth of food coupons, redeemable for groceries at a future—and financially stable—date. When the Boston Food Co-op moved from its room on the Boston University campus to a rehabilitated tire warehouse, members of the community plunged in to scrape off years of grease and oil, seal leaky roofs, and heave tons of second-hand milk and meat coolers. The pioneering spirit of the new co-ops came not from nostalgia but from economic necessity. "Local bankers," one Washington co-op organizer said, "wouldn't touch us with a hundred-foot pole."

Sprouted in such spartan and hostile soils, neighborhood food co-ops have achieved some remarkable results. One of the major objectives of the new-wave co-ops is to cut food prices, and despite the supermarket chains down the street, many co-ops have succeeded on a considerable number of products. When I stopped by a Safeway in Washington, D.C., in late 1977, for instance, shoppers were loading their carts with half-gallons of milk for 81¢ instead of only 72¢ at the Bethesda co-op around the corner. Oatmeal at Safeway was more than twice as expensive, eggplants and cabbage cost two and a half times as much, and some cheeses were selling for a good 10 to 50 percent over the co-op prices. These differences are not unique to Washington, or to the time I checked. Ronald Curhan and Edward Wertheim surveyed twenty-four food co-ops in the Boston area in 1971; they found shoppers could save a whopping 33 percent over supermarket prices on their fresh fruits and vegetables.[5] Other studies suggest that even with all the other groceries on the food bill—dairy, grains, packaged foods—shoppers still can often save from 10 to 25 percent at co-ops.

Food co-ops sell for less partly because they *don't need* to hike prices to pay for supermarket-style advertising, fancy stores, huge parking lots, and hefty corporate profits. They also make it easier for shoppers to spend less money than at the supermarket. It's the psychological climate: while the basic strategy of a supermarket is to encourage shoppers to spend as much as possible, the philosophy of most co-ops is to help shoppers spend as little as possible. Denver's Common Market, for instance, tags foods with special "price alerts": they publicize not only great bargains that shoppers should purchase but also bad buys that shoppers should avoid.

Most co-ops save money by recruiting members for volunteer labor; customers, in effect, are paying part of their food bill with time rather than cash. The New Haven Food Co-op, for instance, has more than a dozen full-time, paid staff members, but it relies heavily on volunteer shoppers to hoist boxes and stock the shelves and slice the cheese; the co-op will cut about 8 percent from your bill whenever you shop if you volunteer a mere one hour every month. St. Paul's Green Grass Grocery, a storefront launched with the proceeds from a neighborhood festival and a loan from the landlord, is managed entirely by volunteers.[6]

Efforts to lower food bills complement another important co-op goal—to shift consumers away from synthetic and processed foods toward a wholesome, nutritious diet. Conventional supermarkets design their advertising and shelf displays to promote the highest-profit items, which usually are processed foods rich in fat, sugar, artificial colors and other potentially hazardous additives. While most supermarkets were devoting prime shelf space to highly sugared breakfast cereals—the most profitable cereals on the market, according to industry trade journals—the Berkeley co-ops were kicking two-thirds of the sugary brands they carried off the shelves. At the same time, the co-op launched a consumer education campaign against high-sugar breakfast foods—and sales of the extremely profitable products plummeted 50 percent between 1974 and 1976, according to the Berkeley *Coop News.* Sales of nutritious low-sugar cereals "went way up."

During the same period, Berkeley began selling giant bins of irregular, blemished produce for less than half what local supermarkets were charging for more perfect versions; at one point peaches at Berkeley were going for 12¢ a pound versus Safeway's 39¢. Produce sales zoomed 25 percent, according to co-op statistics—which suggests that lower produce prices prodded many shoppers to shun convenience foods and go back to the real thing.

To a considerable extent, food co-ops have offered consumers the possibility of taking control over sales of their single most precious resource, food. Co-op shoppers can't control how the food is raised or processed, but they can at least control which foods are sold and how. At most new-wave co-ops, major policies are formulated by a board of directors elected by the members. How do you become a member? Each co-op has its own criteria. To become a member of Denver's Common Market you chip in a $5 contribution and then volunteer one hour's labor every month (or pay $2 a month instead). You can help elect the Bethesda co-op's board of directors, which rotates every three months, if you merely work three hours in the store during the month before the vote. At some co-ops, such as the Common Market, members not only elect the board but decide major policies, too. For instance, when board members of the co-op a few years ago proposed expanding from their small storefront to a vacant supermarket, a controversial move that some members feared would destroy the co-op's informality and warmth, the board referred the decision to the entire membership for a vote. (Members approved the expansion by a wide margin.) And while community activists were picketing major supermarkets such as A&P and Safeway in a futile effort to persuade them to boycott non–United Farm Workers lettuce and grapes, members of the Common Market were calmly instructing their board, through a special binding referendum, to join the boycott. This concern for democratic control has led many co-ops to create a system of worker self-management, whereby employees operate as a democratic collective, not as traditional workers taking orders from a boss. At the New Haven co-ops, for instance, the dozen full-time, paid staff members have decided to divide themselves into three teams—and each team manages a different part of the store as an independent unit. The teams get together to vote on issues that affect the entire co-op.

The new-wave food co-ops have created still another alternative to conventional supermarkets—an alternative that is less tangible than lower prices on carrots, an exotic variety of whole grains, and an occasional referendum. This alternative is a *spirit* that permeates many co-ops, an almost religious spirit that seeks to satisfy the human needs forgotten in the plastic-coated world of a corporate supermarket. Some of the people who work and shop at co-ops seem almost starved for a sense of communion with the earth and with their food, and co-ops help provide it. Our Store Food Co-op in Fresno, California, boasts in its brochures that it's a place "where a pound of rice is weighed on a scale, not wrapped in a plastic bag"—as if scooping those kernels of grain into a bag with your hands is more nourishing to the human soul. And members of the Coordinated Produce Orders for Maine Co-ops, a buying service for a dozen Maine buying clubs, vie with each other for the bliss of driving two hundred miles to the Boston wholesale market —just so they can experience the din and the colors and smells of an old-time produce market.

For many co-op members, working once a month in the store fulfills an emotional need: "I can't tell you how much joy I feel working here," one Minneapolis co-op volunteer said. "In a way it's brought back the days when a grocery was a social event—people around the wood stove, drinking coffee, talking. We do the same thing here, slicing up wheels of cheese, drinking herb tea, and talking. And maybe it sounds corny, but I feel I'm doing something important for my family and community."

Reading literature on new-wave food co-ops, you get the sense that relationships between people in the stores are far more important than the relationships between sales and profits. The Safeway 1976 Annual Report, for instance, ends with the note that "Capital expenditures for 1977 are expected to approximate $270 million. . . ." A recent report on the Boston Food Co-op ends with the observations that "Relationships among staff members have always been more intimate than what one would expect to find in a traditional job" but that "Staffers need to be open, to confront others with minimal emotion, and to make themselves confrontable."

In some ways, then, the co-op movement seems to be both successful and growing. Minneapolis and St. Paul boast more than a dozen alternative food stores. There are more than two dozen warehouses across the country formed just to supply the buying needs of new-wave co-ops. Along the West Coast, Midwest, and East Coast there are several interstate co-op trucking networks. Some co-op networks are growing strong enough to establish their own small processing plants: in Vermont and Canada, for instance, a federation of about ten co-ops called the New England People's Cooperatives has joined forces with an organic growers' organization and established a co-op organic grain mill. "We get about 150 letters a month," said one top official at CLUSA, "most of them asking, 'How can we start a food co-op?' "

But despite these signs of success, the long-range prognosis for food co-ops in America is more sobering. Economically, food co-ops are in trouble. Individual co-ops are succeeding, and individual cities are building strong co-op networks—but co-ops as an economic *movement* confront a difficult and uncertain future. It's uncertain because co-ops are suffering an identity crisis: ask twenty different co-ops to describe their most important goals and strategies for achieving them, and you'll get twenty vastly different answers. The future will also be difficult because many co-ops are fighting just to survive. While the Washington area's Bethesda Community co-op earned a $35,000 surplus in 1976, the nearby Fields of Plenty co-op tottered on the brink of bankruptcy. Denver's Common Market has suffered such chronic losses that its members have voted to lend the co-op $10 per year each, until the store gains financial stability. The Berkeley co-op, one of the few survivors from the thirties, expanded to three new stores in recent years—but in 1977 its directors issued a "Member Alert! Our cooperative is facing a financial crisis of declining member patronage and increasing [monetary] losses. . . ."

"Whenever I speak at a conference of co-op organizers," says Art Danforth, former secretary of CLUSA, "I start out my speech saying, 'If we hold this conference again next year, eighty-five percent of you won't be here.' "

Why are co-ops in trouble? "When we decided to open this store," said the organizer of one food co-op in the Washington, D.C. area, "we naïvely figured all we had to do was eliminate the profit margin and we'd have the cheapest food in the world, and people would flock to the store. It all seemed so easy.

"If I had known one-tenth about the crushing realities of the food industry as I do now," he said, "I never would have tried to start a food store, not in a million years."

The single most crushing reality is this: while co-ops attempt to create an alternative food system beyond the control of the food-industry octopus, they need precisely the same nourishment that Safeway does. That's money—lots of it. And the key to accumulating money is adequate size. Yet from the first day a food co-op forms, its fundamental nature guarantees that money and size will be painfully beyond its reach.

Consider Stone Soup, Washington's first antiprofit, alternative food store. The store is not technically a "co-op," since members of the community can't vote for the store's directors, but its troubles are typical. Crippling labor costs were the first problem. Since the store was so small—about 1,600 square feet, common for a co-op storefront—there wasn't much shelf space to stock food. Workers had to restock items constantly. As sales volume increased, the stocking problems got worse; even with volunteers helping out, the store had to keep hiring more workers, driving labor costs so high that it couldn't accumulate a financial cushion. When sales slumped suddenly the first summer, the store plunged into a financial crisis. "We started bouncing checks and suppliers cut us off," an organizer named Steve Clark remembered. "We had to cut salaries and had to go out borrowing money again"—from rich friends—"just to stay alive."

Since most co-op storefronts are so small—compare the Bethesda Community Food Store's 2,600 square feet to the 28,000 square-foot Safeway down the street—they are unable to handle much sales volume. And in the U.S. food industry, big sales volume is the key to operating a financially sound business. "Del Monte wouldn't even look at us twice when we called them," Washington's Clark said, "because to buy direct from Del Monte you have to buy in semi-trailer lots." That means small food co-ops (and most co-ops are small) have to buy from local wholesalers by the case, at a premium price. Even at Denver's supermarket-size Common Market, store coordinator Kathy DePaola said, "We've had to pay two percent higher at the wholesaler than bigger markets because our volume wasn't high enough." The co-op can't buy on credit, because the wholesaler demands a $30,000 cash deposit—a mammoth sum the store has not been able to afford. And *that* means the co-op can't accumulate crucial financial reserves, a potentially fatal weakness should sales begin to sag. Even the two dozen new-wave co-op warehouses across the country, which buy in bulk for the co-op stores in their areas, can't generate enough volume to bring the co-op stores more than modest savings. "Lots of brokers of prepackaged foods come in and scoff at us," one worker in Washington's Community Warehouse said. "They don't want to waste time with someone like us who buys in less than carload lots." The Community Warehouse handles less than $10,000 worth of food per week; a typical supermarket-chain warehouse handles weekly sales of at least $500,000.

These economic problems are inherent in the food business,

but they are made worse by difficulties that might have been avoided. Co-op history is littered with the carcasses of food co-ops whose organizers had plenty of enthusiasm and commitment but little or no business experience. "When we made the move [from a storefront to a supermarket] I didn't know anything about running a supermarket," Common Market coordinator Larry Hotz said. Within six months after opening, the Common Market had plunged $20,000 in debt—partly the result of "a poor meat department, lack of organization, and untidy shelves," according to Jonathan Klein, a worker with the North American Student Cooperative Organization. And after a jubilant first year in which they earned a $35,000 surplus, staff members of the Bethesda Community Food Store suddenly discovered they were on the brink of a financial crisis. Why? A board of directors committee decided to inspect the chaotic financial books, and found that costs had soared while income had dropped. "I have absolutely no idea what the money situation is now," the co-op bookkeeper said with a shrug. "We're not into the establishment-accountant thing of keeping official records of every little financial detail."

All these economic difficulties add up. They mean, for one thing, that many co-ops cannot sell all their food products as cheaply as co-op devotees imagine. While Bethesda Community co-op offers some stunning savings over Safeway prices on many vegetables, cheeses, whole milk, grains, and spices, for instance, you'll pay 6 percent *more* at the co-op if you're a skim-milk drinker, 10 percent more for butter, and 38 percent more for eggs. Bulk oils at the co-op cost considerably more (26 percent more for corn oil) than at Safeway—and even among the grains and produce the savings are not constant. Shop at the co-op and you'll save on kidney beans, unbleached white flour, and brown rice—but you'll lose on Great Northern beans and, ironically, whole wheat flour. You'll pay far less at the co-op for onions and zucchini but more for broccoli and oranges. You won't find any canned goods at the Bethesda co-op, but if you drive a few miles to the Fields of Plenty co-op you'll pay double the Safeway price on canned tomatoes; when it comes to processed foods, co-ops just cannot compete. As for meat: not one of the alternative food stores in Washington sells it. "It's partly because so many of us are vegetarians," said one co-op worker, "but it's mainly because we can't handle it economically."

In the cold, ruthless world of shopper comparisons, this means that few if any shoppers buy most of their groceries at the co-op. They merely pick up the best bargains and then desert to Safeway or A&P for the rest. "I like to come by once every month or so when we run out of honey, grains, peanut butter, herbal tea, and stuff like that which is so cheap at the co-op," one woman shopping at the Bethesda co-op said. "I'll pick up some vegetables, too, if they're looking good. They're really cheap; it's a shame they're so often bedraggled." Wilted produce is an eternal co-op dilemma; most co-ops, such as Bethesda or Boston Food Co-op, can't afford produce-display coolers. ("Chances of spoilage, rot, and wilting are great," according to one former worker at the Boston co-op, "especially in the hot summer months.") Many co-ops do themselves the added injustice of forgetting such establishment-style amenities as frequently mopped floors, nicely painted walls, and sparkling clean cheese bins: "It's a little dirty here," one shopper at the Bethesda co-op confided, "and if I'm in a queasy mood I just stay away."

The co-op food stores, far from their visions of replacing the supermarkets, have become specialty stores. And so they become locked into a vicious economic circle: low volume, higher costs, not enough top-quality foods at low enough prices, fewer customers, low volume . . . Workers in the food co-ops get understandably distressed as they watch customers buy $6 worth of groceries and then head for the corporate supermarkets to load up their carts with $40 worth. "It's really frustrating to see that people who shop here won't support us simply because they believe in us politically," said a worker at Washington's Fields of Plenty storefront, which tottered last year on the brink of bankruptcy. "They should understand that if they support the store now politically it will serve them better in the long run." But few people pinched by climbing food prices can afford to indulge in the luxury of paying higher prices for some items just to support a correct political line. And the shoppers who can afford it don't care to, if the price of their political support is a wilted head of lettuce.

In an effort to attract more consumers and increase their income—and survive—many food co-ops have felt compelled to compromise or even forsake their original goals. "It's a trade-off," as one Washington co-op worker put it, "between political purity and economic survival." For instance, while co-ops have viewed their role as a means of economic self-defense—protecting workers from inflation by offering food at lower prices—many co-ops have badly exploited their *own* workers in a desperate effort to keep costs down. Typical wages in the Washington area nonprofit stores hover around a paltry $2.50 an hour; the Bethesda co-op, the most successful nonprofit food store in the Washington area, pays its six staff members only $4.50 an hour, compared to a possible $6.73-an-hour-plus-benefits at the Safeway supermarket down the street. "The only reason we can even compete with supermarket prices is because our wages are so low—not to mention all the volunteers we need," one co-op organizer said. "It's really kind of a scandal. But the fact is, if salaries were raised across the board, most of the nonprofit stores would fold."

A good number of co-op stores are also abandoning their original visions of carrying only wholesome, healthful foods. Store workers believe that too many shoppers are turning away when they can't find their favorite processed foods amid the soy grits and wheat flakes. "We don't have stuff like Cap'n Crunch breakfast cereal [a heavily sugared brand] right now, but we plan to," one worker at the Fields of Plenty said. "We think that's a reason why more working-class people in the community don't shop here . . . We think more working-class people would come if we carried more junky foods." The Common Market long ago resolved a heated debate over whether the new supermarket-sized store should carry processed foods with potentially harmful additives. "The current position of the Board and the Business Coordinator," wrote co-op organizer Jonathan Klein, "is that unhealthy products . . . must be carried both as a service to the neighborhoods and to keep the co-op alive economically."[7] The co-op makes peace with itself by posting signs to steer the customers toward the more healthful items.

Swept up in pursuit of economic survival, it becomes easy for even the most ardent co-op activists to shunt more ideological goals aside. Worker self-management was once a crucial aspect of the Common Market co-op, as at many new-wave co-ops—the co-op's major organizer, Larry Hotz, had been leader of the Denver chapter of Students for a Democratic Society (SDS). But when the co-op expanded to its supermarket quarters, the group's leaders decided the store could survive only with the "efficiency" of a more traditional, hierarchical staff. "Today, the store is operated on a much more linear model than ever before in its history," Klein reported—a development which other co-ops concerned with economic survival report as well.

Co-op workers preoccupied with credits and debits tend to forget one of the major reasons why so many new-wave co-ops were formed in the first place—to take food stores away from the control of private corporations and make them truly community-controlled economic institutions. When the New Haven co-op was still a small storefront struggling to "establish the volume of business necessary to survive in competition with more conventional stores," reports former co-op worker Winston Dines, "the organizers had little energy left to publicize the ideals and motives of cooperative business and to develop new strategies for membership participation." As a result, said Dines, the co-op "tended toward a hierarchy of centralized power and decision-making, leaving most members feeling excluded."

New-wave food co-ops have tangled with the realities of doing business in the United States. The result: even the most politicized and radical co-op activists are becoming more pragmatic. In fact, many of the new co-ops are raising the same battle cry of the corporate food industry they are struggling against: get bigger. Build bigger co-op stores, build more co-op stores. "Scale is the key," one co-op organizer in Washington, D.C., said. "It doesn't make any sense to open more [storefront-sized] stores. We have to concentrate on supermarket-sized stores.

Mom-and-pop-type stores are more romantic, but they just can't survive."

The battle cry is provoking sharp controversy in the movement. Look at any co-op that has expanded from a storefront to a supermarket: you'll find a clash between co-op members who said the move was crucial for survival and those who charge that "bigness" means selling out. The New Haven co-op's move to its current supermarket location was stiffly opposed, according to Winston Dines, by members who felt the large scale was "too impersonal" and "too much like a replica of the food industry [rather] than an alternative to it." Five years ago it would have been hard to find a member of the new-wave co-ops who didn't ridicule the Berkeley and Greenbelt co-op chains, survivors of the New Deal, for precisely those reasons. "We don't even talk with those people," one Washington new-wave activist said in a 1972 interview. "We might as well talk with somebody over at Safeway." Four years later the same activist approached officials at both co-op chains for guidance and help.

So far, talk of growing and expanding in the new-wave co-ops is little more than a dream, for there are few ways the co-ops can get financing to expand. A report by the House Committee on Banking, Finance, and Urban Affairs (May 13, 1977) chronicled how banks have stymied co-op growth. "Outpost Natural Foods, in Milwaukee, is bursting at the seams," the report declared. "Yet three blocks away there's an abandoned Kroger store—large enough to make a small co-op shopping center possible." But the banks won't lend any money. A food co-op in Port Washington, N.Y., had enough business to justify building a warehouse, but they were "stopped cold by lack of a capital source," according to the House report. Even the Berkeley co-op chain—a titan in the co-op world with its thirteen markets, 86,000 member families, and annual sales topping $70 million—was turned away by ten banks and several other financial institutions when it went shopping recently for a mortgage on the co-op's choicest property.

History suggests that the only successful co-op movement was financed by the U.S. government—the farm marketing co-ops, nourished by the network of co-op banks established in 1933. Now many co-op food-store activists say they have learned the lesson. "The ultimate answer to our financial difficulties, the only way nonprofit food stores are going to grow and become a significant social force, is to have public money," said Mark Looney, co-director of the Washington-based Strongforce, Inc., which gives technical assistance to co-ops and other alternative food stores. One bright hope for many co-op leaders is the Consumer Cooperative Bank Act, passed by Congress in 1978. The act established a government-controlled consumer co-op bank, with substantial amounts of Treasury cash to lend to co-ops and to provide both technical assistance and seed money. Eventually the bank is to become self-sustaining, nourished by loan interest and stock sales, and control will pass from the federal government to the borrowers, meaning the co-ops themselves. If the bill works out in practice as its proponents hope, it will do for food stores and other consumer co-ops what the Farm Credit System did for marketing co-ops—propel them from the periphery of the U.S. economy to status as a powerful economic movement. At this writing, however, it is too early to tell what the result will be.

Without government assistance, is there any way food co-ops could gain economic strength? The only possibility, many co-op workers agree, would be for co-ops to join forces—to form large networks that consolidate their wholesale orders, build more and larger warehouses, and create interstate trucking networks. "If you have a bunch of separate co-ops, they can't generate the capital resources to open new stores," said former CLUSA secretary Danforth. "I'm always saying to co-ops, 'Consolidate, consolidate. That's the only way you're going to grow.'" And how much will co-ops have to grow in order to wield clout? "If you have much less than $20 million wholesale business per year," says Danforth, "you can't run a wholesale business in normal food-industry terms—which means you don't have the buying power to order food to your own specifications." Twenty million dollars means pooling the buying power of twenty co-ops the size of Common Market.

Efforts to unite food co-ops on this scale will confront formidable odds. The major obstacle is this: the food co-ops across the country, even the food co-ops within a single city, do not share the same political and philosophical visions and goals. Most co-ops share a common desire for cheaper and more nutritious food, and a belief in community self-help. But beyond that, there is no clear movement of co-ops that share a common political vision of what is wrong with the U.S. economic system and just how food co-ops fit into the strategy for changing it. Co-ops in America have never shared a common political base—in fact, political and economic theories were anathema to co-op leaders in the first half of the century. In 1928, in an era of roiling social, economic, and political ferment, the congress of CLUSA passed a resolution banning any *discussion* of "Communist, Socialist and other political or economic theories" because they were "fields of divisive, controversial opinion." How would co-ops lead America toward economic utopia without a political-economic theory or strategy? Co-ops, the congress assured, would somehow find "an evolutionary solution of the people's problems."

The historical reluctance of co-ops to position themselves in an economic and political context set the stage for the dramatically diverse nature of food co-ops today. Seldom has one economic form been adopted by so many different economic and political classes. Some co-ops, such as a $10-a-week buying club in a neighborhood of $150,000 houses in Washington, are content to get a pretty assortment of fruits and vegetables every week. Its members enjoy the weekly outing to the wholesale markets by Washington's spaghettied railroad tracks—a kind of "slumming" which brings the co-op's wealthy members in contact with the grease and sweet-rotten stench of an old-time market. "We don't want any members who are going to rail against grapes because they're non-union, or anything like that," one member explained. "To us, politics in a food co-op are irrelevant."

Yet across town, members of another co-op argue that the ultimate purpose of food co-ops is precisely politics—the politics of revolution. They talk about food stores as "strong, effective organizing tools," for launching "radical programs which will help bring about the demise of capitalism." "Selling food isn't our goal," as one member of the Fields of Plenty alternative food store explained. "It's just a pretext for building living and breathing models of revolutionary change."

How can co-ops as diverse as these ever hope to unite to form a nationwide cooperative system? Even co-ops which do share a common political purpose, such as building models of radical economic change, are notoriously unwilling and unable to unite on any scale essential for building significant economic power. A few years ago, for instance, food co-ops in Madison, Wisconsin, agreed to contribute 1 or 2 percent of their monthly incomes to a "community sustaining fund," which would finance community political and economic projects, but the co-ops fought bitterly over how to spend the money, and the fund fell apart.

"We're anarchistic," one Washington food-store activist said. "The co-ops in Minneapolis are very isolationist," a co-op worker there declared. But the co-ops' contradictory dilemma —anxious to grow yet anxious to remain totally independent— is nowhere so clear as in a letter, sent in 1974 by Washington's Community Warehouse to other co-ops in the southeast. "The possibility of the collapse of the present capitalist economic system in the near future points out the need for anti-profit systems to be strong enough to survive such a collapse," the Warehouse collective wrote. "Someone has to feed the people." Then the collective declared: "We all value local autonomy and seek to avoid the monolithic development of the co-op movement which came out of the last depression. . . . This is a battle that each of us must fight alone."

American food co-ops stand at a turning point in economic history. On the one hand, they have grown in the face of monopolistic food corporations in hundreds of cities and towns across the nation. On the other hand, they can't gain the economic strength necessary to take root in the American economy and build a system that reaches beyond the immediate neighborhoods where they're located. Food co-ops could be on the verge of receiving crucial financial help from the federal government—yet even if co-ops did get large-scale financing, many would not be sure what to do with it.

The new-wave food co-ops do give encouraging evidence that ordinary citizens—with few resources but enthusiasm, vision, perseverance, and plenty of hard work—can create neighborhood economic institutions that provide important, if temporary, alternatives to the corporate style of buying food. Whether these alternatives can grow beyond their neighborhoods will depend to a great extent on whether co-op members can unite in some common political vision.

It's little wonder, then, that the mood of many co-op workers seems to swing so precipitously between what one co-op worker in Ann Arbor, Michigan, calls "illusions of grandeur and burnout." "Some days, when I see all these people in here, I think we really are the vanguard of a social revolution," said a young worker in Washington's Fields of Plenty. "Other days, when the landlord reminds us we owe him rent and we have to throw away a case of squash which is rotting, I think: this is just a game. We're not going anywhere with this tiny store. Then a week later the future seems rosy again."

Co-ops may not yet be the vanguard of a social upheaval. They may not put the supermarkets out of business. But for the people who shop and work there—for the people buying bags of cheap bulgur wheat and filling their recycled jars with natural peanut butter—food co-ops offer the *beginnings* of an alternative way of providing this precious resource, food. Without the food co-op alternative, however fragile it may be, there would be none.

Notes

1. Many of the new-wave co-ops are not legally and technically "co-ops," as CLUSA defines the term. But "food co-op" is used loosely to mean any "alternative" food store which has a large measure of community influence or control and which is not-for-profit.
2. William Ronco, *Food Co-ops—An Alternative to Shopping in Supermarkets* (Boston: Beacon Press, 1974).
3. EPEA press release, announcing publication of *Cooperatives at the Crossroads* (Washington, D.C.: Exploratory Project for Economic Alternatives, 1977).

4. Joseph G. Knapp, *The Rise of American Cooperative Enterprise, 1620–1920* (Danville, Ill.: Interstate Printers and Publishers, 1969).

5. Ronald C. Curhan and Edward G. Wertheim, "Consumer Cooperatives: A Preliminary Report" (Boston University Working Paper, 312 Bay State Road, Boston, Mass., 1971).

6. Ronco, *Food Co-ops.*

7. Jonathan Klein, "Common Market Cooperative—Denver, Colorado," in *Nonprofit Food Stores: A Resource Manual* (Washington, D.C.: Strongforce Series on Worker/Community Owned Businesses, 1977), p. 45.

Communes
in Cities

by Rosabeth Moss Kanter

In the early days of the contemporary commune movement, urban communes saw themselves as wayside inns on the route to the country.[1] City houses looked like country communes once you were past the front door: windows full of plants, batches of drying herbs, tattered oriental carpets, clutter of furniture, pets, smells of incense and marijuana, old barn boards, and rough wood shelves in the kitchen holding mason jars of organic grains. And long-haired people mused about when they'd have their piece of land. But gradually the city commune lost its back-to-the-land nostalgia and attracted a different constituency: young professionals, single parents, and a few middle-class families.

Urban communes now have little in common with their rural or spiritual counterparts. Their purpose is not a return to the land and a retreat from technology. Nor do they plan to build a new community or to further particular spiritual ideals. Urban communes exist to create a collective household, a shared home, an augmented family. Like traditional families, the members of these "domestic" communes often share no specific values beyond intimacy, no activities beyond domestic chores and companionship, and no time together beyond evenings and weekends. Members commute to city jobs like other workers. While they may participate in the urban counterculture, their involvement with city life itself is conventional.

Urban communes have their roots in traditional family values as well as in America's long communal history. Outwardly they resemble nineteenth-century families-with-boarders and twentieth-century cooperative houses. Before 1969, those few urban groups that created communes solely for domestic purposes were virtually invisible. In 1974, the Boston area alone had over two hundred identifiable communal households. One prestigious, countrylike suburb of two thousand families had at least twelve groups in 1973.

The crisis in the nuclear family is often blamed for the rapid rise of collective households. This in turn leads to speculation that future family forms will be radically different from traditional conjugal family structures. I doubt it. I think the outward form is less the issue than the change in underlying relationships among family members, whether communes or conventional nuclear families.

Long-term family trends have made urban communes possible, and at the same time have made traditional families more vulnerable to dissolution. But communes have not invented new family relationships. Rather, they bring into focus and speed up the process of change in family norms that has been taking place over many years. Assumptions of not so long ago no longer ring true for many, perhaps most, American families: "A woman's place is in the home"; "Children should be seen but not heard"; "That's women's work." Communes take these trends beyond what most American families would find comfortable today. But families based on intentionally created relationships of mutual support, rather than rigid roles determined by the biology of sex and age, may well be the norm in the future, whether the families are communal or nuclear. Urban communes may be the forerunners of "postbiological" families, where biology no longer determines status, role, who lives with whom, and how decisions are made within a family grouping.

Urban communes themselves are unlikely to be the family form of the future. They are too temporary, transient, and conflict-ridden. But they do signal shifts in family process, and they are laboratories for new kinds of family relationships.

The first urban communes were in hip-bohemian-student parts of the city. Now they can also be found in quiet suburban and exurban neighborhoods where large old houses provide comfortable settings for eight or ten increasingly affluent people. As often as not, the size of a commune is determined by the number the house will hold. Each adult, coupled or not, generally has his or her own room, and small children often share a room. The amount and use of space in urban communes is important, for they are *places,* settings for family life, more than they are groups of specific people. Most communes take their names from their addresses, like "Cushing Street" or "Greenbrook Road." They refer to their living arrangements as a "house," as in "house meeting," or "friend of the house" (a friend of everyone's), or "I'm taking my house out for dinner."

A few countercultural communes are centered around enterprises (a Cambridge commune runs a bookstore and craft shop) or shared religious tradition (Jewish communes in many cities, Mennonite communes in Kansas). For the most part, however, the house itself is the drawing card. Membership is surprisingly varied, but the young, the uncommitted, and the recently separated are most likely to have the opportunity or feel the need for urban communal living.

The Redbird Street commune was formed by a political group. The renovated multiple-family city building was financed by a married couple with inherited wealth, Sharon, twenty-six, and Carl, twenty-seven, parents of a three-year-old. The other adults are in their twenties and thirties, and include the divorced father of an eight-year-old boy. Two women in their late thirties, both with daughters, left Redbird last year because of life-style conflicts. For one it was too organized; for the other, too disorganized. Occupations of the present Redbirds run from teacher to part-time construction worker. Sharon and Carl have the strongest ideological commitment to communal living. They are thinking of starting a new community on a larger scale, and without them it is unlikely that Redbird Street will survive. Not surprisingly, single people often join communes to meet practical needs couples don't share. Like Sharon and Carl, couples more often join for ideological reasons.

The Brills' commune represents another configuration altogether, the augmented family. Jean and Harry Brill, both thirty-seven and parents of three daughters, fourteen, ten, and six, began to add other people to their rambling fourteen-room urban house in 1969. Several couples and individuals have since come and gone. Present members include a fifty-year-old divorcee, now back in school; two men, a law student and a priest, twenty-six and thirty-six; and a twenty-three-year-old woman artist. The Brills, including the children, enjoy sharing their lives and household chores with other people, and they miss those who leave.

Much rarer is a family cluster such as Blue Stream Farm. It was started in 1970 by five families from a Unitarian church group on fifteen acres in a wealthy shoreline suburb. Ten children, ages four to seventeen, and nine adults, twenty-nine to fifty-six, now live there. Blue Stream resembles a traditional utopian community more than an urban rooming house (one of the outbuildings around the big white farmhouse is even called Utopia), for members have strong beliefs in a committed community. They are very sad when members leave. One night recently they brainstormed eighty-two ideas for their future, and they changed the name from Blue Stream Farm to Blue Stream Community, hoping to attract more prospective members. The commune also responds to mid-life-change rumblings. Two couples have switched partners and one of the new couples plans to remain at Blue Stream.

Communal Styles

Though people seek communal settings for a variety of individual reasons, the communes themselves have in common certain styles of living that anticipate a change in what we mean by "family." Family life is more public, and the boundaries between nuclear families are blurred. The closest human relationships, especially man-woman and parent-child, are less private. Outsiders within a household who are privy to the most intimate details of family life are not new, of course. In the late nineteenth century, taking in boarders was common, and upper-class families have had live-in servants throughout the ages.

But the particular mixture of strangers who themselves try to *create* a family in the city and witness each other's private lives not as outsiders with limited privileges, but as full-fledged members with equal rights, is new. It belongs to the same contemporary era that can broadcast "An American Family" coast-to-coast and turn encounter groups into weekend recreation.

The "publicness" of family is reflected in the way communes use space. For example, the bedroom, a private single-functioned preserve in the ideal, typical, one-family household, becomes a multi-purposed room for sleeping, working, and individual entertaining, since each member has only one private room. Because all members are free to invite guests, if not to the common rooms then always to their own, no individual or "head of household" or nuclear family can control the flow of people in and out of the house. There are frequent grumblings about other people's guests, especially strangers who appear at breakfast. In Greenbrook Road one woman complains that if she makes bacon for herself in the morning and leaves the room, someone else's visitor is apt to eat it. Visitors respond to the public character of the house by treating it less like a home than like a museum (the "house tour" is nearly universal) or a hotel (wandering around the bedrooms looking for a bathroom or opening the refrigerator in search of a snack).

Another theme shared by urban communes is the notion that family feeling can be intentionally created. A basic premise is that a group of strangers or casual friends, recruited from referral services, newspaper ads, or mutual acquaintances, can develop not only the external supports families provide their members but also the special, close, loving feelings. A new technology of instant intimacy developed in the sixties, along with an examination of the pathologies of that "ideal" human group, the family. At the same time, an increasing separation of two classical meanings of "family" developed. One is a set of specific, biologically bonded, age- and sex-differentiated relationships, irreplaceable and obligatory. The other use of "family" is a metaphor for a quality in relationships—supportive, sentimental, warm, loyal, self-disclosing—regardless of the kinds of ties and the kinds of people who share the feelings.

Homosexual marriages, single-parent families, artificial "kin" networks, childless couples: all compete for inclusion in the definition of family through a stress on quality of relationship rather than structure or biological base.

Urban communes deliberately try to develop family feeling within their households. Whatever their other shortcomings, most communes succeed admirably in making dinner a warm, fulfilling event, nourishing in emotional and spiritual as well as physical senses. Many groups begin dinner holding hands in a ritual moment of silence. Members take turns cooking, and ordinarily no one has to cook more than once a week. As a result, much energy goes into preparing dinner, and meals are often feastlike. People linger around the table long after dinner exchanging stories, laughing, sometimes discussing household business.

In most urban communes, members take care of each other in ways common to any family group. To be sick in a commune means there is company around and someone to make chicken soup, which someone inevitably does. Occasionally a member asks for a meeting to discuss a personal problem. Advice, help with tire-changing or painting a room, and transportation are always nearby. Though members of urban communes typically do not pool incomes, they tend to help out-of-work members. Greenbrook Road has its own "medical insurance" that pays members' medical bills. Communes also talk about providing emotional support, but the success of this depends on the particular house. Communal living itself sparks emotional and interpersonal conflicts.

Holidays and celebrations—classic "family occasions"— punctuate the life of the more "together" urban communes. Usually such holidays are for the "family" alone; outside friends are not invited. Greenbrook Road, currently in its sixth year, has four yearly holidays, including an ecumenical Easter-Seder every spring and the celebration of Epiphany, a combined Chanukah and Christmas, every January. By now a rich body of tradition has accumulated: a mimeographed Seder, special foods, a traditional rhythm to the day of Epiphany. Former Greenbrookers often return to be with the "family."

Along with traditions and rituals, urban communes also develop stories, legends, myths, family portraits, family albums, and collective symbols. Greenbrookers' photographs line a kitchen wall. On another wall is a large mandala, a circular painting in twelve parts, each section drawn by one of the members. Another group took a collective name from a television program they watched together early in their existence and became known as the "Swan family." During an evening of joking around the dinner table, one house invented a character, Steve Thoreau, named after their street and a dinner guest. From then on he was the symbolic "head of the family." Postcards from traveling members and internal messages are sent to and from Steve Thoreau. Magazines come in his name, and Christmas gifts are given to and by him.

Negotiation rather than authority is the basis of relationships in urban communes. Role distinctions are blurred, as they often are in communal settlements historically and cross-culturally. Communes try to equalize the status of men and women and the status of adults and children. Decisions are usually made by the whole group at weekly or bi-weekly house meetings, which last until a consensus is reached. One group I visited stayed up all night to agree on admitting a new member. Formal authority is not recognized in most urban communes. Even when some people have more influence than others, that influence has to be negotiated, and it may not even be overtly acknowledged by others. Couples sometimes play a parentlike role toward other members, particularly if they have a special stake in the house, but "parent" is a pejorative word when used by one commune member to another. One group put its cat as "head of household" on census forms rather than single out a member. Another commune, a stable group with several members in their forties, tries to acknowledge each member's influence in special areas and to give each equal credit. I observed several house meetings where Laura played an especially strong role. She checked consensus, restated issues, and generally policed the interaction. Her opinion obviously carried much weight, but when I asked the group who their leaders were, they said that Laura is good at meetings, Jim makes decisions about the kitchen, and so forth. They named every member, including, "John leads us in drinking and having a good time."

Changes in family norms are most clearly reflected in the equal work sharing of communal households. Everyone, sometimes even young children, cooks and does the dishes once a week. Shopping responsibilities are rotated. And everyone has a piece of the house to clean, sometimes a long-term specialty, sometimes a weekly rotation. Work assignments are usually posted prominently near the refrigerator, a common communication center in urban communes.[2] Greenbrook Road has "area committees," like its kitchen committee of two men and a woman. Nightly kitchen cleanup rotates among everyone, but the kitchen committee takes larger responsibility for cupboards, the inside of the refrigerator, and the stove. Denny, self-named "Ecology Man," looks after garbage, trash, and recycling. Other houses mount collective cleanups reminiscent of the work "bees" in nineteenth-century communes. On Saturday mornings the vacuum cleaner hums in the background as men and women interchangeably push brooms and wax floors. Blue Stream combines work with outreach. Every weekend they invite friends and visitors for a workday of repairs and projects, like the barn they are currently building.

Despite attempts to devise egalitarian work systems, however, house-cleaning is the one aspect of domestic routine communes struggle with least successfully. There are more fights about cleaning than about any other single issue in urban communes. Family therapists tell me that cleaning fights also occur with increasing frequency in "liberated" couples. Because relationships in communal households are negotiated rather than authoritative, and because little besides the basic space-in-the-house is shared, the cleaning issue is the principal arena for power struggles—how to make order, whose standards prevail. Proponents of "clean" and "neat" are also proponents of order and collective responsibility. Those who are messy tend to resist order and deny the legitimacy of collective demands. This is a political issue and not entirely one of differing standards of cleanliness. One woman whose own room is spotless, for example, is among the messiest users of common space.

In the Colorado Avenue house, issues of dominance and commitment were played out in seven months' worth of fights over cleaning. Jim was the central figure. At meetings he would declare, "I want this house clean!" Others interpreted this as, "I am committed to this house, and I want it my way." His "commitment" won over two others. His "power move" alienated him from the other three, and the house was split, three-three. Jim finally presented the issue as one of caring. "Do you care about the house? Do you care about me? If you cared about me, you'd keep the house clean." This plea won over the dominant member of the opposition, a man who prides himself on his concern for others. Now the house is much cleaner, though not to Jim's complete satisfaction. This outcome is rare, however, and occurs primarily in highly committed groups. More typically, anarchy drives out order.

Similar themes emerge in house after house. Many commune people respond to the state of the physical house as a symbol for the state of the group, the state of relationships. Sherry of Greenbrook Road reported:

> When I get fed up with people, sometimes I get very down. When we first got back from Christmas, the kitchen stayed in a perpetual mess, and I got so I just didn't want to go there, so I didn't. I'd eat my breakfast in my room and just go up there for dinner, and by then it'd be cleaned up. When it started to get cleaned up, I felt better and better about people, and then I started to feel good about the house again.

People also respond to the cleaning issue in terms of equity, a difficult problem for a supposedly participatory group. The "clean" people resent the fact that they must do more to make a comfortable environment for themselves than the "messy" folks. Said Don:

> I assume that in any communal situation I am going to have to do a hundred-and-ten or a hundred-and-twenty percent of my share in order to make it work. When it gets to be three and four hundred percent, I start to feel bitter. Also when I feel like someone else is doing only fifty percent.

Kids as People

Living in an urban commune is a mixed blessing for kids, but the egalitarian ethos seems to be a good thing for them. Children of school age and even younger are treated as separate people able to make their own decisions, obey the norms of the group, speak for themselves, contribute to the work of the household, confront, and be confronted. Parents in communal households tend to set few directions for kids other than self-discovery and learning to trust. More than one parent stressed in interviews that adults should be honest and open with children but that the children are entitled to form their own relationships. Says a mother of two small girls, "I want people to really care about the kids, to be straight with them. I don't care *how* they deal with them—that's their relationship, and I don't get involved." Another mother of a six-year-old boy sees her child's separate relationships as a problem for her, but feels she cannot interfere. "I lack control over other people and how they relate to him. Living here means he can learn anything from anybody, and I can't tell them how to relate."

The parent's role as intermediary for the child declines. People are encouraged to go directly to the child if they have an issue with him or her: "He's a human being and doesn't need me to intercede." Further, commune parents try to influence their children, but rarely coerce them to do something for their own good. "Benjamin's a fussy eater," one mother reports about her nine-year-old son, "but I finally stopped shoving food down him. It's his body, I decided. I've told him what's healthy, and now he's got to make the decision."

Formal demands on children and adults tend to be equal. Children have their chores to do from an early age and may be included in the regular job rotation. In the Brill family commune everyone, age six to fifty, cooks once a week, though each child has an adult assistant. On a recent visit, six-year-old Barbara was making cheeseburgers for dinner. At suburban Hilltop House, chores are divided by spinning a job wheel with

Benjamin's as well as everyone else's name around the periphery. His favorite room to clean is the living room, and he sometimes volunteers three times a week to do the dishes (to his mother's dismay, since she is his back-up person). No less but also no more is demanded of Benjamin than other house members. According to his mother,

> He's not going to do the living room as well as I could do it, but I think it's important to give equal responsibility. Unfortunately, all the adult members don't do their jobs, so it's hard for me to say, "Benjamin, this house is clean except for your room." I can't come down hard on him when he looks around and sees others haven't finished their jobs.

Children have a public role in urban communes, and they also have a public voice, or at least learn how to make their voices heard. They are encouraged to attend house meetings, and they learn to bring up their issues directly with other members of the household. Seven-year-old Mary came to a house meeting in her nine-person suburban commune to complain that adults were eating the ice cream and cones, supposedly "kids' food." She confronted people individually and responded to one person's remark that he never eats ice cream by insisting, "But that's not the issue. There is never enough. . . ." And later, "Don't be defensive with me!" She won her point. Benjamin routinely brings up house issues at meetings, like when the living room needs new light bulbs. Roger, six, knows he can go to house meetings when he wants to but usually doesn't. "It's boring," he says. "They just talk and make rules."

Experienced commune kids develop a noticeable ease in relating to people, especially adults. I first met five-year-old Janet when I arrived with a friend for dinner at the commune. No one was on the first floor except two adults and Janet. At first she looked coy, didn't come too close, and swung her body with her hands behind her back. Then she took my friend by the hand out of the room, saying, "I want to show you something." When they returned she repeated the same routine with me, led me from the dining room, where drinks were being prepared, to the pantry, and pointed out the glasses in the cabinet. Then she took me to her favorite couch and told me to sit in it. "Isn't it comfortable?" I agreed, we rejoined the others, and she brushed my hair until dinner was ready.

Other children seem equally at ease in their relationships with adults. Roger's teachers tell his mother, Linda, that he is a strong but benevolent leader in school. Roger, like most of the children in my research, attends public school. Linda herself notices that the commune has "given him many skills in dealing with people, getting in touch with what his needs are, and asking for things. He's easily accepted into a new group and very accepting of other people." Benjamin, according to other adults in his commune, was "just a closed-up little boy when he came. Now he's more open, more trusting, talks more, and can be drawn out more easily."

Kids in city communes live in adult-dominated worlds. Roger is six and lives with Linda (divorced), eleven other adults, and a newborn baby. The large, cleverly renovated two-family house was formed in 1970 and is in a dense urban area. Since he was two-and-a-half, Roger has been the only child. Sometimes grown-ups do special things for him, such as the candlelight breakfast with boiled eggs two of the women made to celebrate his first day of school. When Linda makes a special request, other people do take him out or put him to bed, but she is reluctant to ask. She feels that others don't really want to do things for Roger, and she complains that the men especially ignore him. Other single mothers also join communes to find father surrogates, apparently a rare commodity thus far. Roger, for his part, feels very close to Linda and feels especially happy "that my Momma makes me breakfast every morning, and when it's her turn to cook, she makes me dinner, and Saturdays we might go out or she might make me dinner here."

The parent-child bond is close and strong in urban communes. The parent is the chief "honcho," as one mother put it, for the care of his or her child. But Roger also feels sad that there are no other children his age living in the house, and that none of the other adults offer companionship. He says that his best friends are the television and the boy across the street.

Benjamin, who is nine, feels lonely sometimes in his house of five adults and two teen-age girls. A football addict, he wanders around the house in his helmet, roughhouses with the teenagers, but finds no one who'll throw the ball around with him. The other mother in the house did take him to a football game once, but the men always seem too busy for Benjamin.

From a child's viewpoint, living alone or virtually alone with many grown-ups means that many more authorities tell him or her what to do. For Roger, communal living is having "lots of bosses." Benjamin sees it as "two mothers, four fathers, and two sisters." Adults make rules, and any adult can call a kid on violations. Some adults, a distinct minority, have little to do with the children in their households except to tell them to be quiet or stop interrupting. Benjamin says that when he breaks a rule, the adults respond by making a bigger one. Commune members seem to release around children otherwise suppressed authoritative, demanding behavior, even if children are supposedly equal. Roger's fantasies of what he would change in the house are revealing:

> I'd want the inside of the whole house to look like a castle, with a throne for me and my mother, because she's the only one that has a grown-up kid, and I'd sit in one and she'd sit in the other, and we'd have servants.

The situation is different when there are more children, older children, or the adults are genuinely interested in children. Some people join communes especially to be with children, like the middle-aged woman new to the city who immediately became a grandmother surrogate to the young children in the Brill family, or the divorced medical student who says, "I don't want to be a father; I want to be an uncle." It is not surprising that people who are or have been parents themselves are generally more responsive to children than younger unattached residents who may not know how to react to a child. When asked who they would go to with a problem, children often name adults with parenting experience.

Kate lives with her five- and seven-year-old daughters in a suburban house where child care works particularly well even though the girls are the only children currently in the house. The other adults include three people in their forties who have had children. The seven-year-old expresses her warm feelings toward the house in essays she writes in school: "A commune is not just one family. It is many families. . . . Dear House, I love you. . . ." Janet and Mary are fortunate in the love and attention they get from adults. After school, they read, paint pictures, listen to music, or help out in the kitchen, with Kate if she is there but with other people if she's not. Some evenings they put on plays after dinner and recruit grown-ups to be the characters, using children's records for the sound and setting up chairs to transform the living room into an auditorium. Kate is especially pleased with how the men in the house treat Janet and Mary.

> I get the impression that the men are really concerned about their relationships with the kids. One man feels closer to them than to his own kids. That must be hard. He told me that the other day, as though to say, "Isn't that something?"

Kate feels that communal living makes her a better parent.

> The house took the pressure off. When I was the only Mommy I lost my temper a lot more. There was no relief. Living alone with them I was terrified that I'd get sick. There was absolutely no one else. Here, if I have some problem, there is always someone to take care of them. So relating to the children is a lot freer. I do it because I want to, not because I have to.

For adolescents, communal living poses a set of problems having nothing to do with the commune itself, but rather with outside attitudes toward it. Several teenagers have reported nearly the same experience.

> My friends thought it was a hippie commune. Everyone thought we were always having an orgy or smoking pot. It took me a while to convince them that it's just a place, and there are just more people there. After a while my friends came over and saw that the place wasn't weird. They weren't put off, once they saw it.

An eleven-year-old was teased by kids in school who assumed that "since we're in a commune, we share our bodies." Pressure from conformity-conscious peers is especially disturbing to some adolescents. One sixteen-year-old girl, living with her parents and sister in an augmented-family style commune in a wealthy suburb, denies to her friends that the house is a commune.

> I tell them that we take in boarders for the money. When they ask me how we can afford such a big house in that case, I say that it is mortgaged to the hilt.

This particular teen-ager is as much bothered by her parents' lack of image consciousness as she is by the presence of other people in her home. Like the many adolescents who wish their parents "looked better" for their friends, she wants a *House Beautiful* home instead of pillows on the floor for seating.

The status and participation of children in urban communes is probably as egalitarian as anywhere in America today, and in most cases the opportunity to relate to many adults seems good for the children. Otherwise, communal households are no different from other permissive families, and children are surrounded by universal middle-class cultural items: footballs, "Sesame Street," gerbils, trips to the dentist, ballet lessons, Brownies, sleeping over at friends' houses, posters of rock stars. Organic food isn't even particularly common.

Tensions and Conflicts

Urban communes have their problems as well as their rewards. Some of these stem from paradoxes inherent in the attempt to translate "communitas" into community: over time, spontaneity gives way to order. Communitas itself, the spontaneous, emotion-laden feeling of belonging together, is inherently unstable as a basis for social organization, and it must be routinized into an ongoing structure, with clear expectations, in order for any group to survive. Emotional "highs" are unpredictable and unreliable foundations for group life, especially when the group must earn a livelihood and run a household in addition to expressing the feelings of its members. Communes that hope to avoid rules, roles, positions, and all of the accouterments of structure, and count only on a brand of naïve anarchism—everyone doing his or her own thing—tend not to survive beyond the "honeymoon," unless they find a way to build and sustain commitment and collective solidarity. They need structure and organization. Benjamin Zablocki wrote of the inevitable movement from spontaneity to order:

> Most communes start out with no restrictions on behavior. Everyone is allowed to do his own thing at all times. It is expected that the gentleness, love, and compassion engendered by mystical drug experiences (or in other ways) will prove adequate substitutes for the moral and legal constraints which all other societies have found necessary. The initial experiences are often encouraging and exhilarating. . . . After a while, however, the strains inherent in such situations begin to reassert themselves. Work may slow down, jealousies may arise, or people may start spending more and more time away from the commune. At the same time, as the commune grows older, it may begin to give its attention to complex tasks such as starting a school, expanding housing facilities, or developing a business enterprise. Increased strain on one hand, and more complex tasks on the other, eventually lead most communes to abandon their absolute anarchism in favor of some more restricted alternative.[3]

The tension between spontaneity and order makes communalism a somewhat unstable social form, and it takes time for groups to strike a balance between strong collective demands and routine organization, and individual freedom of expression. Without some degree of order, a commune can be nothing more than an emotional episode. But for certain people this is fine; they would prefer to see a group dissolve if it cannot live by spontaneity alone.

Communes also face the specter of the tyranny of group pressure for conformity. Group pressure plays a large part in the life of all communal orders, from the large, highly organized intentional community to the small, loose urban commune.

Even in the latter, members often reported great discomfort at "letting down the group." It may be, in fact, that group pressure is more oppressive in anarchistic groups that lack formal statements of rules and understandings; in the absence of clarified standards and expectations, nearly any event is a potential source of anxiety, and those who are loudest and most aggressive may exert the most control over others.

Group pressure also arises around decision-making. Most communes pride themselves on their democratic decision-making procedures in which all members supposedly have an important voice. Yet, as in most groups, some members still exert more influence than other members; the verbally facile can beat out the shy and quiet; and challenging what appears to be the will of the majority, or the sentiment of the meeting, is very threatening and anxiety-provoking for many people. Field observations of urban communes showed that the ideal of decision-making by consensus may break down in reality. In one thirteen-person house, a coalition of three men nearly always got their way on issues, and anyone failing to add one's positive vote was looked upon with disapproval because "we all should agree on everything."

Intentional communities experience pressures for conformity not only in overt behavior but also in feelings. One of the principles of communitas is that it represents a common bond of feeling among all members and that emotions as well as behavior are an important part of the life of the group. But many communes translate this to mean that a unanimity of sentiment must exist at all times. Such unspoken norms make it difficult for members to express challenges to the prevailing agreements or the communal ideologies and myths. It is particularly hard to say that things are not going as well as everyone is pretending. As one commune member wrote:

> Ten or more of us were able to live in the same house in the middle of a dirty, cold, alienating city by playing some pretty heavy games. The game we played most is called Peace Treaty. The object of the game is to hide your feelings enough that you don't have to deal with them, or anyone else's. You play it by

being very polite and considerate toward your cohabitants—smiling at them, asking about their health, activities, etc., while avoiding any of the commitments involved in really being interested in how they're feeling or where their heads are at. You also avoid expressing your own hostilities and fears.

Successful communes value collective solidarity to such an extent that they often attempt to preclude exclusive or private relationships. The nineteenth-century Oneida community is perhaps the most dramatic example of a community that attempted to eliminate all such attachments, while still producing children and having an active sex life. Oneida practiced "complex marriage" and reared all its children together. Yet dyadic ties and mother-child attachments persisted despite community criticisms, occasional punishments such as separation, and strong norms against "sticky" relationships. Members had to work hard to ignore the special feelings engendered in them by a lover or a parent or a child.

More often, communal groups contain special relationships (such as couples), but there are strong pressures against the pair not to withdraw their energy from the group. The need to centralize energy of all kinds on the group and diffuse it among members and group tasks seems to be an underlying dynamic in group life: the more radical the group, the more unstable and uncertain its future and the more sources of outside support unavailable to it, the stronger the need to collect energy. (Many social theorists have written about this phenomenon.) The tendency to *collect energy* is surprisingly universal, even in the loosest communes with the most limited programs and expectations for future existence. A member of a small, loose urban commune of students explained the situation in her house, around a couple:

> There were subtle hostilities from almost everyone being directed at their partial withdrawal from the rest of us into their own world. It came out in criticisms of their relationship by various people. . . . It's true that if you start to get into a heavier-than-usual relationship with anyone, you should have every freedom to let it develop. Living in a commune, however,

carries with it a responsibility to maintain a certain amount of awareness of where everyone else is at and how what you are doing is affecting the total group.

But the group need sometimes conflicts with individual desires, leading to tensions and strain. An example of such conflict arose in another urban household. According to members of the group, they had only one expectation for a member: attention to the group, an attention which could be made up of little things. The crisis for this commune arose over the presence of a couple that met in the house and ultimately left. Their attachment to each other was extremely strong, and he, especially, was jealous of any time she spent away from him. Finally, they were confronted in a meeting about their neglect of the house and the other members. Said one person: "We thought we had no expectations, but in fact we really did. We wanted a time commitment and attention to the house. This was difficult to acknowledge because we hadn't made it explicitly, but we could feel the strain around [the couple]." In group meetings, the meaning of the terms *close, communal,* and *enough time* were discussed; a great deal of pressure was brought to bear on the couple. Finally, they announced their decision to leave before any request was made to them. It was important to the group that it happened that way, for members reported that they would have been hard pressed to expel them. The two people who left, however, said that they felt judged. They said that the group was responding not to them but to the issue of "coupleness"—it simply did not want couples.

Attachments outside of the commune are often as much a source of strain as relationships within, for they may even physically remove the member for periods of time. Conflicts frequently arise, especially in urban communes surrounded by other people, around the issue of how much time members are spending with the group.

Assessment

How well do communes work? As the man in the old story answered about his wife, "Compared to what?" To the best or the worst in our family history? Communes are usually evaluated against an idealized picture of the stable, loving, child-centered family of "and they lived happily ever after" lore.[4] Questions are raised about the problems inherent in communal living as though nuclear families never faced such issues. Rarely are these questions addressed as more universal problems of the society. An example is the issue of how high turnover in communes affects children. Kate, divorced mother of Janet and Mary and refugee from a difficult suburban marriage, talks about the great loss her daughters suffered in their precommune days, when the family with four young kids next door moved away and there was no one else at home to substitute or to help cushion the blow. Now, in their "big family" of the commune, they feel sad when someone leaves but handle the loss with much less storm and stress.

Many people who ask how well communes work seek confirmation of their belief that group living is impossible, unworkable, destroys freedom and privacy, and retards children. There's a not-so-remarkable defensiveness around any proposal to tamper with the family. And commune folks have their own stake in rejecting typical criteria of success like longevity and stability. "We're here as long as we continue to grow together" is a common response to questions about commitment and future plans. "Success is a matter of how much we learn, not how long we last" is another response.

Nonetheless, turnover is an issue for collective households, and is an extreme version of the increasing fragility of families in the rest of society. Of sixty-three Boston-area groups contacted in the summer of 1972, only seven were more than a year old. Thirteen were continuing intact, six breaking up completely, and in thirty-eight houses, two or more people were leaving. (And these statistics are conservative, overrepresenting continuing groups where someone is likely to be available for an interview.) Relationships are often tentative and easily broken, which is reinforced by members' varied backgrounds and lack of shared work. In only a few groups do members seem solidly and deeply committed to one another as immediate family instead of distant relatives.

Indeed, the consensual, negotiated relationships characterizing these households almost preclude longevity. No one can assert too much influence or wield power without the risk of alienating the others. Few routines remain established for very long. Old issues recur and are debated again. New people represent subtle shifts in culture and organization, but old members are reluctant to claim the rights of seniority. All these things generate a feeling of living in an always-changing, complex, emotionally charged atmosphere, where order is only temporarily accomplished and not to be regularly expected. One response is to move out of the house or to withdraw emotionally. The commune thus becomes institutionalized as a transient household where people continually move in and out, with the life cycle of an affair rather than a marriage. Cooperative houses of earlier periods also fit this pattern. Another response to fragility is the establishment of one family at the commune's core. The commune becomes their house, then, with others present at the family's sufferance, like the Brills' commune and those nineteenth-century families that took in lodgers. A less likely response for urban communes is to move toward an organizational rather than familial model, with rules, norms, and commitment mechanisms that make it difficult for people to leave. But the organizational response works only where there is a transcendent ideology to justify the social control and a strong, committed organizational core. Instead, in most of the urban communes I know, the most frequent response to easily breakable relationships is to break them.

Fragility is greater at some times than others, a function of group moods and rhythms that ebb and flow with the seasons (at least in the North). In January and February, for example, nearly everyone nourishes private thoughts of moving out. For two years running, several Greenbrook Road people told me confidentially that they would probably leave the house. None has. The cycles of group highs and lows are cultural: a greater scattering and transiency in the summer; a September sense of freshness; a partying and gift-giving atmosphere Thanksgiving through New Year's; the January-February-March slump accompanied by locked-in feelings of unrest. It is not hard to detect a group low, for its signs are nearly universal: the house is messier than usual; dishes are piled in the sink; communication is by notes left in public places rather than face-to-face; and attendance at dinner drops. Highs are marked by parties and spontaneous gatherings, by little extras such as a special dessert, games and surprises, and by people lingering at the table long after dinner is gone.

Some few people may live communally all of their lives, with or without mates and children. Even though urban communes as a social movement differentiated from rural cousins are less than a decade old, there are a number of people, both couples and singles, who have lived in one household throughout this period and intend to continue into the indefinite future. A somewhat larger group of urban migrants engage in the communal variant of serial monogamy: permanently commited to communal living but moving from group to group. One woman who has lived communally up and down the East Coast told me, "Of course communes work. I'm in my fifth." A surprising number of current commune residents express commitment to the communal way of life even if they are unhappy in their present group. Just as people with bad marriages blame it on their choice of mate and not on the institution, urban commune members insist that the idea is a good one even if their present group contains all the wrong people. In a Boston and New Haven study, which asked members about future plans, even those who were in the process of moving out said that they intend to live with another group some day.

A much larger number of people form communal households in response to a particular life-cycle issue. Young people who are out of school, new to a city, not attracted to marriage or perhaps divorced, find in communal living a way to create a family, live in a nice house, and lead a full, rich, familylike life. The recently separated and the single parent find communes a way to ease the pain of transition, to share the burdens, to develop a new life. People in midlife, perhaps part of a couple, perhaps divorced, with grown or nearly grown children, find in communal living an opportunity to open their horizons, to start a new set of adventures, to focus on self-development instead of the narrower responsibilities of running a nuclear family.

It is unlikely, however, that urban communes will be a dominant household form for more than a relatively few people and for more than a short period of people's lives. In the late 1970s, the romantic, utopian search for community has given way to less intentional "group living," and the desire to think of housemates as "family" has been replaced by the more conventional idea of roommates. In short, the faddish proportions of a deliberate movement have disappeared in favor of more privatized and more hidden temporary group households of convenience. The one exception is spiritual groups that continue to have communal living as a base. But the combination of later age at marriage and high divorce rates continues to make available a population who want the less lonely and more economical option of sharing a house with others, but informally, with limited commitment, and until an intimate relationship comes along. The urban-commune movement of the 1970s did not exactly die; it is just gradually fading away.

Yet descriptions of family structure seldom tell the whole story. The recent discoveries by demographic historians that the typical Western family has been much larger than five or six people does not mean that the character of family life has stayed the same during that period. Similarly, the impact of communes is not in their form, their numbers, or the degree to which they become widespread. Rather, it is in how their existence reflects changing norms and expectations about the way all families, nuclear and otherwise, conduct their shared life. Urban communes reflect a general trend away from assumed biological imperatives of "family": the importance of blood ties, age and sex differentiation, authoritative relationships. If current trends persist, families of the most conventional nuclear variety will become more public. They will continue to minimize sex and age distinctions in favor of negotiated, egalitarian, intentional relationships. The experience and experiments of urban communes may be guideposts on the road that lies ahead.

Notes

1. I define urban communes as households of five or more unrelated adults, with or without children, sharing a common kitchen and household expenses, and who define themselves in collective terms (as a "commune," "collective," or "extended family"). They are located in or near a metropolitan area, and members work in urban institutions.

   I have been studying urban communes for over two years under a grant from the National Institute of Mental Health, MH 23030. Members of five households in Boston and New Haven were interviewed and observed over periods of seven months to two years. Members of another thirty groups were interviewed and/or surveyed. Names of individuals and communes are fictitious. See also Rosabeth Moss Kanter, *Commitment and Community: Communes and Utopias in Sociological Perspective* (Cambridge: Harvard University Press, 1972).

2. An intentional division of labor promotes egalitarianism. When tasks are left to be done spontaneously, they may reflect traditional sex-role socialization. I found in one study no differences in the participation of women and men in household work divided intentionally. But where one person more often than others "fell into" a particular one-time-only job, sex differences emerged. Handling money was more often male. Cleaning the bathroom was more often female.

3. Benjamin Zablocki, *The Joyful Community* (Baltimore: Penguin Books, 1971), pp. 308–9.

4. By narrowly defining opportunities for family along biological lines, people momentarily or permanently without marital or blood ties are excluded from access to close human support. Beyond that, groups that do not fit the official definition of "family" face discrimination, from zoning laws to insurance.

Radical Law: Three Collectives in Cambridge

by Anthony P. Sager

As the 1960s came to an end, seismic changes were shaking American campuses from Berkeley to Columbia. A few even touched the traditionally quiet realms of the nation's law schools. There, activists forced their reluctant fellow students and teachers to confront the issues of the Vietnam War, American racism, and educational reform.

At Harvard Law School, for example, a small group of students found ways to combine their political energies and newly acquired legal skills. As core members of the Committee for Legal Research on the Draft, they prepared briefs for lawyers handling draft and military cases, published a handbook on military law, and took summer jobs with military organizing projects. As founders of the Radical Law Students Association, they went to antiwar demonstrations and organized support for a universitywide student strike after the American invasion of Cambodia. They distributed leaflets urging students not to take jobs with the big law firms that served the worst offenders in the American corporate economy, and they demonstrated against recruiters from these firms. They sought support for a law student who was being disciplined for occupying an administration building with the Afro-American Student Association. They published a radical underground law-student newspaper called *The Outlaw.* Some reportedly hid an AWOL soldier in Harvard Law School buildings for three weeks without being detected. Anticipating the need to defend themselves physically later on, the students even studied karate together.

In 1970 some members of this group graduated and quickly

founded, with the assistance of spouses and friends, the Boston Law Commune. A year later, three other members of the group and I graduated and joined the Commune.

At Boston University at the same time, a similar nucleus of radical students was formed. Its members had organized the student strike after the Cambodia invasion, had worked for educational reforms such as open admissions, and had assisted in the criminal defense of Black Panther party members in New Bedford, Mass. With this group of activists and friends at its core, the Law Collective was formed in 1971.

Similarly, a group of women law students at Boston University came together around feminist activities. Several of them had taught courses on women and the law and other subjects in the "Communiversity," a free university at Boston University in 1970, and in an off-campus free school. Together with other lawyers and law students who had worked with them on a pro-abortion lawsuit, they started an evening law practice which became the Women's Law Collective in 1971.

These new lawyers called their groups "communes" or "collectives" because they wanted to tell the world that they were different from established law firms, that they were a part of the nationwide movements for social change. (Later, the Board of Bar Overseers would force them to drop the terms from their names and to call themselves by their partners' names, as all other law firms must do.) These were exciting times: political goals, personal friendships, and a sense that work could be both egalitarian and satisfying all blended together in a project that seemed to reflect the values of a new kind of socialism. Virtually no other job opportunities in the law seemed to allow the realization of any of these objectives, let alone all three. In government-funded legal-assistance or public-defender offices, attorneys often couldn't represent the most radical groups because of limitations on client income and the inherent politics of the situation. In foundation-funded or Ralph Nader–linked "public-interest" research and litigation projects, the focus was limited to consumer and environmental concerns. Established civil-rights and civil-liberties organizations—and the few small liberal law firms that could be found in some cities—could take on no more than one or two new lawyers a year. The commune members had no doubt that their own work situation was the best of these alternatives. Besides, they wanted to create exemplary institutions for others to emulate.

Like most of the new left, the communards believed that fundamental change in America would come from the growth of grass-roots organizations and movements in communities, workplaces, and other basic institutional settings—and that these local groups would eventually consolidate into a powerful national force. Lawyers, they thought, could help these emerging organizations meet legal requirements as they grew; could defend them against the repression that was inevitable; and could at the same time keep them from relying too heavily on lawyers and legal processes. Their ambitions made the goals of legal-services lawyers—including some of the communards' classmates—pale by comparison.[1] However, in their excitement and inexperience, these new lawyers did not explore their potential differences or the economic difficulties of starting law practices. Prior to opening its office, one group devoted more attention to selecting a telephone system than to comparing political goals or attracting financially solvent clients.

Beginnings: Politics and Equality

When the Law Commune opened for business in September, 1970, its offices occupied the second floor of a run-down walk-up commercial building in the Central Square section of Cambridge, space previously occupied by a karate studio. Although the lettering over the building's front entrance read "Board of Trade Building," the stairway from the street and the second-floor landing were a favorite resting place for Central Square's resident drunks, and the hallways smelled accordingly. Furnishings for the new law office included secondhand rugs, desks, chairs, and couches. The inevitable complement of radical posters and announcements of demonstrations papered the walls.

A year later the Collective moved into the remainder of the

second floor next to the Commune, into an open space half the size of a basketball court. Shortly after that the Women's Collective moved in also, building walls to make a small office in one corner of the Collective's space. The Collective, for its part, decided not to have individual offices for its attorneys. Instead, members built open desks from plywood sheets and two-by-fours along the walls. The purpose was to convey a sense of openness with each other.

From the outside, the groups were seen simply as "the law communes." But to themselves, there were differences of political emphasis, at least at the beginning. The Commune aimed to provide legal services to antiwar activists and grass-roots organizers, including defense against governmental repression. Its members also wanted to challenge the myths of lawyer professionalism and to participate personally in political activities (like demonstrations) designed to make people aware of the need for radical changes in America. The Collective's goals were to provide high-quality legal counsel for the working poor, both black and white, while bringing out the larger issues implicit in each case. Its members also sought to participate as activists, not simply as lawyers, in radical movements. The Women's Law Collective shared the other groups' goals, while also aiming to be a successful law office staffed exclusively by women. Its first duty was to assist women's organizations and to handle cases involving women's issues.

In all three groups, however, the work style was to be strictly egalitarian. Decisions would be made collectively, less desirable tasks shared, and the appearance of professionalism avoided. Clothes were casual and office furnishings "homey" at best—creating an overall informal image that all would later regret. There was no self-protective professional detachment from clients' concerns, but often a close emotional involvement. All the members of every group—lawyers, law students, paralegals—were equal in status and responsibility. They were determined to avoid the destructive egotism and competitiveness of the "star" system that plagued well-known radical lawyers in other cities.

To realize this equality, the groups had no secretaries or

receptionists: each attorney or legal worker was to do his or her own typing, copying, and filing. Telephone answering and reception duties were rotated; so were the jobs of cleaning the office and buying supplies. Nobody enjoyed the scutwork, or thought that it was efficient to do it that way. But all believed that hiring someone to do the firm's dirty work would be unethical—and probably also that it was a "culturally revolutionary" act for lawyers to do the nonprofessional work. Those who failed to perform their assigned duties were criticized by their collectives, and assigned extra telephone duty for repeated failure. Telephone duty was an especially effective sanction.

Each group met together at least once a week, ordinarily for three or four hours in the evening. At these meetings, members reviewed pending cases, potential new cases, group tasks, and other business, political, or personal matters. Every member of each collective had an equal right to participate and to vote. Volunteer law students or investigators, however, were not considered "members." Collective decisions covered everything from what new cases to accept to salary levels and current interpersonal disputes.

New cases in particular were subject to endless discussion—from a political as well as from a legal perspective. A tenant union seeking representation in opposing evictions or going on rent strike, for example, would be examined carefully. What was the class composition of its membership? What were the group's roots in the community? How capable and responsible were its organizers? Would the union continue to exist after the immediate crisis was over—and if so, would it seek objectives other than the self-interest of individual tenants? The examination sounds more rigorous than its results were in fact. Enough potential clients—tenants, prisoners, workers, etc.—showed promise, dedication, and need to keep the lawyers busy representing them.

In the Collective and the Women's Collective, the whole group would decide whether to take on *every* new case—and if so, on what terms. Even in routine fee cases, like uncontested divorces, the group would screen, set the fee, and assign one or more lawyers to the case. The Commune, by contrast, reviewed only those new cases that involved political issues, that raised ethical problems, or that were likely to require a lot of time for little or no fee. Otherwise it trusted each attorney to decide what cases he or she took on. Sometimes the Commune refused cases on political grounds. Among those turned down were accused rapists, a hard-drug dealer who was not himself a user, and men in divorce or child-support cases who (in the Commune's opinion) were essentially seeking to shirk their responsibilities. The Commune, like the other two groups, typically assigned more than one lawyer to each case. Whenever the lawyers actually adjusted their busy schedules in order to work together, this partially compensated for the general inexperience and led to a sharing of judgment and skills.

The collective decision-making process also applied to administrative and personnel matters—most memorably, to salary levels. All these groups were committed to becoming financially self-sufficient and providing basic but adequate salaries for their members. To provide funds at the beginning, the Commune sought capital from members and contributions from wealthy friends. The Collective relied on member contributions, on low (or nonexistent) salaries, and on income from members' outside jobs (waitressing, for example, or driving a cab). The Commune expected its expertise in draft and military law to be the mainstay of its private practice; the Collective expected its senior attorney's expertise in criminal law to do the same.

The principles for determining salary levels emerged slowly from the painful process of consensus. In the Commune's early days, salary levels were proposed by each member based on an estimate of "basic need." Basic need, a flexible concept that was to evolve over the years, was initially supposed to take into account how many people lived in the member's household, how much they all earned, and how much they required overall for a modest standard of living. In all the groups at the beginning, people without any financial need for a salary—because of their own financial resources or their spouses'—took no salary.

Practicing Radical Law

In their first few years, the law communes met many of their initial goals. They represented progressive and grass-roots groups such as the Black Panther Party, state prisoners protesting inadequate treatment and conditions of confinement, tenant unions, individuals and communities suffering from police brutality, and antiwar demonstrators. Some of their attorneys successfully defended draft resisters in federal court and assorted felons in jury trials in state courts. But the bulk of the Commune's and the Collective's cases initially were criminal and landlord-tenant cases. Most of the Women's Collective's were divorce, separation, and custody cases. All three groups also handled residential real-estate transactions, workmen's-compensation claims, the formation of small corporations and partnerships, dogbite injury claims—in short, the typical potpourri of small private practice.

The mixture of cases and the successful results in many of the political ones continued over the next few years. By 1975, the three groups had represented clients such as the Puerto Rican parents' organization that intervened in the historic Boston school-desegregation case; an independent restaurant workers' union in its organizing drives; insurgent caucuses in the laborers' union; and a statewide citizen action group, Massachusetts Fair Share. They successfully prevented the deportation of a leading Vietnamese activist from the United States, and they won the return of a politically active prisoner who had been transferred to a federal penitentiary in Georgia. They stopped construction of commercial high-rise buildings in residential neighborhoods, diverted thousands of dollars of withheld tenants' rent to much-needed repairs, and pioneered tenant collective bargaining that won tenants a role in management. They also provided more mundane legal assistance concerning incorporation, tax filings, and permits to groups such as the authors of a women's health book; an inner-city scholarship fund that refused to pay taxes during the Vietnam War; a socialist economists' magazine; working-class newspaper projects; and action groups opposing foreign dictatorships.

Over time, the communes also became a legal resource for the many countercultural and "hip capitalist" ventures that flourished in the Cambridge area: a community film-making and distribution group, a bicycle-repair collective, a gay community newspaper, small recording companies, food co-ops, a homemade ice cream store, and residential communes that wanted to buy a house together. The communards developed reputations as independent, responsible attorneys, comfortable with unusual or controversial cases, and personally sensitive in matters like marital disputes. That reputation, ironically, attracted increasing numbers of middle-class people for whom the lawyers did not have to cut their fees.

Politics were not forgotten in the bustle of cases. Members took part in antiwar demonstrations and prisoner-organizing projects, and each of the three groups organized weekly study sessions. The readings included Volume I of Marx's *Capital,* the Weather Underground's *Prairie Fire,* the history of Puerto Rico and its independence movement, the history of racism and school desegregation in America, and Mao's writings. Even monthly intercommunal business meetings came to include a study and discussion component.

As the three groups' practice grew, money was a little less scarce than it had been at the outset. Early on, two members of the Collective who worked part-time elsewhere dropped their outside jobs and began drawing weekly salaries. All members of all the groups drew at least a minimum salary, and no longer had to lie to their parents about their earnings. In the Commune, after much heated debate, the definition of "basic need," by which salaries were measured, was broadened. Eventually, "need" came to include not only basic living expenses but also psychiatrist fees, repayment of student loans, vacation expenses, and finally savings for a down payment on a house. The groups' new-found financial stability enabled them to hire part-time secretarial and reception help. Still, to keep a steady cash flow, a few attorneys from each collective had to take part-time outside jobs as state hearing officers, for instance, or as prosecutors under the lead-paint-poisoning prevention law.

Staying Together and Breaking Up

When the Commune and the two collectives began, members hoped to combine movement legal work with close friendships and a satisfying work environment. They viewed their communal entities as experimental. Nobody made any explicit commitments in those days, but the tacit understanding was that the young lawyers and paralegals would stay on for the foreseeable future, if not indefinitely, if the communes proved successful.

It didn't take long for that expectation to become unsettled. In the Commune, four of the six founders left within two years of its inception. One left to separate from his wife, also a lawyer in the group. Two more lost interest in the law—one left to have a baby, the other to teach in a free school. The fourth departed because of the extreme anxiety caused by his heavy trial responsibilities as "senior" attorney after being a member of the bar for not much more than a year. Four recent law school graduates joined the Commune during its second year (I was among them), but one left within a few months to pursue Transcendental Meditation full time.

In the Collective, the biggest blow was the experienced senior attorney's departure to a faculty position at a nearby law school. Where would supervision and good fee-paying cases now come from? Later several members of the Collective were doubtful that they would have started the group at all if they had known he wouldn't be around very long. Another founding member had left shortly before, because of stormy interpersonal issues; but two new lawyers joined the group after a couple of years. The Women's Law Collective didn't lose any members until it was a few years old. Then, one founding lawyer left because of conflicts (which some saw as political and others as personal). Another left to work with the National Lawyers Guild (she and her husband were leaving town as well). A third left for a job that would offer both more professional training and more money (she needed to pay off law school loans). Two recent law graduates later took their places, followed by a paralegal worker.

If turnover was a symptom of unanticipated tension, parenthood was a prime cause. Three children were born to members of the Commune and the Women's Collective. Suddenly the lawyers who had become parents had less time to spend on work. They needed more money and had a new focal point in their lives that was more important than their groups. Their emotions were caught up in an experience not shared by all. Some others, meanwhile, not only didn't have children but were not involved with a spouse or lover. The group was still the major focus of their lives—yet, as a result of other members' decision to have a child, more was being demanded of them.

The tension surfaced over money. In the Commune, one member with two dependents was paid more than three times as much as those who were unmarried. Although salary levels had been collectively decided upon, some individual resentment remained. For most members, salaries were about $5,000 per year, and it did not seem that the type of clients attracted to the group would let the typical salary level get much higher. Tempers grew short as the end of a low-income month approached, and differences over individual life styles swelled into resentment over how others were spending their earnings. Ironically, the abolition of the draft in 1972 had eliminated the area of law where the Commune had the most expertise—and which it had thought would be its bread and butter. The departure of the Collective's senior attorney had a similar deleterious effect on that group's financial position.

Although there was an undercurrent of dissatisfaction with the low-paying case load that made up most of the three groups' practice, for a long time little was done to change this, mainly because of the primacy of political concerns over financial ones. For example, the Women's Collective chose not to pursue the potentially lucrative possibilities of bringing sex-discrimination cases on behalf of middle-class women, because they wanted to develop a working-class sex-discrimination practice.

The year 1975 was the turning point: all three groups decided something had to be done to bring in more money. Dropping the term "law commune" from the Commune's stationery the preceding year had not been enough, nor was the change from sliding fee scales (adjusted according to the client's ability to pay) to fees set at the going rates. All three groups moved their offices to a respectable building. ("There's no politics in dirt," one lawyer commented.) All instituted higher standards of appearance—less casual clothing, neater common space, and no dogs in the reception areas. Shortly thereafter came the hiring of full-time reception and secretarial help. The principles that once forbade hiring such employees gave way rather easily, not with debate, but with a vast collective sigh of relief.

By the mid-seventies, the political context in which the communes operated had changed drastically. The left movement in Massachusetts and nationally appeared to have disintegrated or disappeared. There were very few organizing projects starting up in the area, and many existing ones lost momentum or closed down. It was these changes in the political context of the three groups' legal work that affected them most profoundly. As the war ended, different tendencies on the left were reflected in the law offices. Some members were dissatisfied that their group did not focus on working-class issues. Client groups that were once seen as potentially revolutionary, such as the Black Panther Party or militant state prisoner organizations, did not live up to expectations. Some members felt disappointment, if not disillusionment.

On the other hand, an increasing proportion of political client groups had become tenant unions and other community organizing projects with more immediate and modest goals. Many of these did not necessarily need to be served by lawyers with the political approach and views of the communards; other law firms or government-funded law offices could do the job just as well. In representing these clients, the lawyers of the Commune and the two collectives saw themselves acting as conventional lawyers, not as radical ones.

By the end of 1975, the internal problems of their groups had led many members of the Commune and the Women's Collective to reassess their commitments. By this time, initial satisfaction with the new office space had given way to the realization that the new offices themselves were not going to change the communes' public image or attract well-heeled clients very quickly. As the members reflected on the patterns of interpersonal conflict and dissatisfaction that had remained virtually constant over the years, it seemed clear that internal change was not feasible.

In the Commune, divergent political viewpoints merged with differences in life style outside the group. On one side were those who were frustrated that the Commune never came to focus on labor cases and working-class issues, never had the discipline for extended political study on Marxist-Leninist topics, never managed to participate in a nonlegal project as a complete group, and never developed into a group of friends who were as close outside the office as in it. Those who were frustrated by these failings were, by and large, unmarried and childless. On the other side were those who felt good about the diversity of the Commune's political clients, because all were seeking necessary social change. They also thought that the Commune ought to provide for its members' growing families, believed there was no "correct" political line to study and follow, and believed the group ought to adjust to accommodate changes in its members' lives. Those on this side of the line were mostly married and with children.

Both sides were tired of the continuing tension and strain; by the winter of 1976, most Commune members had decided to leave and to dissolve the organization. Individual reasons, of course, varied. One member, a founder, was in the process of separating from his wife and was still depressed by the death from cancer of his closest friend a year before. Looking for a change of scene and a job that would be free of the personal and financial tensions of the Commune, he took a position as managing attorney of a neighborhood legal-services office in Boston. Another member was chiefly frustrated by the lack of internal political focus and discipline in the Commune, the pressure to generate sufficient income from fee-paying cases and the large amount of time spent on those cases, the consequent lack of time for work on political cases, and the group's low interest in his political activities outside the Commune. For a while this member considered starting a labor-law practice in Fall River, an industrial city south of Boston. In the end he moved to California to become managing attorney of a legal-assistance office (and to be near backpacking country). A third attorney, equally political, left not only the Commune but the law itself, and went to work in a factory with the intention of doing organizing work. The only nonlawyer in the group would not have left if the Commune hadn't ceased to exist. After its dissolution, she finished law school at the top of her class and went on to a judicial clerkship. For myself, I felt constrained by the routineness of many of the cases I had to take on. I felt I wasn't learning much, and that lack of professional development and my low salary weren't being counterbalanced by a sense that the group was handling important political cases. I took a job as an assistant attorney general for Massachusetts.

The Commune members decided not to seek new members to continue the practice, because they believed that new members would soon run into the same frustrations the departing ones felt. Also, having viewed the Commune from its inception as an experimental institution, designed to combine various political, interpersonal, financial, and professional goals, its members saw no need to continue its existence when they believed it could not achieve these goals in the present political climate.

The Women's Collective members decided to leave their group for similar reasons. Their practice was not generating much money, and the resulting financial sacrifices were not compensated by political or personal satisfaction. As a group, they did not have the personal affinities or supportive relationships they had sought. Lacking that, their interdependence in the collective structure produced too many conflicts, too much competitiveness, and too much anger. However, because there were three women lawyers who wanted to take over the case load and established reputation of the Women's Law Collective, the members passed on their practice in the fall of 1976.

The Law Collective, by contrast, continued its existence. Its members were truly close friends who enjoyed being together both inside and outside their work. None of its members had children. When their political case load grew less satisfying, they responded by separating their political and legal work entirely. They put new emphasis on being better lawyers and more successful financially. They also acted together in the Puerto Rican Solidarity Committee and were bound together by their study group, whose topics closely reflected their political activities. Although they were dissatisfied with their earnings and the routine nature of many of their cases, they remained committed to each other and optimistic about the group's chances for success.

In retrospect, even members of the disbanded communes do not regret their experiences. We successfully defended antiwar protesters and other militants, helped to build radical and countercultural projects, and learned to work democratically in small groups.[2] We did high-quality legal work, although we felt more self-doubt than self-confidence at the time. We also had a good time with each other. Where else would we have happily worked all night together preparing legal briefs, or closed our office for the afternoon to go to a Bob Dylan concert in Providence?

If we had it all to do over again, we would be more professional and serious in learning to practice law. We would study legal as well as political issues and would have a senior attorney and a structure for supervision to help build self-confidence and skills. We would be more realistic about salary needs, personal compatibility, family changes, and interdependence. Maybe some of us will be senior attorneys in postcommunal experiments in the future.

As students who were then deciding what to do with our lives, many of us were tricked by the sixties into becoming lawyers, because then there was a movement that needed us. After that movement faltered in the changed circumstances and moods of the seventies, we responded by altering the structure of our working lives, but not our values. Although we are functioning more traditionally in our professional roles, we still are looking for ways to be progressive and skilled as lawyers, egalitarian in our work relationships, and close with our friends, wherever we are now.

Notes

1. It should be noted that the federally funded program of legal assistance for the indigent was not created to achieve similar political goals. Its purpose was to provide free legal services to the poor, who were unable to pay for representation by members of the private bar. It provided individual case assistance in poor people's problems with creditors, landlords, governmental-aid programs, abusive or nonsupporting spouses, and the like. However, most legal-services programs did not address the question of how to change the system that created these problems, and became swamped with far more individual cases than they could handle. In the eyes of the law communes, the legal-services program was inherently apolitical for several reasons. Most of its cases were on behalf of individuals, not groups, and did not seek to remedy the cause of their problems as a class. Even though its class-action law-reform cases might expand the rights or benefits of many poor people, these would not increase poor people's power within the American system, weaken the institutions that kept them powerless, or build grass-roots organizations for social change. On the contrary, legal-services lawyers, even when successful in litigation, were seen as encouraging poor people to rely on "their" lawyers and on change through the legal processes, thereby discouraging the growth of self-help political organizations. In addition, some believed that the poor who were served by legal services constituted an underclass which was too oppressed and too dependent on government-assistance programs to initiate new movements for basic social change.

2. My impressions are certainly based largely on my own experience. From conversations with former coworkers, however, I think that most of them share these reactions.

Part Two
Issues

Alternative Services and the Crisis of the Professions

by Larry Hirschhorn

Alternative service organizations in many different areas of work proliferated in the sixties. Many have disappeared, some have become innovative mainstream services dependent on the usual complement of public and private funding sources, while others remain as viable alternatives. The people who founded alternative services did so for many reasons. The political climate, the search for better jobs, and the desire to create communal and participatory settings were all significant.

Yet in analyzing the sources of alternative services, we cannot ignore the underlying moments of change, crisis, and transformation in the mainstream service sector. We must stand back for a moment and examine the growth of alternative services in the context of the social-services system as a whole.

Here striking parallels emerge. Professionals, clients, and managers in mainstream services were also searching for new models and ideas. As with all powerful currents of change, there were many proximate causes. Hospital administrators found that they had to develop "teams" of health professionals to deliver effective preventive service. Mental-health professionals discovered that self-help groups were sometimes the most effective way to help poor people change their lives. Administrators found that simple "bureaucratic" management and personnel procedures were no longer enough to run their agencies effectively; instead, they had to develop job-mobility, enrichment, and training programs to keep the professionals in their employ satisfied. Finally, members of agency boards discovered that they had to perform more than a perfunctory oversight role. Client pressures for high-quality service, combined with neighborhood groups' and government agencies' demand for accountability, required that boards of directors intervene ever more actively in the ongoing work of their agencies and organizations. In short, the emergence of alternatives was part and parcel of a period of *general* transformation, testing, and development within the established social services.

This mainstream service crisis raises critical questions for professionals and others working in alternative services. Often people who founded alternatives did not have a concrete enough conception of the evolving tensions affecting all services. They posed abstract goals for their agencies (e.g., participation of clients in the service system, democratic decision-making within the agency, free services, etc.), without asking how these goals might be translated into the language of mainstream conflict and politics. This disregard for established social services considerably weakened the impact of the alternatives. Too often they remained isolated at the fringe of the service system, burdened by their own marginality and unable to function as effective testing grounds for the productive resolution of the general social-service crisis.

In this essay I want to examine the dimensions of the larger crisis, so that people in alternative service can increase the impact of their own efforts and experiments on the direction and course of conflict within the mainstream. The essay is divided into five sections. Section I argues that the social-service crisis emerged as the result of a general social crisis in the work system and the family. Section II examines the new form of social-service organization that arose in the "turbulent" federally financed service system. Section III analyzes the crisis of professional practice as a function of these trends in organizational form and social life. Section IV shows how the crisis of the professions can lead to unproductive responses based on rationalization and "one-dimensional" measurement technologies. Finally in Section V, I return to the alternatives and propose a model of service that reflects the experience and goals of the alternatives and also responds directly and concretely to the crisis of the mainstream.

I. The Social-Service Crisis

The 1960s saw a number of strains on social services. Welfare clients in many cities demanded more money and insisted that welfare workers no longer intrude into their personal lives. Hospital administrators and doctors were pushed by both client groups and federal agencies to expand the range of preventive and community-based programs. Public-school teachers were attacked by community groups on the one side and by their students on the other. They could not teach children to read and figure, which enraged parents; students assaulted them verbally and in many cases physically. Finally, university students pushed faculty and administrators to change curriculum and to involve student and community groups in decision-making in the areas of research funding and university development.

The struggle over the control of services signified at a deeper level that services were failing in their historic and classic functions—they could no longer adjust clients to social life and urban institutions. Teachers could not prepare the young for jobs, welfare workers could not find jobs for their clients, doctors could not improve the health of the communities where they worked, and universities graduated students into underemployment. Social services were not coordinating individuals with the requirements of social institutions.

The Crisis in Historical Perspective

Modern social services arose to help individuals cope with a complex and stressful urban system. Yet they could perform effectively only insofar as the key institutions of social life— most importantly the work system and the family—possessed sufficient resilience and depth to organize and control individual actions, plans and impulses. Thus, a crisis of the family or a crisis of work can throw social services into disarray. Without the benchmark of work and family, social-service professionals can neither adjust their clients nor rationalize social institutions. Instead, they find themselves in a no-man's-land, pressed on the one side by decaying institutions and on the other by individuals dispossessed of social status and function.

The history of modern social work is relevant here.[1] The settlement-house social workers who worked and wrote at the turn of the century based their practice on a careful analysis of work, family, and community institutions. They launched some of the earliest comprehensive studies of city life, industrial jobs, immigrant culture, and health conditions. Using such studies they developed a practice (including both casework and social reform) through which individuals could be adjusted to social life. They correctly argued that work and family were basic institutions. A rational work system would give every family an income and a sense of place and status, while a stable family would ensure a well-balanced moral and emotional life, particularly for children. Social workers then tried to mobilize community resources to enable people to adjust to their work and family situations. Thus they might try to secure a better job for a father, decrease tensions between immigrant parents and their Americanized children, improve the vocational skills of a teenager, and organize a satisfactory and moral social life for young women.

The Decay of Work and Family in the Sixties

In the sixties, however, work and family were subjected to great pressures.[2] Structural unemployment for the unskilled and underemployment for the educated put strains on the work system. The unskilled no longer took any job, however dirty or low-paying, just to become "dignified" workers.[3] They wanted social mobility and were unwilling to sacrifice everything for their children—whose success, in turn, could justify their own misery. Educated blue-collar and professional workers were increasingly dissatisfied with their jobs. Young blue-collar workers found it hard to submit to the discipline of the factory, while professionals found that they could not employ their full talents and capacities in often stultifying and bureaucratized jobs that offered few chances for growth or advancement.[4]

The family, too, was subjected to great strains. The rise in the divorce rate and the growth of the women's movement indicated that the nuclear family was not organizing people's intimate lives effectively.[5] Divorce indicated that a new "developmental ethic" was permeating the culture. People were willing to leave their marriages if they could not grow and change in tandem with their spouses. Similarly, the women's movement destabilized nuclear-family sex roles as men were forced to support their wives' drive for competence and for sexual pleasure.

These strains on the nuclear family pushed people into new and different household arrangements. Increasingly they lived in single-family, two-adult childless communal or female-headed households. While at some point all people might live in a nuclear family, it no longer dominated people's passage through life. The crisis of the family was leading to a more variable life cycle.[6]

The Developmental Ethic

Looked at in broad historical perspective we can say that *developmental* needs and tensions were undermining the power of work and family to organize social life.[7] People accepted jobs willingly only insofar as they promised social mobility and professional growth, and they accepted marriages only insofar as the requirements of intimate life did not limit the chance for personal growth.

Yet, social change does not proceed in a straight line free of conflict and social regressions. While people sought new forms of work and social life, they often held tenaciously onto the old. Some could not bear the insecurity of searching for meaningful work and stayed with old jobs, though with increasing anger and resentment. Similarly, some defended stale marriages and increasingly dysfunctional sex roles in the face of their own latent dissatisfactions. The result was a general milieu of crisis, a feeling of deep dissatisfaction with the way things were, unaccompanied by a vision of how social life might be changed. The sense of crisis was amplified by a sense of stalemate.

The Pressure on Services

This was the context in which social-service professionals worked as the sixties unfolded. No social service was free from the pressures of institutional decay. Thus for example, the decay of labor markets in old cities made welfare workers obsolete. They could no longer adjust the poor worker to the lousy job. Consequently their claim to expertise, based on their ability to represent the stable mainstream of steady work commitments, was completely undermined.

Similarly, the stress of social change, reflected in the decay of labor markets for the semiskilled, underemployment for the educated, and the breakup of family life, affected people's health. Yet, doctors and hospital administrators could not organize preventive services that allowed people to cope creatively with these stresses. Suicide among young people rose, while stress-related diseases such as heart ailments, glandular malfunctions, and even infectious diseases (which grow when stress reduces the strength of immune responses) increased in significance.[8]

Finally, the lack of good jobs for the poor and jobs with growth potential for the educated helped to undermine teachers' authority in the classroom. They could not control their students because the work world promised little after graduation. Schools appeared as hollow institutions with little function, operating primarily as warehouses to keep students off the job market.

The social-service crisis, at its heart, was not a function of inappropriate or inadequate professional behavior, nor was it caused simply by fiscal imbalances. These factors certainly contributed and continue to contribute to the breakdown in many cities. Most importantly, however, the decay of services was a sign of deep changes in the organization of social life itself. New relationships between men and women and between people and jobs put great pressure on the capacity of those institutions that historically adjusted individuals to the mainstream of life. The social-service crisis was itself a sign, an indicator of a more general social crisis.

II. Social Services and New Forms of Organization

The service crisis unfolded against a backdrop of decisive changes in the organization of such services. Three interrelated trends predominated: the increasingly dominant role of the federal government in organizing and funding social services, the continued decline of the independent professional, and the rise of agencies and organizations that cannot and do not function as strict bureaucracies. Let us briefly examine each trend.

The Federal Role: A Historical Perspective

The social upheaval of the sixties exposed the weaknesses and inadequacies of older service-delivery systems. In response, the federal government expanded its already extensive intervention into the area of social services, by funding programs, creating new organizations, setting standards of performance, and integrating social services into a more national framework.

A historical perspective is helpful here. The classic urban agencies at the turn of the century drew their legitimacy and strength from a combination of local philanthropic elites and professional associations. The former supplied the funds and political support, while the latter provided the personnel, the direction, and the ideology of service. By the end of the First World War, this structure had been fully consolidated.

Philanthropic elites organized their giving through local community chests, while the professional associations consolidated their control over service content by dominating local charity boards and federated agencies. The two groups together developed a system for generating and allocating funds that was relatively free of political influence from city councils, workingmen's groups, and other interests.[9]

This began to change with the Great Depression. The local federated charities could not possibly support the thousands upon thousands of poor families, and instead were forced to turn to the federal government (though many resisted doing so for several years after the crash). Federal relief programs began to dominate local charity giving as well as other forms of social casework. This did not, however, reduce the power of the social-service professions. If anything, professional agencies became more powerful as they gained a national presence and could influence the size and composition of large federal spending programs.

After the Second World War, the professions and private foundations continued to initiate major programmatic changes in service delivery. The Ford Foundation, for example, in tandem with social work theoreticians at Columbia University, launched comprehensive community-development programs in selected "gray areas" of New York to solve the problem of juvenile delinquency. This comprehensive strategy, in turn, became the model for community action and community development in the sixties.[10]

The Changing Balance

The balance between the federal government and the professions began to change decisively in the sixties. After the ghetto riots it became increasingly clear that the scale of effort required far exceeded the resources of the foundations and the organizing capacity of professional associations. Instead, the federal government entered into the war on poverty on a grand scale and in the process placed itself at the center of all social action.

Consequently, federal programs and money created an increasing number of agencies and careers. For example, the Community Mental Health Act of 1963 and 1965 altered the practice of mental-health delivery throughout the country.[11] Cities were divided up into mental-health catchment areas, and many psychiatric departments and clinics changed the populations they served in order to receive public monies. In addition, since the federal program mandated or encouraged a specific set of programs if agencies were to qualify for funds (e.g., short-term therapies, community outreach, and group work), many clinics had to change their psychiatric practice. Finally, the shift to community mental health was increasingly integrated with states' attempts to close down their large mental hospitals and so had an important effect on the overall balance between inpatient and outpatient treatment. Many clinics, particularly those based on classic psychoanalytic practice, could not adjust and simply closed down. They could not develop other service modalities nor readjust to a new and often poorer clientele. The federal program thus had a decisive impact on the overall structure of mental-health practice.

Legal, medical, and teaching services were similarly affected by federal intervention. The federal government created the present community legal-services structure. The old Office of Economic Opportunity supported neighborhood legal-service offices, which proved instrumental in changing appeal procedures throughout the welfare bureaucracy. During the Nixon presidency, OEO itself was disbanded and legal services became a separate federal corporation with agencies in most major cities. It has become an important service for poor people and a critical step on the career ladder for most lawyers interested in public-interest law.

Health-care organization was also changed by federal spending. The post–World War II Hill-Burton act financed the construction of large numbers of hospitals; Medicare and Medicaid legislation substantially increased poor and old people's access to doctors; and the present Health Systems Agency legislation will enforce a more rational, if gradual, redistribution of medical facilities and technologies in the many overbedded and oversupplied hospital systems in large cities. Finally, federal support for prepaid plans, the emergence of mandated Professional Standards Review organizations, and cost controls that will be introduced with any health-insurance legislation—all have had and will continue to have a decisive impact on the way doctors are paid, the managerial structure in which they work, and the way they practice medicine.

Teaching too has been affected. Federal support for facility construction and, most importantly, for research, has shaped the rate and patterns of university growth and development. Government spending has had an equally important impact at the elementary and secondary levels. In particular, the significant growth in compensatory education (which is fast emerging as the new avenue of professional development and employment for large numbers of teachers entering the job market for the first time) for poor children, preschool children, and learning-disabled children (e.g., retarded, dyslexic, hyperactive, and emotionally disturbed) is creating an entirely new sector of elementary education for the child with special needs and disabilities.

Large Organizations

Federal intervention has both shaped and been affected by a new form of social-service organization. The growth of these organizations has reinforced the historic half-century decline of the independent professional. The history of medicine is relevant here.[12] Up to the early twentieth century and prior to the famous Flexner report on medical education in 1910, medicine was a disorganized profession composed of large numbers of independent doctors who represented a wide range of skills and approaches to the treatment of disease. But as the large, established universities organized to control medical education, many small medical schools were decertified and medical education was standardized. This development was reinforced by the rise of the hospital as a center for the treatment of the middle class (a trend under way by the turn of the century) as the predominant hospitals and universities combined to form the first medical complexes for delivering medical services. These two trends were cemented and integrated by the emergence of the AMA as the single organization for mobilizing the political power of doctors. The AMA regulated the relationships between the doctors, the hospitals, and the specialities and was able to resist further federal and state intrusion into the organization of medical care.

The balance between the federal government and the medical profession began to change with the rise of federal financing for construction, medical research, and reimbursement for services (reinforced by the cost pressures on the insurance companies). The AMA is losing power and legitimacy (it is not enrolling its historically large proportion of medical-school graduates), and corporate organizations are gaining increasing control over the practice of medicine. As we have argued, health planning itself will rationalize the distribution of medical instruments within and between catchment areas, and the likely rise of prepaid plans supported by private corporations, insurance companies, and large public employers (e.g., universities) will create a corps of salaried doctors dependent on organizations, state governments, and the federal government for their livelihood, technologies, and modes of practice.

Other professions have experienced a similar transformation. The solo-practice lawyer has not disappeared, but the growth of administrative law on the one side and the growing number of lawyers hired *as staff* in many public-sector organizations (universities, social agencies, hospitals, etc.) have created an organization-based job structure for lawyers. In particular, the increasing struggle over entitlements (e.g., rights to jobs, discrimination suits), the increasing pressure by clients and consumers on providers of goods and services (e.g., malpractice and consumer class-action suits), and the increasing complexity of interorganizational transactions particularly within the public sector (grants sharing, facilities sharing) have created a very complex *negotiated order* within and between organizations. All kinds of institutions both within and outside government find that they need permanent staff lawyers to handle their normal daily transactions with suppliers, employees, and recipients.

Finally, the teaching and mental-health/social-welfare professions were based in organizations from the start. Yet even here certain trends are of interest. While I have no statistical evidence, it seems that the rise of community mental-health centers and the emergence of nonpsychiatric mental-health techniques and theories have placed sharper limits on the number of psychiatrists who can successfully pursue an independent practice. Psychiatrists themselves are increasingly becoming salaried professionals.

Beyond Bureaucracy

Nevertheless, the rise of organization cannot be equated with the traditional rise in bureaucracy. The term *bureaucracy* conjures up the image of an organization with well-defined decision-making protocols, career ladders, and budgetary procedures. Today we are beginning to realize, however, that the *internal* stability of an organization, so critical to its success as a bureaucracy, depends very much on the stability of its *external* environment or field. The more unstable and fluid the latter, the more dysfunctional do the rigid patterns of a bureaucracy become.

Today, the social-service organization functions in a highly uncertain and "turbulent" environment.[13] It must respond to a wide range of constituencies. Federal funding, for example, often mandates community participation in program formulation. Good politics requires that the agency be tied into a local infrastructure or network of local agencies: it must also have contact with grant officers, congressional aides, congressmen, and state planning offices. Finally, it must keep in touch with the whole range of professional associations, schools, and where necessary, service-worker unions.

This complex of forces creates an uncertain climate for service operation, institutional maintenance, and institutional growth. The end of a budget cycle can lead to the termination of a program, community protests can convince grant officers to withdraw funds, professional practice can undermine the innovative intent of a new service program, and service-worker unions can create unexpected pressures on agency budgets.

Intake Control

The problem of *intake control* typifies this new complexity. Legal-service agencies, mental-health agencies, ambulatory clinics, and (where separately organized) public-defender services are losing control over the rate at which clients are referred to them for services. Instead, the actions and policies of other organizations prove of decisive importance. If, as often happens, this results in cycles of overload and underutilization of the professional staff, the agency finds that it no longer controls its own basic rhythms of work, resource flow, and morale.

A public-defender service, for example, finds that the flow of clients will be determined by the arrest practices of the police, the practices of prosecutors, constraints on plea bargaining, the legislative mandates that determine client eligibility for service, the judges' assessment of the likelihood that a client will be incarcerated, and the courts' expectation concerning case flow. All of these actions are decided outside the defenders' service, yet they are the major determinants of the quality and quantity of professional work within it. If a defenders' service wants to get control over intake, it must work to develop a complex "negotiated order" among these units.[14] Such orders are never stable. Instead, they are subject to change and pressure from even more complex "systems," so that the defenders' commission will find it is constantly adjusting the distribution of work between functions or, what is more likely, it is developing additional services and capacities (e.g., preventive services, based on a more integrated coordination with social-work and rehabilitation agencies) to buffer itself against this unwanted variance in its environment. Both developing such a negotiated order and managing within it require that the service be more fluid than strict work protocols and bureaucratic job ladders and definitions would ever permit.

Internal Turbulence

The internal life of these agencies is also increasingly turbulent. Today, managers of social-service agencies can no longer rely on professional discipline and norms to create reliable and predictable practice among professional workers.

The service crisis of the sixties undermined professional norms and the inherited concepts of practice. Professionals cannot draw to any great extent on their education and early experience to guide them. Community mental-health professionals, for example, are exposed to such a wide array of techniques—through official educational and clinical settings, alternative institutions, client-initiated practices, and federal demonstration programs—that no single educational program provides a firm orientation from which the array of practices, norms, and ideologies can be examined and judged. Thus, community mental-health managers cannot predict how their therapists will respond to federal program initiatives, nor can they be sure that the center is equipped to specialize in new program areas. Consequently, managers compete for program funding in an almost random way, hoping that good grantsmanship will substitute for a "point of view" or orientation in securing a direction and future for their agencies.

The managers of medical services in hospitals and clinics are under similar pressure. There is a growing realization that medical practice does not generally affect the cycles of health and disease in patients. Epidemiologists in particular are showing that in contrast to the old infectious diseases of the nineteenth and early twentieth century, diseases today lack specific agents. Instead, *stressful* situations weaken a person's body defenses and then, depending on cultural and hereditary disposition, or the random accumulation of certain viruses in or around the body at that particular time, a person will come down with a particular disease. Diseases, in other words, have their origins in social-psychological stress mechanisms that interact with cultural and hereditary dispositions.[15]

Doctors, however, are trained in a "linear" cause-and-effect model and still look for specific causes. Since, in addition, they are trained primarily to "cure" disease, they are not generally capable of developing good preventive programs of health care. Moreover, they are proving less capable at disease management. Today's complex of diseases—heart disease, cancer, and hormonal and glandular dysfunctions—are bound up with many body systems, so traditional drug management based on the concept of a single disease spot and a single cause produces the growing legion of "side effects." Physicians are therefore coping less effectively with both disease prevention and disease management.

This is an unstable situation. There is growing pressure— from the federal government and from the insurance companies and corporations who fund health plans—for effective preventive service programs. In response, research physicians and hospital administrators have tried to develop new "team" approaches to medical care, integrating medical specialists and other professionals within a unified delivery system. But team treatment is a complex undertaking, with little theoretical foundation as yet; it meets with resistance both from the doctors, who fear that their own position will be weakened, and from the other professionals, who do not want to be dominated by doctors. Thus, hospitals, clinics, and medical complexes face a turbulent situation in which skills, prerogatives, and models of effective service are up for grabs.

Professional Development as Turbulence

There is another source of such "internal turbulence." As conventional career lines are integrated into the federal social-service complex, professionals are turning to their own agencies for advancement opportunities as well as for professional growth. Two forces push them to rely on their organizations. First, as professional practice in mental health, juvenile justice, social work, teaching, vocational counseling, and medicine becomes detached from the worldview of a self-conscious and autonomous profession, practitioners mark their advancement in terms of the numbers and kinds of innovative programs in which they can participate. But since new programs emerge out of a political interplay between federal programming, national politics, and client lobbying, the professionals depend ultimately on the political strength of their organizations to provide them with a chance at new opportunities and career lines. When program planners in HEW funded child-abuse programs, for example, they created opportunities for quick-responding agencies to attract funds, hire new professionals, and retrain old ones.[16] If such agencies were successful in attracting money, the professionals within them could build entirely different career lines and become national experts in a few years. A professional's career thus depends on the politics of problem definition on the one hand and the entrepreneurial capacities of his or her organization on the other.

Second, it seems that professionals, paraprofessionals, and administrators within social-service organizations are no longer simply content to do a well-defined job competently. Rather, many want to move up in the organization as well as increase their overall capacity to get other jobs with more responsibility and pay. The same "developmental" pressure in the culture that leads to the periodic testing of close relationships leads also to a periodic testing and renewal of one's skills and competencies. *Learning* and *mobility* are replacing the idea of *craft* as a framework for organizing professional life. Managers discover that if they simply stand still, if they provide a range of services to clients effectively and efficiently, however that may be defined, employee morale declines. It appears that a permanent change gradient must be built into organizational life. Unless professionals are constantly presented with new opportunities, expressed concretely in both horizontal movement between lines of responsibility and vertical movement up the line of authority, their level of satisfaction falls. Managers find that they must design "learning institutions" which teach, upgrade, and retrain staff at the same time that they provide services to clients.[17]

The Interdependence Between Professional and Organization

The contingent environment faced by these new social agencies combined with the professional's dependence on them to negotiate programs, career lines, and standards of service with federal and state funding sources creates a complex interdependence between professionals and their organizations. In traditional service organizations the professional always had two affiliations: one to the organization and one to the profession. The manager then had to coordinate the professional worker's desire for autonomy with the organization's requirements for service and output. The professional, in other words, "resisted" bureaucracy in the name of autonomy, while the manager resisted professional autonomy in the name of organizational effectiveness.

But today the relationship between the two is more complicated. Professionals find it harder to claim autonomy and an independent career line. Yet, at the same time their demands for development grow stronger every day, nourished not by an autonomous profession but by the developmental ethic. Managers, for their part, can no longer rely on simple bureaucratic stances and procedures. The contingent environment in which they operate requires flexibility, while the uncertain services environment (i.e., which kinds of services will be favored today and funded tomorrow) requires that professionals in their employ be given maximum freedom for self-development. Managers also have to ensure that each individual's career plan is consistent with organizational strengths. Thus, the conflict in the "new social agency" becomes less one of the bureaucrat versus the professional and more one where groups fight over the appropriate level and quality of mutual interdependence in an organization that in turn operates in a highly contingent setting. Bureaucrat and professional become dependent on each other for a successful definition of both the organization's and the individual's mission. This reciprocal dependence increases the overall level of tension in the organization, since the once-opposing sides can no longer draw on outside referents and associations to buttress their own position. They all sink or swim together.

How can the two coordinate their efforts to create a more viable framework for professional practice? To answer this we must explore the crisis of professions in greater depth.

III. The Crisis of the Professions and the Collapse of Distance

Stable professions provide their members with professional "armor," with techniques and rules of action that allow them to minimize their emotional and psychological involvement with their clients. From the professions' point of view, such armor is essential to good practice. An overinvolved practitioner can neither objectively assess client needs nor employ professional techniques in the most efficient way. Moreover, professional armor also protects service workers from being overloaded by clients' complaints. In particular, workers who deal with poor people or those suffering from emotional or physical disorders need some distancing mechanisms to block their own instinctive involvement in their clients' troubles. Professional codes sanction such distance on the grounds that excessive identification can limit the professional's capacity to give help.

Historical Distance

The history of social work can be analyzed in this context.[18] The early charity workers of the 1870s and 1880s derived their armor from a theory of the moral inferiority of the working class. They represented the bourgeoisie, with its special code of behavior, and thus felt superior to the poor people who came to them for money, food, and shelter. Their sense of superiority enabled them to work with poor people while preserving a protective emotional distance. They were, after all, doing the poor a favor. They were instructing them in more productive ways of behaving: if the poor remained poor, they had only themselves to blame.

Social-work ideology changed by the turn of the century as the settlement houses developed more modern theories of poverty. Settlement-house workers, journalists, and others argued that poverty was the result of unemployment, poor housing, and poor health. Social-work theoreticians developed "casework" as a method for helping clients improve their working and living conditions.

Caseworkers became "scientists" in the urban laboratory. They were taught how to interview clients, how to discern and record a family's problems, to analyze its budget, its health problems and practices, and the quality of its housing. Finally, they were taught to examine the range of urban service as a system of aid, so that community resources—the church, the charities, the employer—could be mobilized to assist the client. A broadened arsenal of scientific tools replaced a sense of superiority as the new armor of the social work professional. While theorists were wise enough to stress the importance of empathy as one tool of effective casework, they put primary emphasis on the techniques of interviewing, reporting, recording, and resource mobilization.

Finally, psychoanalysis restructured social casework after the First World War and provided a new source of professional armor.[19] The psychoanalytic theory of human development and the analytic process allowed the professional to delve deeply into clients' intimate lives while at the same time maintaining a proper emotional distance. The theory of human development allowed workers to see their clients as objects of study, while the theory of analysis required that caseworkers be as "neutral" as possible toward them. Empathy, to be sure, became more important than ever. But in the degree that it became more central, theoreticians warned of its negative consequences. Caseworkers were trained to watch for their "countertransferences," that is, the projections of their own needs and wishes onto their clients. They became more intimate in their relationship with their clients, but simultaneously they had to become more guarded. Thus, as social workers probed more deeply into their clients' lives, viewing them first as inferiors, then as victims, and finally as the objects of universal neuroses, they simultaneously built up a more complex professional armor to protect themselves from their clients' problems.

The history of social work can be read as the history of the interplay between new social problems, new theories of adjustment, and new professional armor. A similar history could be written for other social-service professionals. Doctors, for example, could preserve their distance on the assumption that they were treating objective and agent-specific diseases. Bedside manner was valued, but the best doctor was one who could most effectively examine the patient as a piece of physical-clinical material. The problem of the subjective interaction between doctor and patient—increasingly important today—was minimized. Similarly, teachers who entered the public school at the turn of the century could control their empathetic responses to the low-status and impoverished lives of the immigrant children they taught by presuming that as representatives of Protestant culture they could effectively "uplift" the poor. Empathy was modulated by the sense of class and cultural distance on the one side and by missionary feelings on the other.

I am not arguing that such feelings of distance were inappropriate. Indeed in the age of infectious disease and large-scale immigration, doctors and teachers and social workers could find reasonably *authentic* sources for professional armor and the accompanying techniques. The material situation of life gave such techniques an authenticity and legitimacy. Rather, I am arguing that professionals as a rule must find and periodically renew such distancing mechanisms if they are to function effectively.

The Collapse of Distance

The crisis of the sixties undermined the theory and practice of the social-service professions. This development destroyed professional armor and exposed many to the emotional strains of overinvolvement and a feeling of "burnout."

Ann Swidler has described the dynamics of this phenomenon in her brilliant study of free schools.[20] Free schools were set up in response to the crisis of authority in the public schools during the sixties. Curriculum appeared irrelevant to students, teaching methods seemed oppressive to teachers and students alike, and it became increasingly difficult for teachers to enforce discipline in the classroom. Free schools were organized to break away from the old pedagogies and develop in their place a freer system of learning and teaching.

Yet free-school teachers found themselves in an almost impossible position. Since they lacked authority and did not believe in their own skills and techniques, they could exercise authority only through the sheer forcefulness of their own personalities. There are always a few teachers with commanding personalities who can push their students to the limits of their own potential; such teachers hardly need to learn pedagogic techniques. But these are the gifted few. Most teachers need professional armor, a host of techniques, a code of behavior, and a prescribed role, both to make them effective and to structure the appropriate distance between themselves and their students. The schooling crisis robbed them of these rules and roles, and those who tried to substitute a manufactured charisma for lost techniques within free schools were soon overwhelmed by their own emotional struggles, as well as by the projections of their students. They soon burned out and became ineffective teachers. Many free schools predicated on the free interaction between students and teachers thus quickly degenerated into centers of disorganized behavior in which the boundaries between personal impulses and organized social life were dangerously transgressed.

Many social workers faced the same conflict. As the family system and labor market lost their power to organize social life, welfare workers lost their capacity to adjust people to mainstream institutions. Simultaneously, poor people began to attack them. Since key urban institutions were decaying, poor people could detect neither an order nor an authority that placed their status in any comprehensible framework. Welfare workers, who represented the authority of these institutions, came under attack as illegitimate purveyors of cash and in-kind benefits. The standard eligibility interviews and home visits appeared as invasions of privacy. If there was no way to escape from poverty, if the authoritative urban institutions had no moral force or discernible function in the organization of social life, then the poor should receive both mandatory services and benefits without eligibility tests.

Welfare workers had two choices. They could either "identify" with poor clients, and encourage them to demand more money and benefits free of all strings and preconditions, or they could withdraw further from their work into an unyielding cynicism. The former choice led, as in the case of the free school, to the problem of overload. Welfare workers became deeply and emotionally involved in their clients' plight, yet they were limited by the level of resources committed to the welfare system. They could become "activists" trying to pry more money from the system, but the scope and pace of their activism depended in the end on the militancy of their clients. Only a collectivity of clients could change the system. Thus, the more active the welfare workers became, the more passive they felt. Their attempt to define a new professional role depended ultimately on the posture of their clients. All this resulted in feelings of frustration, bad faith, and often mistrust between clients and workers.[21]

The second option, withdrawal into cynicism, had its own costs. The workers lost all respect for their work and competence and saw themselves as simply mechanical conduits for the flow of money in a system committed to supporting poor people at near-subsistence levels. In both cases, the collapse of professional armor and identity exposed the welfare worker to the raw realities of client needs that could no longer be met or manipulated by professional techniques. The worker was overwhelmed.

Mental-health workers faced similar problems. The cultural explosions of the sixties undermined the unitary paradigm of psychiatric thought and practice based in classical psychoanalysis. Instead, the general demands for cultural participation in all spheres of life on the one hand, and the spirit of "acting out" and "doing one's thing" on the other led to therapy styles that encouraged much more active client involvement in the therapeutic process. Encounter sessions, gestalt techniques, psychodrama, and role-playing all pushed the client-cum-patient to act out repressed emotional material. Classical psychoanalysis and classical insight theory controlled the pace at which emotional material was released. The controlled disengagement of the therapist and the fact that the patient was seen alone limited the intensity of emotional release.

But the new therapies valued intensity and put great strain on the therapist. Therapists were forced either to assume greater control than ever before, exercising the force of their personalities as well as their skills, or to join with the group in the exercise of emotional expression. In either case, burnout could result. Indeed as in the case of free-school teachers, the most successful therapists were those who possessed the greatest natural charisma. They became supreme managers of group processes, masters of a many-ringed circus, capable of controlling the rhythm and pacing of group experience. As their charisma was projected they became gurus to some and thus could draw about them assistants and helpers who became their arms and legs. But this happened to only a few. Many others were soon burned out by the intensity and instability of the new therapies.

Finally, doctors also face the problem of distance, though here the forces and tensions pull in a different direction. As health and disease are interpreted as functions of stress levels, doctors are progressively pulled into the psychological "management" of their patients. Most doctors are ill-equipped to do this: they are trained to function as medical technicians. Yet insofar as they resist the pull of psychology they become poor managers of disease.

The social results are complex. Patients need doctors but they trust them less and less. The rise of malpractice suits indicates how deep this mistrust is today. The cultural myth of doctor superiority (if not infallibility) is unraveling, and patients are willing to treat their doctors as "contracting parties" in a market exchange. Just as they feel that doctors treat them as things to be administered to, so do they treat their doctors as objects in the cash-nexus. (Some theorists argue that we must resurrect the family general practitioner, but clearly the role of large organizations in health-care delivery makes this implausible.) Thus, doctors are caught in a crisis of "appropriate distance." If they do not change their practice, they become parties to the vicious cycle of mistrust and malpractice (one cause of the inflation in health costs). If they do change their practice, if they enter the arena of life-style management, they must find new distancing tools if they are not to be burned out by the intensity of psychological interchange.

The loss of distance between the professional and client imposes great strains on them both. The client no longer trusts or respects the professional who is clearly unsure and in need of approval, while the professional increasingly regards the client as an "enemy," as a disrupter of the daily flow of work. Professionals realize that they cannot give their clients the help they need, but to maintain their posture, to protect their facade, they must try to manage and manipulate them so that their potential explosiveness is cooled out. Clients resist such manipulation and professionals grow cynical. How is this new antagonism between the client and professional restructuring professional behavior? This is the subject of the next section.

IV. The New Service Rationalization

The collapse of distance places professionals in an impossible bind. If they try to maintain their classical postures and techniques they lose legitimacy. If they identify with their clients, however, they are soon burned out by the complexity and stress of mutual interdependence and emotional interchange.

This situation is unstable, and there are strong indications that the general climate of fiscal austerity, client dissatisfaction, and professional malaise will push both professionals and their managers into a regressive solution based on the watchwords of "efficiency" and "rationalization." Two forces are operating here: the growth of professional unions and the pressure from the federal government for numerical standards of service delivery and service effectiveness.

Professional Unions

As the service crisis of the sixties unfolded, professionals felt increasingly beleaguered by government, clients, and taxpayers. Since few groups still believed that they were experts, professionals had to fall back on another line of defense to protect their interests. Consequently, teachers, social workers, university faculty, and others turned to unions to protect their social status and working conditions.

The AFL teachers' unions were instrumental in setting the tone.[22] The community-control struggle and subsequent teachers' strike in New York in 1968 pointed to a different role and function for professional unions. Teachers in New York were under attack by the foundations, the mayor, and community groups. More fundamentally it had become painfully obvious that teachers were unable to teach and discipline their students. Dropout rates were high, racial tensions were on the rise, and violence against teachers was increasing. Teachers were pushed against the wall. When a community board in an experimental district insisted on transferring certain white teachers, the union called a strike and waged a successful struggle against such community-board prerogatives.

But the struggle over the transfers was only a pretext for the more general issue. In a period of social decay, teachers needed the muscle power of a strong union to protect their threatened status. While many left the old professional association (the

National Education Association) before the strike, the conflict made clear to others that the NEA could not adequately represent them. The teachers were now acknowledging that they were becoming just "workers" intent on protecting their piece of the social and economic pie against all comers. If their claim to expertise was not respected, then a union would protect them.

To be sure, teachers deserved protection. Their failure in the classroom was hardly their fault. Social conditions in the slums and the job market made it difficult for students to learn. Yet, as the teachers turned to unions, they also signaled that they would no longer take responsibility as professionals for the transformation of school conditions; that they would no longer be leaders in the development of more viable schooling alternatives. Instead, they would be antagonists, resistant to change, intent on protecting their turf.

Unions and Austerity

Today professional unions are the product of an even more complex set of forces. The qualitative pressures on unions are now intertwined with the straightforward threat of professional unemployment. (The teachers' strike of 1968, however, took place when job prospects were still good. At that time college graduates who were looking for draft deferments could get teaching jobs without any credentials, particularly if they taught math, science, or foreign languages.) University professors have unionized at a rapid rate in face of the growing fiscal crisis at both public and private universities. Similarly, doctors have been organizing in response to malpractice suits and pressure from insurance companies. Both threaten their ability to practice medicine in the way they see fit.

But ultimately battles over strict quantitative issues (e.g., the *number* of jobs and rates of pay) are not separable from qualitative conflicts (e.g., decision-making prerogatives, skill structures, and professional credentials). University administrators are responding to the fiscal crisis both by cutting back on full-time faculty and by trying to *reorganize* the disposition of the remaining faculty resources. Faculty unions are then organized both to preserve job security (or at least to regulate it) and to preserve the faculty's right to dispose of its time as it sees fit. Consequently, the faculty become less and less capable of contributing creatively to the underlying qualitative issues in higher education. The problems surrounding the proper mix of teaching, research, and action-research, the issue of continuing education, the breakup of the lockstep undergraduate education (as more students drop out for some years), and the critical issue of linking education to jobs within a nonvocational setting are not generally addressed by union negotiators. Instead the union often introduces an extra margin of inflexibility and the faculty contributes less and less to the solution of such long-term developmental and qualitative problems.

To be sure, there are exceptions. In particular, unions of professionals who have little job status or security (e.g., interns or assistant professors) are more ambitious in their planning and more global in their programs. But in my experience the union form of organization in universities, legal services, mental-health clinics, etc., imposes unexpected rigidities and limits. Union leadership (particularly at negotiations time) generally insists that management and planning be separated from "production." They must do this because attempts by managers to bring union members onto policy boards smacks of co-optation or simply of a demand for more work. Thus union members are pushed away from the problems of planning and organizational development into a narrow defense of the status quo. Militant members discover that they lose the flexibility they had when they functioned together as a "pressure group." The fluidity of the latter gives way to an institutional bargaining arrangement which limits the capacity of either side to mobilize for reorganization and change. (This of course is also the problem with the union structure in traditional factory settings.)

The Quantitative Emphasis

This defensive attitude pushes leaders of all professional unions to emphasize the quantitative features of the professional workday. Unions negotiate for case loads, classroom size, the specific delineation of responsibilities, and tightly controlled promotion systems based on seniority. As professionals come to rely on these quantitative measures to define their work, they progressively lose interest in its quality and context. Social workers focus on case loads and not on treatment modalities, while teachers enforce pupil-to-teacher ratios rather than develop new pedagogies. (Indeed new methods will upset the carefully crafted set of job definitions.) The more unions emphasize these quantitative features, the less they are interested in service innovation. Instead, they reinforce the crisis of services.

State, Evaluation, and Efficiency

Granting agencies at the federal and state level have reinforced this quantitative approach to service measurement. As they fund an increasing number of social agencies they demand that these agencies be accountable to the spirit of the legislative program which mandated the funds. To this end they insist that their programs be "evaluated," either by outside consulting agencies or by the agency itself.[23]

But evaluation is a complex and treacherous activity. Generally an evaluation should answer the following question: "What difference did program X make to the well-being, social status, economic mobility, etc., of the target population?" To answer such a question, the evaluation and program designer must set up a test group and control group on the basis of various social and economic characteristics, devise measures of program effectiveness (e.g., increase in infant birth weights for a nutrition program), and then apply these measures to each group. Statistical measures of significance can then be applied at the end of the program to determine if it has made a difference.

This is the model of evaluation drawn from classical experimental design, akin to the laboratory testing of the impact of drugs. But the world of social action hardly fulfills the conditions required for such clean and decisive evaluation. First, establishing a control group is difficult. Evaluators cannot control the behavior of its members. They might seek service elsewhere during the course of the experiment. Second, measures of effectiveness are often difficult to devise. How can one quantify improved mental and emotional functioning? What measures can an evaluator develop to examine the impact of a delinquency-prevention program? Clearly, the choice of a measure will have a critical impact on the significance and outcome of the evaluation study. Finally, how can the evaluator decide *when* the program will register its greatest effect on the population served? Lack of results a year after the treatment may mask substantial improvements ten years later. Or conversely, substantial improvements after a year may hide significant recidivism ten years from now.

Thus, while on the surface evaluation appears to be a rigorous methodology for examining program impact, it is in fact a highly subjective and discretionary exercise.[24]

The Pressure for
Quantitative Evaluations

Grants officers are well aware of the subjective nature of evaluation. Consequently, in order to facilitate their contol over social agencies they favor those measures of success and impact that are most quantifiable. Qualitative measures leave too many loose ends, there is too much apparent guesswork, and grant officers are afraid that oversight committees in Congress or legislatures will eye such reports with suspicion. However, people can understand quantitative measures, and it is easy to develop uniform standards of service delivery based on them. Granting agencies therefore favor measures of cost efficiency (e.g., dollars per service hour, case load per worker hour, size of the potential population served, access in travel time to the service) as against measures of cost effectiveness (e.g., dollars per "cure," where cure is distinct from case closing), and social impact.

This quantitative focus has three consequences.

First, it complements the present atmosphere of fiscal austerity. In a period of tight budgets, quantitative measures, particularly the cost-efficiency ones, can be used to allocate resources between programs and agencies. Granting agencies can rationalize spending based on these measures, so that cutbacks appear less arbitrary and the inherent explosiveness of austerity programs can be kept under control.

Second, managers are well aware that evaluation measures are arbitrary and are used as instruments of political control. They become cynical about them and begin to use them as weapons in political struggles to wrest more money from granting agencies. In particular, if managers want to justify a new demonstration program or a pilot program, they will manipulate their own evaluations to buttress their arguments for financial support. This approach, however, corrupts the process of service innovation. Since the managers use evaluations arbitrarily to justify opportunistic decisions, they abandon any search for authentic qualitative standards that might help them develop strong service orientations or theories about the development of their organizations. They become "hustlers," and evaluation measures become their coin in the con-game of grantsmanship.

Finally, the quantitative focus reinforces professionals' retreat from the problems of service innovation. They resort to quantitative measures to preserve their status, while funding agencies employ quantitative measures to consolidate their control. The two groups meet, through the social-agency manager, on this plane of one-dimensional measurement and collude to repress the qualitative issues. Professionals then give up control over service development to protect their threatened positions, and the government accepts their posture because it rationalizes their behavior. Professional groups become predictable variables in the equations of political control.

The Emerging Cynicism

The emphasis on quantitative measures has important consequences. First, the issue of service development, critical in light of the underlying social crisis, is repressed from the collective consciousness. Second, the consequent cynicism of profession and managers corrupts the process of service innovation, turning it into a grantsmanship game. Third, clients are kept in a low-level trap of service dependency and are given no forum to discover collectively the roots of their own dislocation. It is, of course, important that clients be served, and in this limited sense measures of service level are crucial. Yet within the framework of efficiency and rationalization, clients become too dependent on such services. Legal services, for example, provide extensive help to the poor, but the problems that bring them to the service (repossession of autos, evictions, child-abuse proceedings) constantly recur as the underlying social crisis deepens. The client returns over and over again to the lawyer for help and feels more and more passive, just as the lawyer feels more and more frustrated. The client is served at one level but is deeply misserved at another. The service becomes an addiction that, like a drug, suppresses the capacity of clients to confront actively, both individually and collectively, the underlying crisis of their lives.

One-dimensional quantitative measurements and rationalization contribute to the social-service crisis. Yet there are powerful supports for a rationalized social-service system. It solves the short-run crises faced by professionals, clients, managers, and grant officers alike. But these are pseudosolutions. Professionals accept rationalization to preserve their status, but at the same time they feel increasingly stagnant and nonfunctional within their agencies. The developmental ethic pushes them toward innovation, but the risky political environment pulls them back toward a regressive proletarianization. The level of professional malaise, frustration, and cynicism deepens. Clients need service, but the service cripples the self-organizing capacities so essential in a period of general social crisis. Managers accept rationalization as a device to control their professionals, but they in turn are controlled by the granting agencies and weakened by declining employee morale. Finally, the granting agencies achieve smooth control over the allocation of money but must cope with growing subterfuge in the use and treatment of evaluation measures. While on the surface they want to depoliticize resource allocation by using objective measures, the process becomes increasingly politicized, as the use of evaluation degrades its meaning. But this happens "under the table," and controls become even more difficult to exercise. The new cynicism takes its toll.

What role can alternative services play in this mileu? How can they pose creative strategies for transcending the social-service crisis? This is the subject of our next and final section.

V. Whither the Alternatives?

Alternative service institutions have often been stalemated by utopian and abstract conceptions of their role and function. The term "alternative" conjures up the image of radical institutions emerging in the "belly of the monster," free of all pressures from mainstream life and strong enough to pose as a complete alternative to mainstream services. However, in today's federal social-service complex such independence is impossible. Without exception, successful alternative institutions apply for grants; get money from the feds, general or special revenue-sharing programs, or private foundations; employ professionals with career lines that straddle mainstream and alternative institutions; and, if successful, are very often co-opted by the adventurous professional schools which institutionalize their innovative approaches and discoveries.

On the surface this looks like a scenario of continuous failure for those committed to building new centers of power. But that is too simple. Those who work in or theorize about alternative institutions often fail to appreciate the crisis of the mainstream institutions themselves. They imagine that mainstream institutions are stable social systems that can control their internal contradictions. The main palace with all its treasures is on solid foundations; the alternatives must settle on areas of the social landscape far from the centers of habitation if they are to survive. As they thrive, it is presumed that people at the center will abandon it wholesale because at long last a workable and more satisfying alternative has been developed.

Such an image of the relationship between the alternatives and the mainstream is decidedly nondialectical. In fact, the crisis of established social services feeds the growth of the alternatives, and the success of the alternatives will depend on whether they can pose solutions to the mainstream's crisis. This process must be based on a continuous flow of information, resources, and people between the two sectors. The achievements of the alternatives will be judged not by their growth, size, and independence, but rather by the degree to which they can break through the stalemate of the mainstream services and unleash new developmental conflicts within and around them.

To do this, however, people who work in alternative institutions must develop a more concrete and problem-focused conception of the social-service crisis. Often alternative services begin with highly abstract ideas regarding their role and function. They will build participatory institutions based on the free exchange of information between client and helper, charge little money for services rendered, and generate a sense of cooperation and communal feelings through their work. All these goals are appropriate if not highly relevant. Yet they are too abstract and lack historical referents. The same goals have nourished the building of utopian communities and projects since the industrial revolution. *If alternative institutions are to unlock the stalemate of the mainstream, they must base their principles of operation on a concrete conception of the present social-service crisis.* They must develop solutions that directly and empirically address the expressed, as well as the unexpressed, tensions of the mainstream.

Toward a New Conception of Professional
Work: The Professional As Environmental Designer

What overall direction can alternatives take? What new principles of service organization and professional work can they embody that address the crisis of the mainstream? Here I can only be tentative. I want to propose a model of services that speaks to the problems of the mainstream that has already been introduced piecemeal in certain service settings and that is consistent with the alternatives' own goals of participation, effectiveness, and equity.

Let us return to the dynamics of the social-service crisis itself. I have argued that the social services entered a period of crisis in the sixties as a new developmental ethic undermined the power of work and family to organize social life. This developmental ethic is expressed concretely in people's desire to construct the forms of their social life—how they work, how they live—with self-consciousness and with a life plan that reflects an estimation of their own potentialities and limits. In other words, the developmental ethic leads people *away* from the older life path through which people grew into prescribed roles and *toward* a path through which they individually or with others define a role structure most appropriate to their own stage of life. (The growing diversity of household arrangements can be interpreted as one sign of this approach to social roles.)

The emergence of the developmental ethic must clearly shape professional-client interaction. The professional's skill used to be based on his or her capacity to adjust the client to social roles. Today clients want to shape their own roles, they want to participate in the planning of the form and content of their own life trajectory. This is the sense in which professionals are pushed away from direct interaction with clients.

But is there a role for the professional in this process? I suggest that there is. It is clear that clients must be helped to plan. Professionals must become experts in the *process* of role definition, life-course planning, and the collective definition of mutual responsibilities. They must learn how to establish the necessary and sufficient *conditions* for client learning. Professionals design the environment within which clients develop their own conceptions of satisfactory roles. To design such settings, professionals must become experts in how clients learn, clarify, plan, and decide. Let us give some concrete examples.

It seems increasingly that the most successful teachers, teachers that can effectively raise the competence of their pupils without burning out, are those who replace themselves with a range of *materials* (physical materials, books, electronic instruments). Such materials are chosen with great care to maximize the chances that students will discover a broad range of unexpected competencies, combinations of skills, and sets of sensory stimuli. The student ranges through the designed setting, and the teacher stands back as a consultant and guide to the student. The teacher becomes an environmental programmer, and the student becomes an investigator of environments. The teacher simultaneously distances himself or herself more than ever from direct contact with the student (there is a minimum of "transference," in psychological terms) yet at the same time he or she must understand better than ever the elements of learning if the environmental design is to maximize the chances for independent student learning. Students are able to exercise their own choices in the learning process and can, if they should so desire, learn individually or collectively, free of the teacher's intrusion. Such an approach pulls the teacher back to a more abstract level of teaching (in which theories of "learning to learn" become central) and simultaneously enables students to mark out their own learning paths.[25]

Mental health presents similar examples. Self-help groups are becoming popular and effective vehicles for dealing with a range of behavioral dysfunctions (child abuse, marriage problems, and, of course, alcoholism). In such settings the professional becomes a *facilitator* of group processes. He or she must design the setting for the group (where it takes place, how many members there are, the range of professionals that can be called on) and then function as a *consultant* to it. The primary exchange takes place between group members. Methods for self-evaluation and behavior change are enforced by the group. Again, the professional acts as a programmer, mobilizer of resources, and consultant to a self-exploration and learning process on the part of group members.[26]

Social-work agencies are also looking for new models of social-service delivery along these lines. Thus, for example, the Community Service Society of New York City, a leading social agency with a long history, reorganized its services away from traditional casework and toward a *consultation* model for client and community groups. Rather than treating individuals and families, it locates funds for community groups, trains community leaders in service development, and mediates between community groups and other public and private institutions. Again, the emphasis is on establishing the institutional conditions within which clients can draw on their own individual and collective energies to solve their problems.[27]

Finally, the role of self-help groups in medical services displays similar properties. The doctor helps the client or group of clients (as in women's-health clinics) learn to detect changes in their bodies, to anticipate and manage stress, and to become sensitized to their own limits and capacities. Within this framework the doctor acts as a consultant to people's attempts to develop their own conception of health (and there can be many such conceptions, depending on preferences for physical activity, diet, the role of acute stress, etc.).[28]

The Model As an Approach to Several Mainstream Tensions

The model of the professional as environment designer responds to several aspects of the present crisis of professions.

First, it addresses the problems of professional distance. As an environmental designer the professional must give up the power he or she enjoyed in direct face-to-face interactions. Yet this loss can hardly be mourned. As I have argued, the professional's direct involvement has become intolerable to clients.

But as professionals become more distant they nevertheless remain integrally involved. The present regressive solution to the crisis of professions, the professional as unionized worker, solves the problem of distance by simply confirming it. Since professionals can no longer instigate change in their clients, they become recalcitrant pawns in the client-professional interactions that are manipulated by managers or the state. In contrast, the function of environmental designer gives a new expert role to the professional while at the same time respecting the constraints imposed by the emergent developmental ethic.

Second, this new role for professionals helps clarify the relationship between the professional and the organization. Environmental design is a problem in *teamwork,* requiring large resources and effective organizing and mobilizing capacities. Teachers who design their classroom require a wide range of assistance, from technologists to learning theorists, media specialists, and psychologists. This effort can be coordinated and evaluated only through a competent and effective organization. Similarly, the therapist who designs settings for self-help groups must coordinate group-process facilitators, experts in particular substantive problems (e.g., child abuse), physical designers, and managers who have contact with other organizations relevant to the problem at hand (e.g., lawyers and courts with child-abuse self-help groups). In other words, the reciprocal dependency between the professional and the organization can be expressed and developed through the concept of the professional as environmental designer.

Finally, the professional's changing position parallels developments in other sectors of the society. Increasingly, managers and administrators of large corporations are focusing not on the internal operations of their organizations, but rather on their overall shape, on their boundary properties, on the regulation of the regulators. They are being trained in systems *design* rather than in systems operation.[29] This development suggests on the one side that the professional as environmental designer is part of a general structural response to the problem of expertise in a developmental culture. But it also argues on the other that radicals, the alternative institutions, must become expert in these new means of administration if they are first to compete successfully with the power centers, and second, to reveal when and where the potentials for expertise in this new role are repressed by old elites who fear too much client and worker learning.

Clearly, this model of the professional is a tentative one. Other solutions and designs are possible. But I argue that certainly the form of any other solution should follow the path laid out here. An effective model for alternative institutions must be based on a dialectical conception of the relationship between the alternative and the mainstream; it must be shaped by a consideration of the substance of the social-service crisis; and it must speak to the present stalemate of the professions within social agencies. Only such solutions can effectively break the logjam of crisis that is presently eroding morale throughout the services.

Notes

1. The history of social work is examined in my essay "The Social Service Crisis in Historical Perspective." It is Part I, and "The Social Crisis of Work" is Part II, of *The Social Crisis,* Institute for Urban and Regional Development, Working Papers no. 251 and 252 (University of California at Berkeley, 1975).

2. To establish that the changes I review in this section are permanent trends rather than temporary disruptions would require a separate essay. For supporting evidence about the nature of the social crisis and its relationship to the crisis in services, see my *Social Crisis.*

3. Susan Gray and Louis Bolce report on their research, from which they estimate that 16% of all New Yorkers go on unemployment or welfare rather than take jobs that do not suit their skills and interests. (See their article "Not That Job, Thanks," *New York Times,* 25 Dec. 1977, p. 39.) Their findings are consistent with much of the theory of the "dual labor market." The nonunionized sector of the labor market is characterized by a great deal of voluntary turnover.

4. See, for instance, Judson Gooding, *The Job Revolution* (New York: Walker and Co., 1972). For a good discussion of professional discontent, see Seymour Sarason, *Work, Aging, and Social Change: The One Career–One Life Imperative* (New York: The Free Press, 1977).

5. I have discussed this at some length in my article "Social Policy and the Life Cycle," *Social Service Review,* Sept. 1977.

6. **TABLE I. CHANGING HOUSEHOLD COMPOSITION 1950–1975**
   Household Composition (% of Total)

	HW(O)*	HW(I)†	PI‡	FHF§	Total‖
1950	59.4	19.6	10.8	8.4	98.2
1955	54.2	21.7	12.8	8.8	97.5
1960	51.2	23.2	14.9	8.5	97.5
1965	47.0	25.6	16.7	8.7	98.0
1970	41.6	28.9	18.8	8.8	98.1
1975	36.6	29.2	21.9	10.0	97.7

SOURCES.—Data for HW(O) and HW(I) through 1970 calculated by combining tables from U.S. Bureau of the Census, *Statistical Abstract: 1974* (Washington, D.C.: Government Printing Office, 1974), p. 40; and U.S. Department of Labor, *Manpower Report of the President: 1972* (Washington, D.C.: Government Printing Office, 1972), p. 40. Data for PI and FHF through 1970 calculated from *Statistical Abstract: 1974,* p. 40. Data for HW(O) and HW(I) for 1975 from U.S. Department of Labor, Bureau of Labor Statistics, *Special Labor Force Reports,* no. 183 (Washington, D.C.: Government Printing Office, 1976), p. 53; and data for PI and FHF for 1975 from U.S. Bureau of the Census, *Current Population Reports,* Series P-20, no. 282, table 5 (Washington, D.C.: Government Printing Office, 1975), p. 5.

*Husband-wife families with wife outside the labor force.

†Husband-wife families with wife in the labor force.

‡Primary individuals.

§Female-headed families.

‖Total adds up to less than 100 percent because of rounding errors and omission of male-headed families. Their inclusion would change the percentages by only insignificant amounts. Family category includes subfamilies.

7. I have developed this theme at some length in my paper "Social Services and Disaccumulationist Capitalism," *International Journal of Health Services,* forthcoming.

8. The theory of stress, mortality, and disease in a socioeconomic context is developed by Joseph Eyer and Peter Sterling, "Stress Related Mortality and Social Organization," *Review of Radical Political Economics* 9: 1 (Spring 1977): 1–44. They show that death rates for males age 20 to 24 rose 21% from 1961 to 1968. In the same period, deaths for black males of that age rose 26%. Motor-vehicle accidents, suicides, and homicides were the leading causes of death. All these causes, as expressions of violent feelings directed inward or outward, are determined in part by stress levels. Table II, taken from their article, gives the relevant data for this age group.

TABLE II. CAUSE OF RISING DEATH AMONG MALES AGE 20–24
YEARS, 1961–1968*

	Motor Vehicles			Suicide			Homicide		
	'61	'68	increase	'61	'68	increase	'61	'68	increase
White	73	95	30%	11	15	36%	5	11	120%
Nonwhite	62	89	44%	12	14	17%	67	115	72%

*Numbers are deaths per 100,000 population. Vietnam War deaths are not included.

9. The rise of the social agency is discussed in Roy Lubove, *The Professional Altruist* (New York: Atheneum Publishers, 1969).

10. Peter Marris and Martin Rein discuss the role of the Ford Foundation in establishing the model for OEO in their *Dilemmas of Social Reform* (Harmondsworth, England: Penguin Books, 1972).

11. For a brief synopsis of the legislation and its context see Seymour Sarason, *The Creation of Settings and the Future Societies* (San Francisco: Jossey-Bass, 1976), pp. 104–9.

12. An excellent text that surveys the emergence of modern medicine is Rosemary Stevens, *American Medicine and the Public Interest* (New Haven: Yale University Press, 1971).

13. The theory of "turbulence" was first developed by Fred Emery and Eric Trist. See their "The Causal Texture of Organization Environments," in Joseph A. Litterer, ed., *Organizations* (New York: John Wiley, 1969).

14. For a discussion of the concept of "negotiated order," see Robert Day, "A Review of the Current State of Negotiated Order Theory: An Appreciation and a Critique," in J. Kenneth Benson, ed., *Organizational Analysis: Critique and Innovation*, Sage Contemporary Social Sciences Issues, No. 37 (Beverly Hills: Sage Publications, 1977).

15. For this concept of disease, see John Cassel, "Social Science in Epidemiology: Psychosocial Processes and 'Stress' Theoretical Formulations," in Marcia Guttentag, ed., *Handbook of Evaluation* (Beverly Hills: Sage Publications, 1975).

16. This observation is based on my own interviews.

17. The concept of learning systems and learning institutions is developed by Donald A. Schon, *Beyond the Stable State* (New York: W.W. Norton, 1973). The problem of professional growth and development in service settings is also discussed in Sarason, *Creation of Settings*.

18. See my "Social Service Crisis"; also Robert Bremner, *From the Depths: The Discovery of Poverty in America* (New York: New York University Press, 1956).

19. For the emergence of the psychological perspective in social work, see Kathleen Woodruffe, *From Charity to Social Work* (Toronto: University of Toronto Press, 1962), chap. 6.

20. Ann Swidler, *Organization without Authority: Dilemmas of Social Control in Free Schools* (Cambridge: Harvard University Press, forthcoming).

21. I have described this process at greater length in "The Social Crisis of Work," 121–38. The demoralization of welfare workers is also discussed in Roy Bailey and Mike Brake, eds., *Radical Social Work* (New York: Pantheon Books, 1975).

22. For a brief (though biased) discussion of the strike, see Martin Mayer, *The Teachers' Strike: New York 1968* (New York: Harper and Row, 1969).

23. An introductory text on evaluation that also specifies some of its limits is Carol Weiss, *Evaluation Research* (Englewood Cliffs, N.J.: Prentice-Hall, 1972).

24. A critical view of evaluation by authors sympathetic to the enterprise is Peter Rossi and Sonia Wright, "Evaluation Research: An Assessment of Theory, Practice and Politics," *Evaluation Quarterly,* Feb. 1977.

25. See, for instance, Maya Pines, *Revolution in Learning* (New York: Harper and Row, 1966), especially chaps. 5 and 6. Also Buckminster Fuller, *Education Automation* (Carbondale: Southern Illinois University Press, 1962), gives a utopian projection of this tendency.

26. See the special issue on self-help, *Social Policy,* Sept.–Oct., 1976.

27. See Harry Gottesfield, et al., eds., *Strategies in Innovative Human Services* (New York: Behavioral Publications, 1973), pp. 283–89.

28. This is the political framework within which women's self-help medical collectives have emerged.

29. For a good description of the new systems view, see C. H. Waddington, *Tools for Thought* (New York: Basic Books, 1977).

The Agony
of Inequality

by Jane J. Mansbridge

The ideals of a radical democracy [include] an equality in which no one is
allowed to dominate others even by such intangible qualities as verbal facility,
flashy personality, or strength of ego.

Bread and Roses Collective
The Old Mole, 1971

Perhaps the most persistent problem confronting the alternative organizations and radical collectives of the late 1960s and
early 1970s was their inability to ensure that every member
exerted equal power over every decision. Political inequality is
not, of course, unique to radical collectives; it arises in all
groups that make decisions. But political inequality poses a
serious problem in groups that view it as illegitimate or im-
moral. Most recent American collectives have gone to considerable lengths to eliminate inequality. When their efforts were
only partially successful, they engaged in orgies of self-blame
and recrimination, attributing the inequalities that persisted to
their members' misshapen personalities.[1] The vision of complete equality has thus helped destroy a large proportion of the
collectives that espoused it.

Radical thought has never been very helpful in dealing with
inequality. Anarchists, adolescents, and other "idealists" have
insisted that complete equality was possible if only enough
effort were made to achieve it. Leninists, adults, and other
"realists" have usually abandoned the ideal entirely. The collectives of the last ten years have generally fallen into the former
camp. But even when they sought workable compromises between the two extremes, they seldom had any coherent theory

to tell them how much equality to seek or to require in any specific situation.

This article proposes some guidelines for such a theory, based on an analysis of the ideal of equal power itself. The analysis was prompted by the experience of an urban crisis center that pursued egalitarian ideals, satisfied the egalitarian impulses of its members, and survived the general collapse of similar organizations in the mid-1970s. If experience leads to theory and theory informs experience, the next step would be to test these guidelines in practice.

I argue here that the anguish of radical collectives over the ideal of equal power derives from a confusion between ends and means. Because the ends for which we value equal power are so rarely achieved in the modern nation-state, we seldom experience a time when equal power is not useful. It therefore easily appears as an end in itself. Traditionally, however, equal power has been seen as a means to other ends.

The arguments for equal power can be reduced to three:[2]

1. *Equal protection of interests.* When interests conflict irreconcilably, the only legitimate way to make a decision is to weight each individual's interests equally, choosing that course which accumulates the most weight. A vote derives its legitimacy from the equal weight of every individual in the outcome, but unless a vote represents equal power, voting does not protect everyone's interests equally.

2. *Equal respect.* An equal vote symbolizes, helps create, and helps maintain equality of respect.

3. *Personal growth.* Equal power encourages the participation in public affairs that is necessary for personal development, to make one fully human, broad in outlook, and conscious of one's own interests.

In all three cases, equal power is a means to some other end. These ends of equal protection of interests, equal respect, and personal growth can, in some cases, be achieved by other means. They do not necessarily require complete equality of power.

1. An organization where everyone's interests were identical would not require equal power to protect everyone's interests equally.

2. An organization where respect derived from sources other than

personal power would not require equal power to maintain equal respect.

3. An organization where each member was taking as much responsibility and handling as much conflict as he or she could manage would not produce more personal growth by distributing power more equally.

The conditions in which equality of power is unnecessary, in this analysis, are identity of interest (to meet the first end) and the separation of respect and growth from power (to meet the second and third ends). No organization meets these three conditions all the time. The *more* these conditions hold, however, the less important it becomes to reduce inequalities of power. Suppose, for example, that the older members of a collective have more power than the newer members. (That is, they are more able than the newer members to get the collective to do what it otherwise would not do.) Then on any given issue the more the old and new members have the same interests, respect one another equally, and have the same opportunities for growth, the less important it will be to devote collective resources to reducing the older members' greater power.

Conceiving of political equality as a means to the three ends of equal protection of interests, equal respect, and personal growth allows a collective to move beyond simple condemnation of any inequality of power to more probing questions:

1. How frequently do interests conflict? When they do, to what extent is everyone's interest represented equally? In many collective decisions, individual members can have similar interests. In this case members do not need to protect their own interests against those of others. However, when interests conflict often, or when individuals do not have equal power in these conflicts, a collective needs to redistribute power—by instituting referenda, for example, or representation with formal accountability.

2. Does equal respect pervade the group? If not, does respect derive from power? Often, when respect is unequal, a collective can generate more equality by bringing the members together in situations where their resources are more equal, or where those who usually have the fewest resources have more.[3] However, when unequal respect derives

in large part from unequal power, then a collective needs to redistribute power.

3. Would more equal power in the organization make the members grow in responsibility, breadth of view, and consciousness of their interests? When some members have such limited responsibility that they atrophy, see only through their own small window on the world, and do not see clearly even through that, a collective can often break this pattern by introducing variety, teamwork, and greater responsibility in individual work. However, when such growth requires more equal participation in central decisions, then a collective needs to redistribute power.

To return to the example of the older and newer members: when members of a collective discover that the older members have more power than the new, they should look then at the interests, respect, and growth of the newcomers. If the interests of the older members do not differ from those of the newcomers, if the older members do not garner greater respect, and if giving the newcomers more power will not hasten their taking responsibility or coming to understand their interests, then the newcomers will not suffer from the old-timers' greater power. The more interests diverge, status differences grow, and disadvantaged members are deprived of opportunities for growth through participation, the more seriously a democratic collective should consider making the power of the two groups more equal.

A Case Study

In the era that developed these ideals of radical equality, I belonged to four egalitarian collectives (a women's group, two political groups, and a block food co-op) and interviewed the members of another food co-op, a research organization, a free school, a radical university, and a women's center, all of which tried to eliminate inequality. Of the collectives with which I had come in contact, I wanted to study the most successful both in meeting its external goals and in satisfying the democratic expectations of its members. My theory was that the lessons learned in such a collective would have general applicability. If patterns of inequality persisted even in the most democratic collective I could find, they would be probably be the most difficult patterns to erase. If participants were bitter or disillusioned, they would be so after having tried a large number of practical experiments in promoting equality. My general strategy was to explore the problems of equality by looking at the deviant—extremely egalitarian—case. This was the same strategy I had followed in choosing a participatory democracy for study in the first place. For the same reason I excluded from consideration in the organization I chose the questions of equality among the volunteers and equality between the volunteers and paid staff. Differences in members' other commitments are so great in voluntary organizations that political inequality is inevitable. Nor, usually, can any volunteer give the time to an organization that a paid staff member can give. Because my strategy was to examine political equality under the best possible conditions, I compared the power only of those individuals who started with approximately equal organizational positions —the paid staff.

The organization I chose, Helpline, an urban crisis center, had forty-one full-time paid staff members and several hundred volunteers.[4] The organization ran a twenty-four-hour switchboard for drug and crisis counseling, a medical-emergency van, a house for runaways, and a commune counseling and placement project. It got money from small foundations, churches, and federal research grants, and from contracting its services to the city, consulting with other towns, and eventually selling some services to individuals (the fee varying with the client's income).

Conceived in 1966 by a charismatic leader but subsequently influenced deeply by the participatory egalitarianism of the later 1960s, Helpline had overthrown its original organizer and sharply curtailed the power of its fund-raisers in the seven years between its inception and the time I arrived. All forty-one staff members took the same salary, with standard increases for particular cases of need. They divided up routine chores equally; there were no secretaries.

The staff strove also for political equality. In the question-naire that I gave them, 89 percent said that they thought "equality of political power in internal decisions" was "very crucial" or "fairly crucial" to making the organization what they wanted it to be. To pursue this goal, they delegated most decisions to five small work groups of six to twelve members, made major policy decisions in full assembly (Community Days), instituted a system of mandated representatives to a central committee, made decisions by consensus, and brought their group and counseling skills to bear on the processes of participation in the workplace itself.

Decentralization to the level of a small work group meant that in the crucial areas of hiring and firing, conditions of work, job definition, and leisure time, every member could hear and be heard. The work groups also gave their members practice for participation in the full assemblies, and served as support groups when real conflict emerged in the larger organization.

Mandated representatives attending a central committee brought every conflictual issue back to the work groups for discussion. This system attempted to lessen the inequalities that developed under an earlier, pure-assembly, "town-meeting" form of government. When the staff had made all their deci-sions in assembly, the less fluent, more isolated members had been distinctly less likely than the others to attend. So the staff finally decided that supplementing the assemblies (Community Days) with a representative committee that took all important issues back to the work groups for discussion would give every member a more equal input. For the same reason they always broke large assemblies into small groups for discussion.[5]

The entire community decided issues by "consensus." Under this procedure dissidents ordinarily went along with the group, but if convinced they were right they could veto any proposed action. This procedure encouraged the group to seek out every-one's opinion, since one person who felt ignored could delay or even stop a decision.

A widespread understanding of the way groups work also helped spread power. Because the organization's task involved counseling or mediating in some way between a person in trou-

TABLE I. POWER, PARTICIPATION, EFFICACY, AND SATISFACTION BY INDIVIDUAL CHARACTERISTICS[a]

Power and Participation	Length of time in organization	Physical proximity to social center	Age	Race (Bl., Wh.)	Sex (F., M.)	Class — Parents' class (working cl., oth.)	Class — Own education (controlled for age)
Speaking at meetings	.26*	.25	.20	−.02	.11	.37**	.25
Attending meetings	.30*	.31*	.30*	.09	.17	.46**	.20
Ranked high in "power" by other staff	.28*	.34*	.22	.17	.06	.26	.35*
Feelings of Efficacy and Satisfaction							
Reports self as high in "say" and "power"	.29*	.30**	.25	.11	.21	.36*	.17
Reports satisfaction with decisions	−.17	.26	.17	.07	.25	.31*	.36*

[a] These calculations are Pearson product-moment correlation coefficients based upon forty-one cases, with some variation for nonresponse. For example, if every man spoke once but no women spoke, this perfect correlation would be represented by +1.00. If men and women were equally likely to speak, this absence of any correlation would be represented by .00. (The correlation between education and income in the United States is about .40.) As many of these variables are noninterval and some may have nonlinear relationships, the correlations should be understood as approximations. Helpline is not representative of worker-controlled organizations. I chose it as having, on its face, the greatest degree of political equality of any of the organizations I had encountered. Tests of statistical significance using, as these do, the entire Helpline staff therefore have meaning insofar as the reader can imagine a universe composed of organizations similar to Helpline. They also indicate the likelihood that an observed association between the two variables appearing among the variables under study, and not to chance alone. Statistical significance is indicated by asterisks. If the probability of the indicated association is due to some systematic causal relation among the variables randomly in a sample this size is less than five in one hundred (p = <.05), one asterisk (*) will follow the correlation; ** indicates p = <.01; *** indicates p = <.001.

"Speaking at meetings" combines a questionnaire report of how frequently one speaks at meetings with observed measures of speaking in the major representative committee and at Community Days. "Attending meetings" combines questionnaire reports of attendance with observed measures of attendance in four committee and at Community Days. Activities ... derives from an exercise administered at the end of the interview. "Reports self as high in 'say' and

ble and a multitude of city agencies, the work itself helped develop the skills needed to hold one's own in public. Moreover, three-quarters of the staff had had specific training in "group process." They had learned how to pause in a meeting when an urgent issue had some people crowding the ends of others' sentences, how to ask—without pressuring—if anyone hadn't spoken, how to check that what they heard was what another had said, how to recognize panic, hurt, and discomfort, and how to speak openly of all these things in themselves and others. In redistributing power, the staff relied heavily on the skills they had developed in group training, and on the attention to each member required by the consensual model. People whose backgrounds had led them to take command learned to listen; those who had previously held back learned they would be listened to.

This commitment of word and deed produced results. Only two of the forty-one staff members missed both full assemblies during the six months I was at Helpline. Among those who attended, all but two or three spoke out. All but one of the staff members who had been in the organization more than a year and a half had acted as representative on one of the two major committees. More than three-quarters of the staff reported that "decisions around Helpline are made by a process of give and take among a number of groups and individuals" in differing combinations, as opposed to being made "by a small group of people." Indeed, of the six major decisions I studied closely, only one person figured prominently in three. Another figured prominently in two. The nine remaining major actors appeared prominently in only one decision each. Mutual choices of friends within the organization did not produce an interrelated governing clique.

However, even Helpline's elaborate paraphernalia of democracy was not enough to guarantee equality (see Table I). Newcomers and members with working-class parents were significantly less likely than their colleagues to participate in Helpline decisions, less likely to perceive themselves as powerful, and less likely to be perceived as powerful by other members of the organization. The same was true of those who reported lower verbal skills or not liking to take responsibility. It was even true of members who worked away from the central social axis of the building and of those who were young. Women participated almost as much as men and were ranked by other staff members as equal in power to the men, but remained less confident about their participation. The three black members of Helpline seemed almost as likely as the whites to participate and exercise power.

Old-timers/Newcomers

The reasons for the old-timers' greater power and participation áre not difficult to decipher. Like many organizations that employ only young people, Helpline had a rapid turnover among its staff.[6] Newcomers took a while to become familiar with the system of making decisions, to gather the confidence to influence decisions, and to become interested in the organization as a whole. They did not understand the meaning of in-house abbreviations, issues with a long history, and terms that had come to have loaded meanings. They did not recognize all the opportunities for participation. Conscious of their lack of background, they restrained their comments and even their questions. As one newcomer put it,

> The meetings I go to? I try *not* to go to them! Because I usually don't say anything. Because everyone else seems to have something they want to say. And maybe it's because I haven't been here that long. And I don't know that much about the organization itself—where their head is at. So I sort of keep my mouth shut at meetings—unless I feel it's necessary.

Familiarity with the organization gave old-timers at Helpline not only more courage than the newcomers but also the advantage of contacts and inside knowledge. They knew more people and were known by more. They were more likely to know whom to contact on any problem and to be the ones others contacted.[7] They had built up the social networks that made the process of mutual influences easier. When the staff members explained to me the reasons behind the inequality they saw in their organization, they cited longevity more frequently than any other reason.

Physical Proximity

Helpline was decentralized—in work, in decision-making, and in emotional commitment. This decentralization increased the members' participation and satisfaction,[8] but it pulled their loyalties away from the central organization. More than half the staff members reported that their best friends in the organization were in their own work group. The more friends at Helpline individual staff members had outside their work group, the more they were likely to participate and exercise power in central decisions.[9] In fact, any circumstance that increased people's chances of associating with other staff members outside their own work group also increased their chances of participating or exercising power in the central organization. As a consequence, staff members who worked at the bottom of the stairwell, right by the front door, had more power than the average member of Helpline, while those who worked away from the central building had less.[10] This "friends and neighbors" effect on power is most common where political organization is informal and unstructured.[11]

Blacks and Women

In 1973, when I measured participation in Helpline, the civil-rights and women's movements had given salience to the disadvantages of blacks and women in acquiring power. The external political situation thus encouraged the thirty-eight whites and twenty-four males to avoid obvious domination, and the three blacks and seventeen females to try to participate more. The women suffered from lower verbal self-confidence;[12] the black staff members suffered from their perception of the "counter-culture" as irretrievably alien.[13] Yet both groups managed to participate almost as much as the males and whites. The disadvantages of blacks and women at Helpline, so long as they were not combined with the problems of class and longevity, had proved easier to reduce than the effects of organizational placement and the deeply embedded disadvantages of class.

Social and Economic Class

Only three of Helpline's forty-one-person staff described their parents as "working class." One of these three was a woman; another was black. All three participated less and had less power than the average staff member at Helpline. Not one of the three, for example, attended both of the two Community Days I observed—compared to 75 percent of the rest of the staff. Not one reported attending "all" or "almost all" Community Days since they'd joined—compared to 72 percent of the rest of the staff. Not one attended any of the representative meetings that I observed—compared to 58 percent of the rest of the staff. Only one had ever been a representative to one of the major committees—compared to 72 percent of the rest of the staff. All three reported speaking less than average at meetings, and when they attended Community Days, they spoke an average of 1.9 times each, compared to an average of 3.6 among the rest of the staff. All three achieved lower than average scores in the power rankings.

These three members attributed the others' higher participation and power to their greater verbal skills. The first, who had worked at Helpline more than three years, argued that the difference in verbal skill created a hierarchy quite parallel to that in less participatory organizations:

> Once I worked in a sales office, and things were imposed on me because of a certain hierarchy. . . . I think that same thing happens at Helpline, only here people's power is used verbally.

The people who are most powerful in the organization, he told me, "can verbalize; they twist things around." The second explained the low power of two fellow workers by saying, "He's like I am, not very articulate," and "He's kind of thick, like me —he won't argue with their big words." The third interpreted inequalities at Helpline the same way, telling me that the most powerful people at Helpline "know how to talk," have "a quick wit," are "very articulate," and "use a lot of wall-to-wall words!"

Unlike the other members of Helpline, these three members were quite conscious of the effects of class, particularly as it expresses itself through education. The first had opted out completely. "The people who think Helpline is attractive," he told me, "are people with verbal skills." As for himself: "*I'm* not participating, I'm just observing!" The second no longer had much hope for her participation: "The way things go at Helpline, it's like meeting with an encyclopedia going to one of their meetings! The words they use!" "To me," she added,

> that ties in with money. Most of the people you see up here had enough money to go to college for four years, or wherever they went, and learn how to use a lot of big words. [Laugh] That has a lot to do with it! You really have to play word games!

She had thought of getting active in politics, but had concluded, "I couldn't do it. First, I'd have to go to school for twenty years to learn how to talk the way they talk; and by then it wouldn't do any good." The third, asked if he had ever thought of going on Helpline's major representative committee, answered,

> No. I never liked talking ideas. I really have a hard time. I can talk to you, you're only one person and I only have to deal with one head, but where there's a lot of people, like, I find myself repeating myself.

He avoided the large assemblies as well.

> Some people don't *feel* like standing up in front of sixty people and saying things. Me too, so that's why it was good to get out of that meeting! [Laugh] I find that with me there is a question of education involved. Like most people at Helpline come from an academic background; they feel confident with papers and pens.

Verbal Self-confidence; Enjoying Power and Responsibility

In a consensual process, the members make all their decisions by talking about an issue until they reach agreement. Verbal skills therefore become essential. Verbal self-confidence "explained" a lot of the difference in power and participation at Helpline due to class, and more than explained the slight differences due to sex.[14] The training Helpline's staff had in interpersonal communication may have reduced but clearly did not eliminate these perceived differences in verbal skill or their effects on participation.

In a fluid organization like this, people who like responsibility and enjoy power are more likely to particpate and actually exercise power. Men at Helpline were no more likely than women to report on a questionnaire that they enjoyed power, and the children of middle-class parents did not do so more than the children of working-class parents. Responding positively to the self-description "I enjoy power" or "I like responsibility" simply had a strong independent association with both participation and power.[15]

Discriminating Among Inequalities

Even with Helpline's elaborate set of procedures for spreading participation, the greater power attributable to longer membership, geographical centrality, age, class, verbal self-confidence, and attraction to power and responsibility proved difficult to eradicate. If Helpline had tried to follow an ideal of perfect equality, this would have opened the way to agonies of self-recrimination. If it had adopted a "vanguard" elitist form of organization, this would have reduced the extent to which the collectivity could work together as friends, under conditions of equal respect. Without formulating the ideas explicitly, however, the members at Helpline seem to have thought of their situation in terms of ends and means. Because they had achieved the ends they desired by other means, they could live relatively comfortably with the existing inequalities of power. If they had made their analysis explicit, they could have gone even further to isolate and work on the instances in which the desired ends were least fully met. Applying an ends-means analysis allows one to set priorities in a situation of scarce resources and directs attention to the inequalities that are most important to reduce. Looking at the inequalities between different groups at Helpline, for example, one would ask in each case to what extent the interests of the less powerful were not protected equally, to what extent the less powerful suffered a loss in respect, and to what extent they had lost the opportunity for growth.

At Helpline the differences in interest between newcomers and old-timers and between young and old were negligible. The long-established policy of equal salaries meant that pay and promotion could not depend on seniority or age. Nor were the older staff more interested in maintaining the organization than the newcomers, as organization theory suggests they might be.[16] I discerned only one difference in interest. The newcomers, having joined the organization in the early 1970s rather than the late 1960s, held ideas that were somewhat less "countercultural" and more "political" than those of the older staff. They were less interested, for instance, in building internal community, and more interested in affecting the outside world directly. But despite the old-timers' generally greater power, the advocates of countercultural values were collectively no more powerful than anyone else. In regard to the second criterion, equal respect, the old-timers often did not want to go through the full explanations and the rehashing of past decisions that would have made the newcomers truly equal. As a result, the newcomers sometimes felt left out and relegated to a more passive position than they would have liked. But because the newcomers were never in this position more than a few months, the negative effects on their self-esteem were neither serious nor long-lasting. As for the third criterion, the opportunity for growth, Helpline often thrust newcomers immediately into positions of more responsibility than the newcomers themselves felt comfortable with. They found no dearth of opportunities for personal growth.

Differences in geographic centrality coincided somewhat more with differences in interest. One work group, geographically isolated from the rest of Helpline, had a separate interest in the preservation of its own program and staff, and a philosophic orientation slightly different from that of the rest of Helpline. The members of this group were not, however, deprived of respect or the opportunities for growth.

As for personal characteristics, the people at Helpline who reported that they expressed themselves well in words or enjoyed power had a lesser interest than the other staff in maintaining equal power in internal decisions.[17] But on other actual or potential issues their interests differed little from those of the rest of the staff. In my estimation, they also seem to have received no more respect than their less verbal and less power-oriented fellows, for at Helpline therapy was the most important task, not administration or talking at meetings. (In a school or consciousness-raising group, where talk is the major product, verbal self-confidence might be more linked to respect.) Even in regard to personal growth, the less power-oriented and less verbal staff at Helpline probably did not suffer, for the organization not only provided opportunity but put pressure on its members to take administrative jobs and speak at meetings. The staff seemed to be growing as much in these areas as it could.

Of all the readily identifiable groups with less than equal power at Helpline, the three members who described their parents as "working class" had interests that seemed to differ most from those of their fellow workers. They valued organizational efficiency and accountability distinctly more than the other members.[18] They also were more likely than others in the organization to place a high value on equal power and equal influence.[19] Because it is impossible to measure objective interests, I can only speculate on the interests the members of Helpline with working-class parents might have had, but either were not conscious of, or did not express to me. These three could reasonably have had a greater interest in higher salaries, although they gave me no indication of this. They could also have had interests in Helpline's hiring more working-class people, trying to attract more working-class clients, instituting a high-school equivalency program for its staff, or making it easier in other ways for its working-class members to get jobs after they left Helpline. Moreover, as members of a social group whose power in the outside society was lower than the average, these three might well have lost more self-esteem than the other staff members through lower participation at Helpline, since their lower participation would corroborate an external stereotype. They were respected at Helpline for their counseling skills, but their own comments about their verbal ability suggest that this may not have been enough to generate a sense of equal respect. Finally, although each of them firmly expressed a desire not to participate more in the central Helpline governance, structural alterations that made it easier for them to take a more active part in the determination of central issues at Helpline (e.g., a working-class caucus, or more referenda) might have made them more aware of the ways in which their interests differed from those of other members.

As a rule, however, the interests of the staff at Helpline were not in great conflict. And as regards equality of respect and the potential for growth, Helpline was lucky enough to have these even without absolutely equal power. Respect in the organization derived largely from one's reputation as a counselor, so that unequal power in central decisions did not lead to unequal respect. The opportunities for participation of all kinds were so great as to have driven a good many members almost to the point of being "burned out." Each staff member carried immense responsibility and probably could not have used more. The conditions requiring equality of power were therefore largely satisfied at Helpline, and a large proportion of the staff could say that they felt "comfortable" with the inequalities that remained.[20]

If Helpline were to devote even more of its scarce resources to promoting greater equality of power, this analysis of the three ends of equal power suggests that it should have tried to increase the power of the working-class members, just as it had earlier focused on the special problems of women and blacks. It might also have given attention to the slightly lower power of the most geographically distant work group. In both of these cases, the members' interests might not have been represented in proportion to their numbers, while the working-class members might also have lost out in the realms of equal respect and personal growth by participating less than others in the decisions.

Conclusion

What this collective learned from its seven-year experience, most collectives never learn before they collapse in agony over their internal inequalities. Helpline learned to decentralize, radically, to groups of five to twelve. They learned some basic lessons of group process. They learned to listen, and how to say when they felt they had not been listened to. They learned the perils of a large public assembly, augmenting it with representative committees and breaking the assembly down into small groups.

But they were lucky. By self-selection and good fortune, these forty-one people had also come together in circumstances that fostered the three conditions of identity of interests, equal respect, and personal growth. When all their techniques did not produce perfect equality of power, they could be genuinely comfortable with the still quite noticeable inequalities that remained.

Because, by and large, the staff all strongly supported the common task, they had similar interests on most issues that came before the collective for decision. They had practiced, and therefore did not have to learn, conscious techniques of promoting equal respect by means other than equal power—by sharing intense common experience, by redistributing valued skills, and by publicly valuing attributes held equally among the members. They had also, without planning it, created for each member a course of development that would generate both greater responsibility and a more accurate understanding of one's interests.

The lesson of this analysis is that collectivities should look to the ends, rather than fixating on the means. They should insist on equal power only if it is the easiest available way of generating equal respect and opportunities for growth. As for the protection of interests, participants should always ask themselves to what extent their interests are really in conflict. This is not an easy question to answer, but it is the right question. In many instances the interests of participants are in fact extremely similar. When they are not, however, attempting to struggle through to a consensual, unitary decision will only produce either deadlock in favor of the status quo or social coercion. When interests differ, a collective ought to recognize this fact and deal with it by distributing power as equally as possible on that issue—by taking turns, or by making a bargain in which each party loses and gains equally. This obvious truth in couples' relations has not yet been applied to larger groups.

When interests diverge frequently in ways that become irreconcilable, an organization that takes equal power seriously must revive much of the paraphernalia of liberal democracy. Majority vote, formally accountable representatives, and referenda—with all their implied confessions of failed negotiations —must come into play to protect the interests of those least likely to participate in an informal system. Individuals must become aware of their interests by engaging in conflicts, and that conflict must have formal avenues of resolution in which, as much as possible, each individual counts for one and none for more than one.

Notes

1. For example, Bread and Roses, a women's organization in Boston, attributed its failure to achieve its egalitarian ideal to the "competitive, fearful, and privatistic" thought patterns of capitalist society. See Bread and Roses Collective, "Getting Together," *The Old Mole,* 1971; reprinted in Richard Fairfield, ed., *Utopia, U.S.A.* (San Francisco: Alternative Foundation, 1972), p. 184.

2. A detailed, philosophical exposition of the following argument appears in my "Acceptable Inequalities," *British Journal of Political Science* 7 (1977): 321–36. The argument does not attempt to refute the claim that

equal power may be an end in itself, since arguments of this type are generally irrefutable by nature. It asserts only that past justifications for equal power have all treated equal power as a means to one of the three ends in the text.

3. Consciousness-raising groups, where each member's personal experience can be as powerful as any other's, equalize resources among women who in other situations hold unequal status.

4. The name of the crisis center is fictitious. My observations of this organization form part of a larger study of egalitarian decision-making, which includes data from a New England town meeting.

   I attended meetings at Helpline for six months in 1973, taking notes on the extent as well as the content of each member's participation. I interviewed forty of the forty-one members in a generally unstructured format for an hour or more, and received responses to a written questionnaire from every member. Toward the end of each interview I asked the staff member I was interviewing to participate in a power-ranking exercise, from which the measures "Ranked high in 'power' by other staff" and "Reports self as high in 'power' " (Table I) are drawn.

5. Dividing the assembly into small groups did give every member a greater chance to participate. It also perceptibly increased both the satisfaction of the members and their ability to engage in what they considered productive conflict. It did not, however, have any effect on the most salient inequalities. The correlations between (a) speaking and (b) length of time in the organization, proximity to the central building, age, working-class parents, race, sex, reported verbal self-confidence, and reported attraction to power and responsibility were no smaller in the small discussion groups than in the full assembly.

6. The average staff member had been at Helpline only a year and three-quarters, and most expected to leave within two more years. When I returned to Helpline in January, 1977, four years after my original observations, only six of the forty-one people I had known and interviewed in 1973 still worked there.

7. The correlation between a staff member's length of time in the organization and the percentage of the staff each member knows is .432 (N=30; $p = < .01$); the correlation between a staff member's length of time in the organization and the percentage of the staff who know that member is .521 (N=41; $p = < .001$). The correlation between length of time in the organization and feeling sure about where to place others on the power-ranking exercise is .597 (N=41; $p = < .05$).

8. Simple arithmetic indicates that the smaller the group, the greater the chance of each individual member to speak. Down to five members, the smaller the group, the greater the reported satisfaction of the participants. See A. Paul Hare, *Handbook of Small Group Research,* 2nd ed. (New York: The Free Press, 1976), pp. 216–17.

9. The correlation between answers to the question "How many people in Helpline *outside* your service group do you feel personally close to?" and the index of attendance was .555 (N=37; $p = < .001$), the index of speaking .449 (N=37; $p = < .001$), and the power ranking by other staff .499 (N=37; $p = < .001$). The correlation between answers to the ques-

tion, "How many people *in* your service group do you feel personally close to?" and attendance was only .095, speaking .103, and attributed power .111. The causal direction here is not completely clear. It might be that those who for other reasons had acquired central power also came, by virtue of their work, to have friends outside their own group.

10. Festinger's study of an MIT housing project also showed that the simple accident of living at the bottom of a stairwell, or at some other point of physical and social communication, increased a student's chances of becoming involved in the internal politics of the project. Leon Festinger, Stanley Schacter, and Kurt Bach, *Social Pressures in Informal Groups* (Stanford: Stanford University Press, 1950), p. 112. The same is true of living in the central village in a small Vermont town. See my "Town Meeting Democracy," *Working Papers for a New Society* 1 (1973): 9.

11. See V. O. Key, *Southern Politics* (New York: Alfred A. Knopf, 1950), p. 37; J. David Greenstone, "Political Norms and Group Process in Private Government: The Case of a Local Union," *Midwest Journal of Political Science* 9 (1965): 350; and Paul E. Peterson, "Forms of Representation: Participation of the Poor in the Community Action Program," *American Political Science Review* 64 (1970): 502.

12. On a checklist of traits, the men of Helpline were significantly less likely than the women to report that "Articulate people intimidate me," ($r = .520$; $N = 32$; $p = <.01$), and significantly more likely to report "I express myself well in words" ($r = .368$; $N = 31$, $p = <.05$).

13. One of the black members told me later that dealing with the "group-talk" and counter cultural norms at Helpline "was an enormous cultural shock! I mean, they talked a different language. . . . It wearied me out at times. I'd say to myself, 'What am I doing here?' This place is *strange!*" Another put it, "I know this is not my trip, OK?. . . . I don't feel safe here."

14. The measure of verbal self-confidence used here combines responses to two questionnaire items: "I express myself well in words," and "Articulate people intimidate me." Controlling for verbal self-confidence reduces the standardized coefficient of class when predicting attributed power from .376 to .086, and when predicting attendance from .512 to .310. Controlling for verbal self-confidence makes the standardized coefficient of sex when predicting attendance and attributed power a negative number.

15. The correlation between responses to the questionnaire item "I enjoy power" and the central power others assigned to one at Helpline was .383 ($N = 29$; $p = <.05$); and with attendance at meetings .237 ($N = 29$; $p = <.05$). The correlation between responses to "I like responsibility" and assigned power was even larger: .599 ($N = 31$; $p = <.001$), and attendance .261 ($N = 31$; $p = >.05$). The index of liking power and responsibility reported in Table I is composed of these responses, as well as responses to the questionnaire items, "I hate to tell others what to do," "I enjoy planning things and taking charge," "I like competition," "I don't like to 'operate'," and "If you had your choice, would you rather have a job where you gave the orders or a job where somebody else told you what to do?"

16. On this point, see Joyce Rothschild-Whitt, "Problems of Democracy," *Working Papers* 4 (1976): 41–45.

17. The correlations between responses to the questionnaire items, "I enjoy power" and "I express myself well in words," and considering "equality of political power in internal decisions" crucial to the organization were $-.313$ ($N=28$; $p=>.05$) and $-.224$ ($N=30$; $p=>.05$) respectively.

18. All three members who identified their parents as "working class" said that they thought "efficiency of decision-making" and "accountability—ensuring that people do their work well" were crucial to making Helpline what they wanted it to be, compared to only 29 percent and 45 percent of the other members.

19. The three members who identified their parents as "working class" all considered "equality of political power in internal decisions" and "equal influence in all internal decisions" in the organization crucial, compared to only 59 percent and 29 percent of the other members.

20. After the power-ranking exercise in the interview, I asked the staff whether they felt "comfortable" or "uncomfortable" with the inequalities they had just portrayed. Eighty-five percent of those who did the exercise (72 percent of the total) said they felt comfortable with the inequalities. The reasons they gave me provided the starting point for my analysis of acceptable inequalities.

Conditions for Democracy: Making Participatory Organizations Work

by Joyce Rothschild-Whitt

Weber's forecast that every domain of social life would become progressively rationalized as Western society became more modern is, today, a coin of the sociological realm. For Weber, the inexorable process of rationalization, and its main locus of expression in bureaucracy, is due to the technical superiority of bureaucracy over all other modes of organization in history, and to bureaucracy's indispensability as an instrument of power for those who head it. Once firmly established, bureaucracy renders revolution (i.e., a fundamental change in the *structure* of authority) impossible, and replaces it with mere changes in *who* controls the bureaucratic apparatus.

Many social scientists have agreed that bureaucratization removes the locus of control over the organization from the individual, and thereby entails a loss of individual freedom and control. Firmly rooted in the work of Weber and Michels, the literature on social-movement organizations is replete with case studies that indicate both the fragility of participatory-democratic systems and their tendency to develop oligarchies that displace original goals. Various explanations are offered:

1. Organizational goals may become increasingly accommodated to values in the surrounding community (such as the TVA).

2. Organizations (like the March of Dimes) may practically accomplish their original goals and then shift to more diffuse ones in order to maintain the organization per se.

3. Organizations (such as the Women's Christian Temperance Union) may find it impossible to realize their original goals and will then develop more diffuse ones.

4. Procedural regulations and rules (organizational means) may become rigidified in their use by members until they are converted, in effect, into ends in themselves.

5. Maintenance and growth of an organization may be transformed into ends in themselves (as in the German Socialist Party) because it is in the interest of those at the top of the organization to preserve their positions of power and privilege within it.

These processes of oligarchization and goal displacement—taken as near-constants—represent no small problem for the social-movement organization, for they may destroy its *raison d'être*. The theoretical model introduced by Zald and Ash is the exception in that it views these transformation processes as conditional.[1]

More recently, the question of whether democracy is possible within bureaucratic organizations has been approached from a different direction. Bennis and Slater, for example, argue that democratic modes of organization are *inevitable* if organizations wish to survive in a society experiencing rapid technological change.[2] Organizations will have the intellectual resources to adapt to changing and complex technological problems only if they direct the talents of specialists from many disciplines into project groups that are run democratically and dissolved upon completion of the project at hand.

In sum, the debate about the prospects of democratic organization has come full circle. It begins with the tradition of Weber and Michels, which stresses that democratic control over bureaucracies is not possible, and ends with the Bennis forecast that democracy is inevitable in the bureaucracy of the future.

I wish to argue that democratic modes of organization are neither impossible nor inevitable. They are conditional. Since "alternative institutions" aspire or claim to be directly democratic, they are ideal locations to investigate the conditions under which democratic aspirations are realized or undermined. This essay seeks to identify the structural conditions that allow at least some alternative institutions to maintain democratic forms of organization, to adhere to their original social goals, and to sustain nonbureaucratic, collectivist modes of organization.

The Research Sites

In the past decade, the United States has witnessed an impressive proliferation of what are now termed alternative institutions. They are important sociologically insofar as they depart radically from established modes of organization. Owing their legacy to the antiauthority movements of the 1960s, alternative institutions may be defined by their resolve to build organizations parallel to, but outside of, established institutions, organizations that fulfill social needs (for education, medical aid, etc.) without recourse to internal bureaucracies or external direction.

Such parallel, oppositional organizations have been created in almost every sphere—e.g., free medical clinics, free schools, legal collectives, alternative media collectives, food cooperatives, research collectives, communes. Some of them grew at a remarkable rate—for instance, in 1967 there were about thirty free schools in the United States; by 1973 there were over eight hundred documented free schools, in spite of declining nonpublic-school enrollments during those six years.[3] Unfortunately, little research has been devoted to this social development. Some studies described one or another alternative institution, but few seek to identify the common traits that link them.

This essay reports some of the findings from a comparative examination of alternative service organizations. It suggests theoretical propositions at the "middle range" about conditions that facilitate participatory-democratic organizational forms. Using a comparative study, rather than a single case study, allows me to highlight organizational properties that are generic and to avoid features that are peculiar to only one type of organization.[4]

The study included a free medical clinic, a free high school, an alternative newspaper, a legal collective, and a food cooperative.[5] All were at least two years old. I tried to choose organizations as varied as possible—some have government funding, some do not; some are relatively large, others are small; some employ sophisticated technology, others' tasks are simpler or undeveloped technologically; etc. Yet all give primacy to operating as a collectivist-democratic alternative to bureaucracy.

A number of methodologies were used, with data from one serving as a check on the other. First, field observations (from six months to two years) were conducted in each of the settings. The resulting information was amplified by intensive, structured interviews with selected members from each group. Questionnaires returned by members of the free clinic, the alternative newspaper, and the food co-op provided further material.

Propositions: Conditions Facilitating Participatory-Democratic Organizations

The capacity of an alternative institution, or any organization, to be directly democratic is conditional. Below I propose a number of conditions to account for the relative ease or difficulty a given alternative institution experiences in moving toward its collectivist ideals. If my hypotheses are correct, these conditions should help an organization to achieve a nonauthoritarian, collectivist-democratic structure. The absence of any condition should constitute a source of tension or contradiction for the collectivist organization.[6] These hypothetical conditions will be posed as antidotes to problems, already referred to, that have been taken to be endemic in organizations: conservatism of organizational purpose (through goal displacement, succession, or accommodation), rigidification of rules and general ossification, oligarchization of power, and maintenance of the organization as an end in itself.

Internal Factors

1. *Transitory orientation*

One basic, but usually neglected, condition that may have a profound effect on an organization and how it changes is the expectation of transience that characterizes many alternative institutions. Since most of the literature on organizations, including that on alternative ones, assumes that permanence is desirable, only rarely has the transitory-permanence dimension been considered as an independent variable in organizational analysis.[7]

A transitory character appears to be taken for granted by many countercultural people. That is, many seem to expect and desire an accelerated pace of social, psychological, and physical change in their lives, and this feeling seems to generalize to their relationships to organizations: they expect them to be temporary. The wider emergence of this sort of transitory orientation has been examined by others who have stressed its implications for the individual.[8]

The point to be stressed here is that this sort of transitory orientation carries with it certain consequences for the organization that have not been fully appreciated. What I have found is that *a transitory orientation profoundly militates against organizational maintenance and goal diffusion as particular forms of goal displacement.* In a transitory organization, member apathy is *not* likely to produce oligarchization and organizational maintenance as an end in itself (contra the Weber-Michels model). For, in the face of membership apathy or inability to move toward its original goals, this kind of organization tends toward purposeful self-dissolution. In the more unusual case where all of their original goals are accomplished, members of a transitory organization would be more likely to admit their project obsolete and disperse than to create diffuse new goals.

The expectation that an organization will be transitory—and the feeling that it is *better* for it to disband than to displace its original goals—was well reflected at the Free Clinic I studied.

There, when faced with the prospect of having to charge patients nominal fees for services provided, thus no longer being completely free, one staff member poignantly said:

> I don't want the [Free Clinic] to go on a heart-lung machine.
> There's such a thing as letting a good thing die, of dying with
> dignity. . . . That's what I want for the [Free Clinic]. . . .
> (February 18, 1975)

A comparable preference for dissolution over goal displacement was voiced at the Food Co-op. Even in a time of growth and expansion, a staff member and founder of the co-op urged that the bylaws be amended to include the following:

> If we do not get a quorum for three general membership meet-
> ings in a row, then the Board should be required to start proce-
> dures for the dissolution of the co-op. . . . I don't consider this
> a "radical" proposal. After all, we started the [Food Co-op] as
> a community-owned and -controlled economic institution. If its
> members don't care enough about it to come to periodic meet-
> ings, then control will naturally fall in the hands of a few inter-
> ested people. If and when that happens, the [Food Co-op] will
> have become nothing more than a cheap Safeway, and it would
> be better to close down, than to continue without real member
> participation. . . . (April 6, 1975)

The point here is not that a transitory orientation is, in itself, either good or bad nor, as others have argued, that it will soon encompass many bureaucratic organizations, but rather that it carries with it important consequences for the organization. At just those times that other organizations would displace goals and develop an oligarchy, these organizations may opt for self-dissolution.

This expectation that the organization will be evanescent holds as well for the programs, personnel, and operations within the organization. That is, members tend to regard the *modus operandi* of the organization as experimental or tentative, as contingent on its outcomes. In this sense, procedures and rules may never be considered established and may, therefore, never carry the weight of formalism and precedent. Such an experimental orientation toward all operations may be needed to support the kind of ad hoc, individualized decision-making toward which these directly democratic organizations aspire, without recourse to matter-of-fact rules and routines. The sentiment that all operations and personnel in an organization ought to be tentative seems to militate against the usual worship of rules that turns means into ends.

As an illustration of the transitory expectations concerning personnel, *all* of the groups under study thought that anyone who had been with the group for nine months to a year had been there "a long time." And anything over two years, as in the case below, might well be considered "too" long:

> [Sally] probably shouldn't be staying here any longer. Not that she isn't good at what she does; it's just that the [Free Clinic] needs the enthusiasm of new people and fresh ideas. . . . (June 17, 1975)

Regarding the tentative ad hoc nature of these organizations' rules and procedures, the following quotation is typical:

> Don't worry, if ⁺here are major objections to our new ID card system, we'll drop it. *All* of our policies and procedures are experiments, in the sense that if they don't work, we change them—fast. (Food Co-op, December 12, 1974)

In contrast to the permanence that characterizes the bureaucratic model, the assumption that the alternative organization will be transitory seems, logically and empirically, to militate against the oligarchies, rigid rules, and goal displacements described so often in the literature on organizations.

2. *Mutual and self-criticism*

A regular and sanctioned process of mutual and self-criticism in an organization, I propose, militates against oligarchization. That is, making the leaders or core members publicly subject to criticism tends to level the inequalities of influence that develop in even the most participatory of organizations. Of course, the leveling effect of one criticism session may be quite visible but short-lived. But when criticism sessions are a regular and accepted part of the organization, the knowledge that one is subject to group criticism helps to curb the assumption of power in groups holding collectivist ideals.

3. *Limits to size and alternative growth patterns*

The face-to-face, personal relationships and direct-democratic forms that characterize the collectivist organization probably cannot be maintained if the organization grows beyond a certain size. Small size has long been held to be a requirement of directly democratic organizations, yet this matter of size is not as simple or straightforward as it appears.

How many members make too many? There was no clear cutoff point in any of the organizations I studied at which collective control suddenly yielded to oligarchy. So I decided to put this question of size to the members themselves, which turned up some interesting results. Of those who say that there *is* an optimal size for collectives in general, almost all take this size to be the number of persons currently in their particular collective, give or take a few. Beliefs about an optimal size are therefore quite consistent *within* groups, and quite disparate *between* groups. This suggests that the actual optimum size for each collective may be contingent on a variety of organizational factors such as technology and the diffusion of knowledge. Indeed, most of the members themselves (from 55 percent at the Food Co-op to 71 percent at the Free Clinic) believe that there is *no* optimal size for collectivist organizations in general. However, members may have answered that question in terms of some shared hidden parameters concerning size. With this qualification in mind, members' perceptions about size lead us to be cautious about generalizing optimum size from one organization to another type of organization. It may be wiser to define optimal size for collectivist-democratic organizations in terms of avoiding "redundancy" of personnel (i.e., when there are more workers than are required for the job at hand), than in terms of numbers.[9]

Complex as the issue of optimum size may be, there are undoubtedly some limits to size beyond which the familial and collectivist nature of alternative organizations is undone. Indeed, members do act as if they believe that such size limits exist. Most notably, this is implied in their inhibition of internal growth, and their unconscious development of functional alternatives to conventional patterns of growth.

For instance, when the Free School found that it was unable to attract any Chicano students and unable to absorb any more students than it already had, it decided to form a coalition with a Chicano community cultural center. This coalition promised to broaden the school's resource base (library, art room, etc., were now shared and enlarged) and to give its students some measure of contact with the Chicano community. The Free School, then, got some of the benefits of growth without growing itself. Thus, building a wider network of cooperative relationships with other small, collectivist organizations is one alternative pattern of growth.

Another alternative "growth" pattern found in collectivist organizations that do not wish to expand is the spin-off of new, similar but autonomous collectivist organizations. At the Alternative Paper, some of the staff envision taking about half the current collective and creating a second collectively run paper in another city in California when this one is "stable enough." But expansion is never imagined as a larger paper or a larger staff.

The Food Co-op plans to double its current store size of 1,400 square feet because

> we already have way too many members for the size store we have. . . . This would be a good size for a store—large enough to allow for a good selection of foods and certain economies of scale, but still small enough to be a real community store. . . . (March 13, 1975)

But after this initial expansion, they envision no more, preferring instead to "start wholly new and independent co-ops with the additional people who want to be members," or to

> build new stores in different locations according to our membership needs. But none of them would exceed 2,500 to 3,000 square feet. . . . If the store gets to be a big supermarket, people would just shop at the co-op because it's cheap and we'd lose our sense of purpose and community.

Rare as they may be, the Alternative Paper and the Food Co-op are not unique in their desire to build new, parallel, but autonomous collectivist organizations as an alternative to internal growth. Schumacher describes a collectively owned manufacturing firm in Britain, the Scott Bader Company, which required this alternative growth pattern of itself when it exceeded 350 members; Kanter describes a similar phenomenon in some of the nineteenth-century communes she studied; and Johnson and Whyte have also observed this sort of deliberate spin-off in the Mondragon system of workers' cooperatives in Spain.[10]

4. *Economic marginality*

Ironically, *the participatory-democratic character of an organization may be facilitated by economically marginal conditions, while surplus financial resources may actually undercut its collectivist form.*

Needless to say, alternative institutions must provide a means of livelihood to their members if they are to be tenable places of employment. But, in paying their workers well, many organizations, be they collectively or privately owned, engender careerism. Careerism, in turn, may lead to hierarchy and to people protecting their own positions of power and privilege within the organization to the detriment of its goals of social change. Even organizations with initially "radical" goals, such as Mobilization for Youth, may find that their goal displacement (in a conservative direction) is attributable to the careerists who head the organization.[11]

Hence, the alternative institutions examined in this study are adamantly anti-careerist. Their rejection of careerism carries with it a corresponding rejection of lifetime career paths, professional certification, full-time requirements, differentiation of areas of expertise, salaries by rank, and advancement in a hierarchy of offices. As in any social-movement organization, work in alternative institutions is construed as a labor of love, not as a "job" or a "career." If work is to retain its value-purposive quality, the alternative must try to avoid the economic incentives that generally encourage the development of careerism. That is, alternative organizations should be structured so that it is *not* economically rational for staff members to seek a career in them.

Accordingly, alternative institutions usually pay their staff members salaries well below those they would receive in corresponding "straight" jobs. On the face of it, they do this because they have less capital at their disposal. On a more subtle level, they do this to ensure that their staff will continue to be made up of people whose dedication is to organizational and movement goals, not to protecting their jobs. Lean salaries assure the organization that its workers are committed.

This condition of economic marginality is also supported by the work of Kanter, who found that an austere life style contributed to commitment in nineteenth-century communes, while affluence diminished it. Likewise, Duberman found that economic precariousness helped to knit the community together and to generate commitment at Black Mountain, a forerunner (1933–56) of the free-school movement.[12]

Thus, economic marginality may have unanticipated but happy consequences for an alternative organization: *A paucity of financial resources averts careerism, and in so doing tends to prevent oligarchization and organizational maintenance from becoming ends in themselves.*[13]

A corollary to this proposition can be stated in the negative: *Financial prosperity tends to undermine the collectivist-democratic nature of alternative organizations.* None of the five alternative organizations in this study were particularly prosperous, so other case studies provide better illustrations to support this corollary. For instance, the *Real Paper,* a collectively run alternative newspaper in Cambridge, was ultimately defeated by its own economic "success." After two and a half years of operation it had built up an impressive circulation and was turning a substantial profit. This made it attractive to private investors, who offered $325,000 for the paper. Like the Alternative Paper in my study, the *Real Paper* was collectively owned by the staff members who had worked there a certain length of time. For staff who were fatigued, disillusioned, or otherwise ready to move on, the $325,000 (or $9,000 net apiece) proved irresistible. Hence, what began as a staff-owned and -controlled collective, is now, by virtue of its financial success, a privately owned enterprise. Similarly, Bernstein describes a collectively owned plywood factory where pressures to sell out to a large corporation mount for a variety of reasons, not the least of which is the attractiveness to the workers of getting their share of the stock at once (between $20,000 and $40,000 apiece).[14]

In trying to avoid the emergence of careerism, with the attendant problem of oligarchization, a collective faces a dilemma. If its pay scales are too high, it will attract and retain staff who are not fully committed to its purposes, and staff will develop a self-interest in preserving the organization as an end in itself. Relatively low pay ensures that staff are devoted to the collective's purposes and people. But, clearly, if the pay is too low, staff cannot subsist and they will leave in spite of their commitments.

If the collectivist organization wishes to retain a committed staff, how much pay is too much and how much too little? Let my try to define these parameters by looking at my two most extreme cases in terms of pay. At the Alternative Paper, staff members (who worked forty to sixty hours a week and whose typical educational level was a B.A.) earned an average of $150 per month (in 1974). Salaries at the paper were determined by the collective as a whole and were given out "to each according to his need." Some staff members at the paper (including some of its most crucial people) were paid nothing; the highest pay was $300 per month to a person with a family. At the Free Clinic, all of the full-time staff (who worked twenty-eight to thirty-five hours per week on the average and whose typical education was a B.A.) earned $500 per month in 1974. Here, all full-time staff members, whether a seventeen-year old secretary or a Ph.D. coordinating the health-education program, earned equal pay. In both cases, there were the nonmonetary "fringe benefits" of working in a collectivist organization—people got more autonomy and control over their labor than they could ever have had in a bureaucratic or even in a professional organization.

The consequences of these two financial situations differ markedly. At the Alternative Paper, a number of capable and dedicated members felt compelled to leave in search of greener pastures. Two of them soon found jobs in journalism for over $800 per month. At the Free Clinic, staff members also came and went, but for reasons other than financial. When the clinic faced the possibility of becoming a fee-for-service agency or dissolving itself, one staff member was accused, with some justification, by the others of "fighting to keep the clinic going just because it represents a comfortable, groovy, and secure job to you—even if it *has* outlived its usefulness."

At the Alternative Paper, staff members generally made about 18 to 25 percent of the salary they could have drawn at comparable, but established, journalism jobs. At the Free Clinic, some staff people made about 50 percent of what they would have drawn at mainstream nursing or counseling jobs for which they were qualified. But the equality principle by which salaries were distributed meant that others made as much as 83 to 100 percent of what they would be paid in comparable "straight" positions. For the latter people, preserving the organization and keeping their jobs became more important. From these examples it seems that "too little" salary could be defined as anything less than 40 percent of the pay for comparable work in a "straight" enterprise, and "too much" salary as anything over 80 percent of that base. Whatever the appropriate numbers, the criterion to remember is that material remuneration should not be so low as to lose committed and capable members, nor so high as to engender careerism, organizational maintenance, and oligarchization.

5. *Dependence on internal support base*

Another internal condition that promotes a collectivist-democratic form of organization is direct dependence of the organization on its members and clients. *Organizational dependence* (economic and sentimental) *on its internal support base tends to support participatory-democratic ideals and to militate against the displacement of original goals.* [15]

Conversely, organizational dependence on an *external* base of support tends to *increase* the likelihood of goal displacement and to *decrease* the level of internal participation. Put another way, where a collectivist organization acquires an independent base of financial support (e.g., a grant), its leaders tend to lose interest in the sentiments and goals of its members and clients, thereby increasing the likelihood of goal displacement.

Ironically, many alternative service organizations regard grants as quite desirable and fail to foresee any problems arising from them. Yet, in the one alternative institution in my study that did manage to get 83 percent of its budget covered by outside grant support, the Free Clinic, paid staff members reported spending a mean of 75 percent of their time seeking continued outside revenue. After writing grant proposals and cultivating the sensitivities of funding agencies, they had painfully little time left to attend to the volunteers and clients. In the thick of grantsmanship, some staff coordinators even temporarily suspended their "components' meetings," the only formal arena for participation and policy discussion that the volunteers at the clinic had.

Dependence on an *external* base for financial support can entail not only a loss in participation levels and in leaders' sensitivity to members' interest, but also more direct forms of goal displacement. As part of the health-education program at the Free Clinic, pamphlets aimed at "demystifying" health care (e.g., on drugs, herpes, VD) were produced for public distribution. One day an important county official deemed the "Medi-Cal" pamphlet, a pamphlet that described plainly how to qualify for California's Medi-Cal program, "too political." Within hours the staff removed the pamphlet from the shelves of the clinic. It was, after all, the season for grant awards. Such co-optations are difficult to avoid when an organization cannot pay its rent without external help.

Agencies that wish to affect the internal operations of an alternative organization need not threaten to withdraw funds to achieve changes. They may decide important matters of organizational policy by simply asserting this as a "right" inherent in giving funds in the first place. The very nature of grant proposals is such that foundations get to choose which part of a budget they wish to fund (if they choose to give at all). One private foundation decided, among many possibilities, to fund a children's clinic. This was not considered a high priority to the staff at the Free Clinic, because there was another children's clinic in town, and the community need for a second one was slight. Yet as one staff member explained: "We're not going to let the five thousand dollars go to waste. We'll sure as hell do a children's clinic now." In another instance a private foundation granted the Free Clinic funds for capital expenditures. This led the staff to create pseudo-needs where other more pressing needs existed (e.g., an elaborate typewriter, acoustic ceiling, photocopying machine). Again, clinic members could not challenge the right of the foundation to earmark funds in this way.

Similarly, in those recent cases where workers, when faced with corporate divestitures and the prospect of personal unemployment, have been able to buy their firms, they have been heavily dependent upon external sources of financing. Since there is no cooperative bank in the United States, they have had, of course, to go to private banks and government agencies for loans. Initial reports indicate that banks have insisted, as a "right" inherent in loaning capital, that the fledging worker-owned enterprise have "responsible management." In effect, this has meant bank-approved managers in some cases, a positive identification with external institutions that have aided the survival of the firm, and little participation by the new worker-owners in managerial decision-making. These organizations are still quite young, and it is too soon to tell what the long-term effects of this external dependency will be.[16]

The converse of this process seems to hold as well. In alternative service organizations which are completely dependent on their *internal* support base, i.e., on the goodwill of their members and clients for financial support (as were the Free School and the Food Co-op), there remains a very high level of responsiveness on the part of the leaders to the goals and sentiments of the membership. For instance, a survey of the general membership of the Food Co-op indicates that fully 74 percent of them consider their elected board of directors to be either "very" or "reasonably" responsive to their needs, while only 29 percent of the volunteer membership at the free clinic believe that their board is either "very" or "reasonably" responsive.

6. *Technology and the diffusion of knowledge*

My observations support the proposition that the egalitarian and participatory ideals of a collectivist organization can probably not be realized where great differences exist in members' abilities to perform organizational tasks. Put more specifically, *a collectivist organization is undermined to the extent that the knowledge needed to perform the organization's tasks is unevenly distributed.* For this reason, some of the alternative service organizations I studied devote a great deal of energy to rotating tasks and to cultivating a *general* knowledge of the work involved in the organization in place of specialized expertise. Evidence for the obverse of this proposition also exists. Stated in the affirmative: *as the knowledge relevant to the operations of the organization becomes diffused, the possibility that some members will develop indispensable and exclusive knowledge, with the usual implications this has for power and oligarchy, declines markedly.*

Sharing knowledge is, of course, easier desired than done, and it seems to require one of the following technological conditions:

1. Tasks involved in the administration of the collective organization must be relatively simple so that everyone naturally knows how to do them, or they must involve a relatively undeveloped technology applied in relatively nonroutine situations.[17] A good example is the Free School. Knowledge of the teaching process is so undeveloped that it can more rightly be considered an art than a science. Furthermore, every student at the Free School is supposed to be treated uniquely. Hence, the issue of knowledge diffusion does not arise in this case, because individuated knowledge does not lend itself to monopolization. It cannot be exclusively held.

2. The technology may be relatively sophisticated and may be applied more uniformly, if the members of the collective are similar enough in ability and interest to learn the technology fairly rapidly. With a more sophisticated technology, the distribution of knowledge can no

longer be taken for granted. It assumes paramount importance here precisely because this type of knowledge does lend itself to monopolization. Alternative organizations routinely using a more sophisticated technology must focus on sharing the knowledge or risk defeating their egalitarian and collectivist principles.[18]

People at the Law Collective, for instance, were very proud of the extent to which their legal workers, people who had little or no previous training in law, learned to do tasks usually reserved for practicing attorneys. As they explain, "legal workers have to learn from doing. . . . We try to put newer workers on cases with more experienced people so they can learn from them." They happily report the case of one legal worker, who after being a member of the Law Collective for only one month, submitted a writ of mandamus to the California Supreme Court that succeeded in overturning local residency requirements for holding city office.

Members of the Alternative Paper also tried to demystify expertise through task-sharing. In part they did this by creating job assignments that combined seemingly unrelated tasks. For instance, a person might be assigned to do twenty hours a week writing, ten hours on photography, and ten hours on production tasks. This sort of division of labor promoted a wider sharing of knowledge, and it meant that no one was stuck doing tedious work full time, just as no one was allowed to do choice work full time. In addition, the paper developed a system of periodic job rotations. As one worker said,

> We know that Gary won't be as good a writer as Sheila was, and that Pat won't be that good at selling ads at first. . . . But people get tired of what they're doing after a while. . . . You can't keep a person on a job as alienating as advertising forever. . . . We think that the long-term benefits of everyone understanding all aspects of the paper, and the kind of equality that comes from that, outweigh the short-run inefficiencies that are involved. (June 18, 1975)

In another alternative organization called Jane—a feminist collective of laywomen that performed some 11,000 illegal abortions with an excellent record for safety— internal education and task-sharing helped the organization to develop and retain its egalitarian form and to provide a high-quality service.[19]

Demystification entails the negation of the processes of specialization and professionalization that occur in most service organizations. The central purpose of demystification is to break down the usual division of labor and pretense of expertise, and thereby to allow all members of the organization to participate more equally in its control.

External Factors

The above six conditions refer to factors within an organization. External factors may also significantly influence its ability to achieve a participatory-democratic form.

7. *Oppositional services and values*

My findings suggest that *members of a collectivist-democratic organization would probably not be able to maintain their resistance to conventional forms of organization if they were producing similar or identical goods or services.* Nonbureaucratic collectivist forms are probably feasible only where the desired outcome of the organization is qualitatively different (in terms of services or goods) than that produced by the dominant, target institution.[20]

All of the alternative organizations in this study tried to provide services or goods qualitatively different in some sense from those provided by the established institutions. The Free Clinic, for instance, was committed to preventive medicine, free medical care, patient understanding of the healing process, and a holistic approach to mental and physical health—principles that it assumed the "straight" medical delivery system did not share. Likewise, the Free School assumed that its loose structure, its focus on learning outside the classroom, its attention to affective development, its critical perspective on social and economic institutions, and its measure of student control over the schooling process, were all anathema to the public school system. The Alternative Paper tried to select and present the news from a progressive perspective to liberalize the local political climate. The Food Co-op sold food at cost, tried to carry wholesome foods and to educate its member-customers about nutrition, and supported other community-owned economic organizations, all of which distinguished it from privately owned, profit-based food stores. The Law Collective, in the cases it sought and in those it avoided, defined itself as an alternative legal service. In the extreme, an organization may be so oppositional in the service it provides as to be illegal, as in the Jane case cited earlier.

Although the actual effectiveness of alternative institutions' opposition to mainstream institutions is debatable, their perception of being oppositional is not. Members' perceptions of being oppositional (and therefore the target of outside harassment) serve to solidify these groups and to justify their existence as "alternative institutions" in an otherwise bureaucratic society.

This sort of oppositional stance vis-à-vis established institutions does not, of course, permeate all cooperative organizations. In cases where worker ownership has emerged as an attempt to save jobs in a plant divestiture, workers may feel very thankful for the banks and government agencies that allow their new enterprise to get off the ground. This sense of identification with the interests of established institutions may inhibit, at least for a time, the development of a sense of group interest and cohesion. Without a strong sense of group cohesion, these groups of worker-owners may not be motivated to challenge traditional managerial prerogatives or to insist upon participation rights for themselves.[21]

We should expect therefore that *the introduction of reforms in the target institution along the lines pioneered by the alternative organization would weaken the once-oppositional organization.*

My data bears out this proposition. For instance, during the Free School's third year of operation, the liberalization of some of the local public-school programs attracted many of the Free School students back to the public system and undercut the justification for having a free school at all.

The converse of this principle operates as well. The Alternative Paper enjoyed a more rapid expansion of its circulation than it ever imagined at its inception. This success is attributable, at least in part, to the conservative cast of the dominant local newspaper, which lends the Alternative Paper a more oppositional quality than it would have if its competition were more liberal.

8. *Supportive professional base*

Although the collectivist organization is strengthened by a hostile target institution that it can oppose, it is also strengthened by having a supportive and liberal professional base in its community. That is, the local environment most favorable to the development of alternative, participatory-democratic organizations would combine the most regressive target institution possible with a large and supportive professional population.

Ideally located between the mountains and the ocean, the city where this study was conducted attracts more than its share of professionals. The existence of a large pool of professionals, though often taken for granted by members, appears to be a significant contributing factor in the growth of alternative service organizations in the area. Such professionals contribute to the maintenance of alternatives in a variety of ways.[22]

Sympathetic professors set up a special course as a conduit through which university students could be channeled into community organizations for course credit. It is not an exaggeration to say that without the steady supply of well-educated volunteer teachers from this course, the Free School could not have existed for long. The Free Clinic recruited volunteer doctors mainly from the ranks of residents and marginally employed doctors in town. This feat, needless to say, would be much more difficult in a city where doctors were encumbered by a higher patient-per-doctor ratio. Another study of free clinics also indicates how important the support of a liberal professional community is to the survival of alternative institutions.[23] The Alternative Paper enlists the talents of several professors who write regular columns and features for it. The list could include some of the quasi-legal ways in which professionals employed in "straight" institutions filter human and financial resources from these institutions to the alternative, participatory-democratic organizations.

In short, sympathetic professionals contribute to the development of alternative service organizations in a myriad of direct and indirect ways. An alternative located in a town without a base of relevant professional support (e.g., a free school in a town without surplus teachers, a medical clinic in a town without many doctors, etc.) would have a much harder time.

9. *Social-movement orientation*

The above two conditions refer to the relationship between the alternative organization and its "straight" environment. However, the environment of the collectivist organization may include many other social-movement organizations, and its relationship to these is also important.

All of the organizations in this study are social-movement organizations. That is, (1) they have goals of social and/or personal change; and (2) the incentives to participate in them are, first, the group's values and objectives; second, friendship and prestige; and only third, material rewards.[24]

I suggest that *the closer a collectivist organization remains to the broader social movement that spawned it, the less likely it is to experience goal displacement.*

Concentrating solely on the organization makes staff members see their own futures as tied to the life and success of the organization, not of the movement, and hence, makes them more likely to pursue organization maintenance as an end in itself. Becoming oriented to the organization per se seems to lead to a narrow emphasis on providing a good service vis-à-vis other organizations in the same profession, but it may also entail a loss of the larger vision out of which the organization was born.

This conservatism of organizational purpose, while not unusual, is not an inevitable transformation. Organizations can remain oriented to the movement into the second generation and beyond. The broader visions of the movement then provide an ideological anchor, enabling the organization to resist a co-optation of goals over time.

The alternative organizations in this study all began with the aim of helping to create an entire "alternative community." Building this mutually supportive network of community-controlled organizations depends on each group's focusing on the movement rather than on itself. Members reflect an identification with the movement not only by providing support services to its people and to new movement organizations, but also by leaving organizations that no longer contribute to the broader goals of the movement and by joining other organizations that do. The latter phenomenon often appears in case studies as instances of individuals getting burned out, but a comparative study reveals a different picture. For example, many of the founders of the Free School left it at the end of its second year, convinced, as one of them put it, that "providing a groovy education to upper-middle-class kids isn't the most revolutionary activity in the world." Although at the time, "burn out" was used to account for this exodus, these same people show up later in my study as committed members of the Alternative Paper, the Free Clinic, and the Law Collective. Their first allegiance was always to the goals of the movement, not to any particular organization that housed them.

To understand this emergent career trajectory from one social-movement organization to another, we must develop a concept of "movements within a movement." Other sociologists have observed a tendency for the personnel of social-movement organizations to flow back and forth among various movement organizations, government agencies, and professional schools that are devoted to a single set of policy issues, and my own data reinforce this observation.[25] For example, a free-school staff member goes on to study "confluent education" in a graduate school of education and shows up later administering a publicly financed "open-classroom" project. However, my study also witnessed a tendency for members of one movement organization to become involved later in organizations pursuing seemingly *disparate* concerns (e.g., switching from a free school to an ecology-action organization to a free medical clinic). This flow of personnel from one movement organization to another can be understood if we conceive of "movements within a movement." That is, at least for some participants, the free-school movement, the ecology movement, etc., are all considered subsidiary to "The Movement" and assume importance only in relation to the broader movement that spawned them. If we employ a "movements-within-a-movement" perspective, then we take seriously the words of some of the participants that they are part of "one struggle with many fronts." When alternative institutions are viewed as entirely unconnected organizations, the notoriously rapid ebb and flow of personnel in and out of them is thought to reflect a fickle commitment. However, to begin to see them, as many of the participants do, as subsidiary movements within an overarching movement, is to recognize a basic coherence and consistency in the actions of individual participants.

Conclusion

This article has proposed nine structural conditions thought to facilitate collectivist-democratic modes of organization. The absence of each of them is said to undermine democratic forms.

Three points are worth underscoring. First, these are *not* traits that *define* organizational democracy. The logical status of these conditions is that they *facilitate* democracy, or put another way, they militate against the development of oligarchies. They are not to be confused with necessary elements that would define workplace democracy.[26] These facilitating conditions are often absent, and likewise, organizational democracy is often undone.

Second, these conditions are thought to affect the ability of an alternative organization to achieve its collectivist-democratic aspirations. Many other reasonable dependent variables could have been used instead (e.g., member satisfaction, organizational longevity, quality of goods or services provided). But

I have chosen to focus on the level of participatory-democracy as my dependent variable. Factors that promote democracy may not promote, and may even inhibit, the achievement of other possible criteria for understanding these organizations. Hence, these organizations confront tensions and dilemmas daily in trying to achieve their participatory ideals.[27]

Third, this list of conditions is certainly not exhaustive. It is my hope that further studies of participatory-democratic organizations will uncover additional facilitating conditions. For instance, I could not examine the independent effect of democratic ideology simply because all of the alternative organizations in this study contained many individuals who had democratic convictions. This is not always the case. Other cooperative organizations might vary considerably on this score. I suspect that, as Bernstein points out, variations in the level of democratic consciousness may have substantial bearing on the ability of an organization to function democratically. This may be a special problem in employee-owned organizations where individuals have not previously developed participatory expectations and habits of behavior, and suggests that education for participation may be an important part of any effective democratization process.[28]

This work has attempted to isolate some of the organizational conditions that support or undermine participatory-democratic ideals. A conditional approach leads me to conclude that these sorts of directly democratic organizations may *not* be as impossible to sustain as Weber and Michels led sociologists to believe, but neither are they easy to achieve. Seen as *facilitating conditions,* they open the door to successfully resisting the usual transformation patterns described in the literature on organizations. Viewed as *limiting conditions,* insofar as they do not always exist, their absence may constitute an internal source of tension or dilemma for the would-be collectivist organization.

Notes

1. For elaboration of these explanations, see Selznick (1949), Sills (1957), Gusfield (1955), Merton (1957), Michels (1949), Zald and Ash (1966).
2. Bennis and Slater (1968).
3. *New Schools Exchange Directory* (1967; 1973).
4. For a fuller description of the comparative method for discovering grounded theory, see Glaser and Strauss (1967).
5. All five of the alternative service organizations selected for this study were located in a small metropolitan area of about 150,000 in California.

The Free School examined in this study was not an accredited school. It was an outside-the-system, Legal Alternative, day school. It contained from 27 to 41 high-school students during the course of this study, 52% of whom were from upper-middle-class families and all of whom were white. The school was staffed by a large number of part-time volunteers, recruited mainly from a nearby university, whose activities were coordinated by a handful of full-time, but poorly paid, staff members. This situation permitted an enviable student-teacher ratio of about 3 to 1, if part-time teachers are weighted 0.5, and classes ranged in size from individual tutorials to seven. Like many free schools, this one stressed learning outside the schoolhouse through work and participation in the community; affective development and its integration with the cognitive; a critical understanding of the cultural, political, and economic institutions in this society; and a sense of control, or an activist orientation, toward changing society.

The Free Clinic examined here was, as the name implies, free to patients. However, faced with economic necessity in its third year of operation, it was transformed into a sliding-scale, fee-for-service. It was run by a paid staff of six, a board of directors, and an army of 60 to 100 volunteers at any given time, who served as patient advocates, counselors, receptionists, lab technicians, and health education speakers. Doctors were largely volunteers, though they were sometimes paid. Besides medical services, the clinic had major health education and counseling programs. The central thrust of its philosophy and purpose was summarized in the clinic's mottos: "Health care for the whole person, mind and body" and "Health care for people, not profit." It also had a strong commitment to preventive medicine. It grew from an average clientele of 130 patients per month by the end of its first year of operation to a mean of 479 patients per month by the close of its third year. Most of the patients (79%) were between fifteen and thirty years of age and were white (86%). Typically, they came to the clinic for venereal-disease testing and treatment (23%), followed in frequency by treatment for the skin (18%) and gynecology (16%). In addition, during the 1974–75 fiscal year, its counseling program reached an average of 69 people per month, and its health-education speaking programs reached an estimated 675 people per month. As free clinics go, this one was very large in the number of patients it saw and comprehensive in the services it provided.

The Alternative Newspaper was just that—an alternative. It was neither "underground" nor "establishment." Conceived in December, 1971, as an agent of social change in a city dominated by one conservative newspaper, its circulation grew to about 22,000. A full-time staff which ranged in size from 14 to 18 put out a weekly newspaper of 28 to 36 pages. In an effort to produce a more progressive social climate in this city, the paper engaged in "advocacy journalism" and presented the news from a liberal-to-radical perspective. Liberalizing local political changes took place after the creation of this paper, but it is, of course, difficult to tie them directly to the impact of the paper. Most of the readers of the paper (74%) were very satisfied with its quality.

The Food Co-op examined here began in 1970 as a buying club for about 100 people, operating out of members' living rooms. In January 1974, it developed into a direct-charge grocery store (for members only) which charged each member a monthly service charge to cover overhead expenses and sold food at cost, and to which each member donated at least one hour's work per month. In this form the Food-Co-op attracted over 1,100 members in a year and a half of operation. It was located in a young, student-dominated part of town. The amount of food it sold was equally impressive: about $35,000 per month during the school year (substantially less during the summer). The membership-at-large decided on major policy changes and elected representatives to a board of directors at quarterly meetings. In between, the nine board members made policy decisions at weekly meetings which were open to the membership, and a paid staff of three or four people ran the store. The ideals of the co-op were "economy, ecology, and community," and it vigorously supported efforts to create other community-owned and -controlled economic institutions in the town where it existed.

The Law Collective in this study began in 1971. It had seven to ten members at any one time. Usually three or four of these were attorneys, and the others were legal workers. Over time, the Law Collective generally changed from defending oppressed individuals in need of legal aid, to defending groups of people, particularly workers. By 1974–75, the latter was a priority, and they had provided legal counsel on contracts to a number of established unions and had helped others to organize (e.g., cab drivers, waitresses, sea-urchin workers). The law collective worked free only on cases judged to be of political significance. However, most of their cases were more or less routine, and for those they received average or somewhat lower fees. This was how they supported themselves. Some types of cases the law collective categorically refused to take. They would not, for example, defend accused rapists because the "prime defense tactic in rape cases is to attack the integrity of the complainant." They also refused to accept the cases of landlords, corporations, and of men in contested divorces. Tasks at the law collective were accomplished in a collective manner. There was no division of labor between, for instance, typists, receptionists, and lawyers. Legal workers entered the collective with little or no training in law, but it was taken as the responsibility of each member to act (through teaching and learning) to close these gaps in knowledge. Thus, attorneys and legal workers alike shared the tasks of typing, reception work, clean-up, legal research, writing pleadings, appearing in court, etc.

Although these five alternative institutions provide very different sorts of services, they are tied together by the primacy they each give to being run "collectively."

All persons and organizations have been given fictitious names in the paper.

6. Each of the nine conditions set forth in this paper has important organizational dilemmas associated with its presence (or absence). For a discussion of these dilemmas, see chapters 4 and 5 of "Organizations without Hierarchy: A Comparative Study of Collectivist-Democratic Alternatives to Bureaucracy," dissertation by the author (University of California, Santa Barbara, 1978).

7. Palisi (1970).

8. See Toffler (1970), Bennis and Slater (1968).

9. Chickering (1971: 214–27).

10. Kanter (1972: 227–28), Schumacher (1973), Johnson and Whyte (1977).

11. Helfgot (1974).

12. Duberman (1972), Kanter (1972: 78–80).

13. A point of clarification: by economically marginal, I do not mean to suggest that these organizations are, or should be, antiprofit. In each case they are struggling to earn enough surplus to provide each worker-member with a livable income. What distinguishes them from capitalist economic organizations is that they have built their organizations around their perceptions of social needs, not around the calculus of profit maximization. Thus, profit becomes a limiting factor: some level of it is necessary for survival, but its maximization is not the prime goal. Profit is also treated as only a limiting factor in the Mondragon cooperatives —cf. Johnson and Whyte (1977)—however there, because they are able to reinvest 85% to 90% of the profits, they have no shortage of capital.

14. Kopkind (1974), Bernstein (1976).

15. Similarly, Eisenstadt (1959) argues that direct dependence of the organization on its members and clients is a condition which facilitates debureaucratization. However, Eisenstadt is concerned with the debureaucratization of already bureaucratic organizations, while this work focuses on new organizations which have resisted bureaucratization from their inception.

16. Researchers involved in the New Systems of Work and Participation Program at the School of Industrial and Labor Relations, Cornell University, are investigating cases of employee-ownership which have arisen out of plant divestitures. The role of the banks in defining responsible management and in limiting the participatory rights of the worker-owners has been suggested by the following research studies: Robert Stern and Tove Hammer regarding the Library Bureau at Herkimer, N.Y. Janette Johannesen on the Vermont Asbestos Group; and Michael Gurdon on the Saratoga Knitting Mill in Saratoga Springs, N.Y.

17. Perrow (1970: 75–85).

18. For an interesting description of the impact that advances in technology may have on cooperative forms of organization, see Russell, Hochner, and Perry (1977). Here the introduction of new packer trucks and

centralized billing procedures reduced the number and complexity of jobs and carried with it less task-sharing and more division of labor in the cooperatively-owned garbage-collection firms in San Francisco. For an overview of this issue, Braverman (1974) shows how increasing differentiation and specialization have historically degraded work, making jobs less skilled and less equal.

19. Bart (1977).

20. In positing an oppositional relationship between the alternative institution and its environment, we assume that the society in which the alternative exists is predominantly capitalist and bureaucratic. Hence, this condition might not hold in a socialist-collectivist society.

21. This line of reasoning was suggested to the author by Robert Stern of the New Systems Program, Cornell University. It seems to fit well with the data of three cases that have been studied there; see note 16 above.

22. For illuminating discussion of the structural bases of this sort of intellectual and professional support for social-change efforts, see Flacks (1971) and Zald and McCarthy (1975).

23. Taylor (1976).

24. Zald and Ash (1966: 329).

25. McCarthy and Zald (1973).

26. For a discussion of necessary elements, see Bernstein (1976). For a model of organization that defines the structural properties of collectivist organization vis-à-vis bureaucracy, see "The Collectivist Organization: An Alternative to Rational-Bureaucratic Models," paper by the author to be presented at the Ninth World Congress of Sociology, Uppsala, Sweden, August 1978. Torbert (1975) has analyzed similar organizations as "post-bureaucratic" in their stage of development. Swidler (1978) has analyzed them as "organizations without authority."

27. For a discussion of tensions and dilemmas, see Mansbridge (1973), Giese (1974), Rothschild-Whitt (1976).

28. See Bernstein (1976). Also, Zwerdling (1977) observed this problem at International Group Plans, a Washington, D.C., worker-run insurance company.

References

Bart, Pauline, 1977. "Seizing the Means of Reproduction: An Illegal Abortion Collective." Presented at the annual meeting of the American Sociological Assn., Sept. 1977, Chicago.

Bennis, Warren, and Philip Slater. 1968. *The Temporary Society.* New York: Harper and Row.

Bernstein, Paul. 1976. *Workplace Democratization: Its Internal Dynamics.* Kent, Ohio: Kent State University Press.

Braverman, Harry. 1974. *Labor and Monopoly Capital: The Degradation of Work in the Twentieth Century.* New York: Monthly Review Press.

Chickering, Arthur W. 1971. "How Many Make Too Many," in C. George Benello and Dimitrios Roussopoulos, eds., *The Case for Participatory Democracy.* New York: Viking Press.

Coleman, James. 1970. "Social Inventions." *Social Forces* 49 (Dec.): 163–73.

Duberman, Martin. 1972. *Black Mountain: An Exploration in Community.* New York: E.P. Dutton.

Edelstein, J. David. 1967. "An Organizational Theory of Union Democracy." *American Sociological Review* 32 (Feb.): 19–31.

Eisenstadt, S.N. 1959. "Bureaucracy, Bureaucratization, and De-Bureaucratization." *Administrative Science Quarterly* 4: 302–20.

Ellul, Jacques. 1964. *The Technological Society.* New York: Alfred A. Knopf.

Flacks, Richard. 1971. "Revolt of the Young Intelligentsia: Revolutionary Class Consciousness in Post-scarcity America," in Roderick Aya and Norman Miller, eds., *The New American Revolution.* New York: The Free Press.

Giese, Paul. 1974. "How the 'Political' Co-ops were Destroyed." *North Country Anvil* (Oct.-Nov.): 26–30.

Glaser, Barney, and Anselm Strauss. 1967. *The Discovery of Grounded Theory: Strategies for Qualitative Research.* Chicago: Aldine Pub. Co.

Gouldner, Alvin. 1954. *Patterns of Industrial Bureaucracy.* Glencoe: The Free Press.

Gusfield, Joseph. 1955. "Social Structures and Moral Reform: A Study of the Woman's Christian Temperance Union." *American Journal of Sociology* 61: 211–32.

Helfgot, Joseph. 1974. "Professional Reform Organizations and the Symbolic Representation of the Poor." *American Sociological Review* 39 (Aug.): 475–91.

Johnson, Ana Gutierrez, and William Foote Whyte. 1977. "The Mondragón Systems of Worker Production Cooperatives." *Industrial and Labor Relations Review* 31 (Oct.): 18–30.

Kanter, Rosabeth Moss. 1972. *Commitment and Community: Communes and Utopias in Sociological Perspective.* Cambridge: Harvard University Press.

Kanter, Rosabeth Moss, and Louis Zurcher, Jr. 1973. *Alternative Institutions,* a special issue of *The Journal of Applied Behavioral Science* 9 (Mar.–June).

Kopkind, Andrew. 1974. "Hip Deep in Capitalism: Alternative Media in Boston." *Working Papers for a New Society* 2 (Spring): 14–23.

Lipset, Seymour M., Martin Trow, and James Coleman. 1962. *Union Democracy.* New York: Doubleday and Co., Anchor Books.

Mansbridge, Jane. 1973. "Time, Emotion, and Inequality: Three Problems of Participatory Groups." *Journal of Applied Behavioral Science* 9 (Mar.–June): 351–68.

McCarthy, John, and Mayer Zald. 1973. "The Trend of Social Movements in America: Professionalization and Resource Mobilization." Morristown, N.J.: General Learning Press.

Merton, Robert. 1957. *Social Theory and Social Structure.* Glencoe, Ill.: The Free Press.

Michels, Robert. 1949. *Political Parties: A Sociological Study of the Oligarchical Tendencies of Modern Democracy.* New York: The Free Press.

Mills, C. Wright. 1959. *The Sociological Imagination.* New York: Oxford University Press.

New Schools Exchange Directory

Palisi, Bartolomeo. 1970. "Some Suggestions about the Transitory-Permanence Dimension of Organizations." *British Journal of Sociology* (June): 200–206.

Perrow, Charles. 1970. *Organizational Analysis: A Sociological View*. Belmont, Calif.: Wadsworth Publishing Co.

Rothschild-Whitt, Joyce. 1976. "Problems of Democracy." *Working Papers for a New Society* 4 (Fall): 41–45.

Rothschild-Whitt, Joyce. 1978. "Organizations Without Hierarchy: A Comparative Study of Collectivist-Democratic Alternatives to Bureaucracy." Dissertation, University of California, Santa Barbara, Department of Sociology.

Russell, Raymond, Art Hochner, and Stewart Perry. 1977. "San Francisco's Scavengers Run Their Own Firm." *Working Papers for a New Society* 5 (Summer): 30–36.

Schumacher, E.F. 1973. *Small Is Beautiful: Economics As If People Mattered*. New York: Harper and Row.

Selznick, Philip. 1949. *TVA and the Grass Roots*. Berkeley: University of California Press.

Sills, David. 1957. *The Volunteers*. Glencoe, Ill.: The Free Press.

Swidler, Ann. Forthcoming. *Organization Without Authority: Dilemmas of Social Control in Free Schools*. Cambridge: Harvard University Press.

Taylor, Rosemary. 1976. "Free Medicine." *Working Papers for a New Society* 4 (Fall): 21–23, 83–94.

Toffler, Alvin. 1970. *Future Shock*. New York: Random House.

Torbert, William. 1975. "Pre-bureaucratic and Post-bureaucratic Stages of Organization Development" *Interpersonal Development* 5: 1–25.

Weber, Max. 1968. *Economy and Society*. Guenther Roth and Claus Wittich, eds. New York: Bedminster Press.

Zald, Mayer, and Roberta Ash. 1966. "Social Movement Organizations: Growth, Decay, and Change." *Social Forces* 44: 327–41.

Zald, Mayer, and John McCarthy. 1975. "Organizational Intellectuals and the Criticism of Society." *Social Service Review* 49 (Sept.): 344–62.

Zwerdling, Daniel. 1977. "At IGP It's Not Business As Usual." *Working Papers for a New Society* 5 (Spring): 68–81.

The Phantom Community

by Paul Starr

The 1960s breathed life into a new generation of what came to be known as "counterinstitutions"—communes, cooperatives, free clinics, free schools, free universities, counseling centers, day-care centers, encounter groups and other forms of collective therapy and "consciousness-raising," "underground" newspapers, grass-roots community organizations, public-interest law firms, and peace, environmental, women's, civil-rights, and consumer groups.

These organizations were by no means without antecedents: America has a long history of utopian communities, cooperatives, reform groups, and other organizations attempting by example and protest to change the society. But the counterinstitutions of the sixties share a cluster of cultural and political features that identify them as special products of their time. Just as the movements of the era had a distinctive style in personal appearance and behavior, in thought, language, and collective action, so they had a distinctive ideal of organizational life. It was a romantic ideal of the organization as a community, in which social relations were to be direct and personal, open and spontaneous, in contrast to the rigid, remote, and artificial relations of bureaucratic organization. The organizational community, moreover, was to be participatory and egalitarian. It would make decisions collectively and democratically and would eliminate or at least reduce hierarchy by keeping to a minimum distinctions of status and power between leaders and members, or professionals and nonprofessionals. Radicals wanted no other basis for organization than consent: People should have the right, they said, to participate in the decisions that affect their lives.

As a movement, the counterinstitutions unquestionably failed. Many died at a tender age. Others have scrimped along like malnourished children constantly begging for handouts. Some have grown sturdy and respectable, only to lose whatever oppositional force they had. A few have established a position for themselves, more or less on their own terms, that may well outlast the movements of cultural and political dissent which originally gave rise to them; even these, however, do no more than occupy niches in the economy and political system. Yet their greatest disappointment was not their failure to go forth and multiply and gain a position of dominance. It was rather the growing realization that even on their own ground, the communal ideal could not be realized, and that insofar as the sought-after forms of organizational life had value, the gains were more modest than their participants had hoped or their theorists had imagined.

It seems useful at this point to assess the whole phenomenon. What gave the counterinstitutions their distinctive character? In what ways have they evolved in orientation and structure from their original form? Why did some survive and others collapse? What has the movement left behind? These are the sort of questions I want to take up here.*

Two Forms of Counterorganization

"Counterinstitutions," as a general sociological category, may be divided into two types. I will call them *exemplary* and *adversary*.

An exemplary institution, such as a utopian community or a consumers' cooperative, seeks, as the term suggests, to exemplify in its own structure and conduct an alternative set of ideals

---

*If I often use the past tense in regard to counterinstitutions, when many of the organizations still live and breathe, it is because the movement they once constituted no longer exists, and there now seems no other way to think of them as a whole, except as a historical phenomenon.

—the ideals, its organizers may hope, of a new society. Compared with established institutions, it may attempt to be more democratic in its decision-making, or less rigid and specialized in its division of labor, or more egalitarian in its distribution of rewards, or less sexually inhibited—or possibly the opposite, if its ideology so requires. Its aim is the direct and independent realization of its ultimate values, within the circumference of its own activities.

In contrast, an adversary institution, such as a political party, a union, or a reform group, is primarily concerned with altering the prevailing social order. Oriented toward conflict, it may not exhibit in its own organization all the values that its supporters hope eventually to realize. Whereas the members of an exemplary organization typically regard its activities as intrinsically valuable, the participants in an adversary organization regard its activities primarily as a means toward an end. For exemplary organization, the goals mainly involve changes in internal structure, while for adversary organization, the goals involve changes outside. The exemplary institution invests its energies in building up a model of what its organizers would like the world to be; the adversary organization expends its resources against the larger world of power.

The two forms of counterorganization cannot easily be combined. An exemplary institution—or rather its membership—may sympathize with struggles against the dominant order, but taking a direct part in conflict would sap its strength and jeopardize whatever freedom it might have to carry on its own activities. Consequently, it generally must make some accommodation with the society and the state. Conversely, the members of an adversary organization might wish to incorporate their ultimate values in its structure, but such a step could impede its effectiveness. For instance, they might prefer it to be open and decentralized, but the conditions of conflict might not allow that kind of organization. In a highly centralized society, effective opposition is likely to be centralized too. Conflict, as Simmel and others have pointed out, tends in some ways to make adversaries alike. Consequently, adversary organizations face incentives toward convergence with at least certain aspects of the prevailing institutional system.[1]

In other words, counterinstitutions face a trade-off between exemplifying ideals and waging conflict. They cannot fully commit themselves to both (unless, of course, their ideals make the accumulation of power a primary value in itself). They can strike different balances between model-oriented and conflict-oriented action, but there is a strong tendency for them to adopt either exemplary organization, without engaging in conflict, or adversary organization, without immediately attempting to realize ultimate values.[2]

The separate development of exemplary and adversary institutions frequently produces a dual structure in radical social movements. Under colonial or repressive regimes, an "underground" organization may be engaged in terrorism or guerrilla violence, while "above-ground" organizations—ostensibly unrelated, but tacitly or secretly affiliated—run schools, distribute food, house refugees, etc. Wherever adversary organizations are by definition illegal, such a dual structure is likely to emerge. In the United States, the opposite circumstances produce the same result—that is, the availability of subsidies rather than the fear of repression causes the separation of exemplary from adversary organizations. Exemplary organizations, such as experimental schools, can often secure resources from the government and private foundations that would not be made available to adversary organizations. The Internal Revenue Code reinforces the split by granting tax-exempt status to nonprofit organizations so long as they do not engage in certain kinds of adversarial activities, such as lobbying or supporting candidates in elections.[3] So even in the absence of repression, creating separate organization maximizes the total resources available to counterinstitutions.

In other societies, the connections between adversary and exemplary activities may be formal and explicit. Adversary organizations such as the established socialist and Communist parties of Western Europe support educational, recreational, and other programs whose purpose is to provide a model alternative to established institutions, as well as to enhance solidarity. In America no left-wing party of comparable strength has emerged; and even if one had, political parties in America do not generally take on the sort of auxiliary functions they do elsewhere.

The relationship between exemplary and adversary institutions is by no means always amicable and collaborative. Quite often they are mutually suspicious. The leaders of utopian communities and cooperatives frequently assert that socialists, communists, and other opposition groups are really "no different" from the dominant parties and institutions—no less bureaucratic, no less power-hungry, no less repressive, etc. Correspondingly, the classic "Leninist" view of utopian communities and cooperatives is that they are destined to fail so long as capitalism endures; they are capable (say the Leninists) only of diverting revolutionary movements from their real tasks. The utopian community and the Leninist party are, in this regard, exact antitheses. In the interests of realizing on a small scale the moral values of communism (in the original sense of the word), the committed utopian withdraws from political opposition. In the interests of gaining the political victory of Communism on a large scale, the committed Leninist defers realizing its values indefinitely and supports a hierarchical, secretive, and centrally directed party organization.

Exemplary and adversary organizations are instances of the contrast between what Albert Hirschman has called "exit" and "voice."[4] By "exit," Hirschman means any form of unilateral departure from an economic or political entity—for example, ceasing to buy a company's product, shifting one's allegiance to another party, resigning from office, deserting from an army, or emigrating to another country. By "voice," Hirschman means any attempt to exert influence on an organization or government by directly complaining to it, grumbling, demonstrating, or even committing violence against it. Exemplary institutions, like utopian communities, are a form of organized exit from a dominant institutional system, whereas adversary institutions are a form of organized voice. The advocates of one alternative quite naturally feel threatened by the other. Many of those who want to change a society by protest—by voice—see the advocates of exit as subverting their movement ("copping out"). Both revolutionaries and reformers often prefer a no-exit situation where those who are dissatisfied are forced to participate in adversarial activities.

In America during the 1960s, the support for exemplary institutions came primarily from the "cultural" wing of the movement, whose members tended to be the advocates of exit, while adversary organizations drew their support from its "political" wing, whose members tended to be the advocates of voice. Their debate over "dropping out" versus protest reflected the exemplary-adversary, exit-voice or, as the psychologists would put it, flight-fight dilemma. The lines between the two camps, however, were not sharply marked. Many political radicals took part in communal, cooperative organizations, partly because of their own need to find arrangements for living and work that made sense to them. Some tried out one organizational alternative and then another. Moreover, nearly all adversary groups attempted to exemplify at least some alternative ideals as they protested against dominant institutions; and some organizations, like the Students for a Democratic Society (SDS), engaged in extremes of participatory democracy, egalitarianism and, in their later stages, self-disclosure and interpersonal confrontation. Just as the radical culture of the sixties rejected the deferral of gratification, so it rejected the deferral of egalitarian and communal ideals. This was partly what distinguished the new left from more traditional communists and socialists. Most counterinstitutions experience some tension about how exemplary or how adversarial they can afford to be, and make the necessary trade-offs and compromises. A few counterorganizations of the sixties attempted to push both to their limits, and burned themselves out in a brief incandescent glare.

Consciousness and Counterorganization in the Sixties

The counterinstitutions that developed in the sixties bore the mark of their era, especially its prosperity and the sense of limitless possibility that it encouraged. Radicals, as well as liberals, had become convinced that Americans lived in an affluent, "post-scarcity" society, and this belief promoted an extraordinary confidence in the benign effects of a complete release of impulses. By its own example and in its criticism of society, the left was continually urging people to abandon constraints of every kind—in language, belief, behavior, sexual relations, family organization, work—on the assumption that America, with its enormous wealth, could afford a degree of human liberation unsurpassed in history. The same spirit infused counterinstitutions, where radicals were similarly unwilling to make cost and constraint a guiding concern. In their exemplary organizations, they put little emphasis on efficiency; and in their adversary organizations, they put little emphasis on discipline. In this regard, the utopian mood of the new left involved two equally important negations: it was not only a revolt against liberal practicality and compromise, but also a repudiation of the "realism" of the old left.

Recent history has seen a transition between two styles of radicalism—one "classical," the other "romantic." The old left, whether social-democratic or communist, exemplified the classical style in its emphasis on reason, its view of science and technology as instruments of human progress, its belief in planning, and its promise of a more rational, orderly and balanced society. In their personal behavior, its supporters upheld the standards of "civilized" conduct, controlling their impulses and observing the conventional boundaries between public and private life. Some radicals continued to uphold the classical style in the sixties, but the predominant temper of the movement was romantic: witness its emphasis on the importance of feeling, its distrust of science and technology, its rejection of bureaucracy and professionalism, its suspicion of conventional roles, its promise of emotional liberation.[5]

The elements of romanticism were ubiquitous in the radical culture of the period. It celebrated the passions and abhorred routine; it explored every route available to "higher," "altered" states of consciousness. Yet in keeping with its fundamental romanticism, its vision of the good life was distinctly pastoral. It idealized the "natural" and "organic," the primitive and the childlike. The fashions of the time—beards for men, long hair for women—spoke of a return to the past, as did the Old Testament names that became popular for children. Thus the movement was simultaneously radical and old-fashioned. It wanted change, but it no longer believed in "progress." The left had always looked to the future for a vision of a better society; now it was looking backward for much of what it wanted.

One aspect of this mixture of radical and traditional sentiment was the concern for "community" and the way community was conceived. Here the left broke with its own past. Of the three terms enshrined in the trinity of the French Revolution—liberty, equality, fraternity—fraternity has historically been the least prominent among the left's concerns. And when the left has alluded to fraternity, it has typically been the human fraternity, conceived as an all-inclusive, international brotherhood. Localism of any kind has been anathema in the socialist tradition. Community and nation were, if anything, the rallying cries of conservatives.[6] But all this changed in the 1960s. The ideal of community (in deference to feminists, the term "fraternity" was dropped) assumed a new priority, and it was now conceived on a small, local scale. The communities that radicals envisioned were immediate and personal. Without even taking note of the change, the left had quietly reduced the scale of life it envisioned in a good society.

Had middle-class youth not emerged as the largest base of support for radicalism in the sixties, "community" would probably not have become the most resonant word in its political vocabulary. For working-class people, still rooted in family life, the ideal of community would not have held the same attraction. It responded to a widely felt sense of homelessness and personal isolation among the young, many of whom were in the midst of a long hiatus in their lives between the families of their parents and the families they would subsequently establish on their own. The ranks of this group, as is well known, had been swollen by the baby boom, the growth of universities, and the postponement of adulthood brought about by extended education and delayed entry into the labor force. Its personal dilemmas were those of alienation and commitment, rather than exploitation and poverty, and it projected these concerns into radical politics, creating a distinct form of socialism whose vocabulary was partly political and partly therapeutic.

The psychological concerns of young radicals were a point of tension in the movement. Blacks and other poor people who were the objects of their sympathy were often wary of the motives that turned affluent youth toward radicalism. As early as 1964, black organizers in the Student Nonviolent Coordinating Committee (SNCC) were denouncing the "bourgeois sentimentality" of middle-class whites who had stayed behind in the South after "Mississippi Summer" to continue their civil-rights work. "Some of the good brothers and sisters," declared a memo circulated at a SNCC staff meeting that October,

> think that our business is the spreading of "the redemptive warmth of personal confrontation," "emotional enrichment," "compassionate and sympathetic personal relationships," and other varieties of mouth-to-mouth resuscitation derived from the vocabulary of group therapy and progressive liberal witch doctors. But we ain't got enough redemptive compassion and cultural enrichment to go around.[7]

Or to put the same point in our terms: An adversary organization ain't an exemplary community.

Against this view, radicals argued that the two spheres of psyche and politics could not be separated. "The personal is political," they insisted. It was to their own forms of distress that exemplary institutions primarily addressed themselves.

The Exemplary Organization

Exemplary organizations took several distinct forms. The main types were communes (rural and urban), cooperatives, restructured businesses (from bookstores and restaurants to a few sizable corporations), and alternative human-service institutions, such as counseling centers and experimental schools. In all of these, the quality of human relationships was a principal concern.

The orientation of communal experiments is a case in point. In her comparative study of nineteenth- and twentieth-century communes in America, Rosabeth Kanter observes that over time there has been a change in their ideological foundation. The earliest utopian communities were religious; then increasingly in the nineteenth century they were politico-economic; and finally in the most recent period they have been predominantly psychosocial.[8] Communes with religious and political orientations still continued to be formed through the last decade, but the prevailing ideology among the communes of the sixties criticized the society not so much for being sinful or unjust as for being "sick."

The new psychosocial conception of community—the desire simultaneously for intimacy and liberation—may not have been "functionally equivalent" to the old religious or politico-economic axes of solidarity. Many of the nineteenth-century utopian communities had substantial achievements to their names; not all were quixotic ventures that ended in penury and disaster. Many of them, on the contrary, proved extremely prosperous and gained a reputation for their industriousness, the quality of their craftsmanship, and their honesty in trade. Moreover, they succeeded in realizing many of their ideals, such as sexual and ethnic equality and the abolition of private property, including property in people through slavery or marriage.[9] Although they were ultimately abandoned in the face of declining membership and an advancing industrial society, some lasted throughout the lifetimes of their founders and into a second or third generation. But as Kanter makes clear in her study, the long-lasting nineteenth-century communities had little in common with the communes of the 1960s. They made exacting demands on their members to sacrifice their wealth to the community, to abstain from sexual and other pleasures, to endure mortification and criticism, and to work long and hard under a strict plan. Kanter calls these practices "commitment mechanisms," on the theory that they were responsible for binding members to the community, and the evidence she has compiled indicates that successful communities were indeed more likely to employ these mechanisms than the communities that failed.[10]

The new rural communes, while also seeking a refuge from society, abhorred such practices, which would have contradicted their ethos of personal liberation. The new communities were looking, in Judson Jerome's well-chosen image, for Eden rather than Utopia, for a garden of pleasure rather than a planned and orderly society.[11] The assumptions that cultural radicals brought to communes ruled out the kind of demands that helped nineteenth-century communities not only cohere but prosper. As a result, the new communes were rarely economically self-sufficient and depended for their survival on inherited wealth or welfare payments. Their life span was typically short, and even in those that lasted for some time, turnover in membership was high.[12] Community proved ephemeral.

Urban communes, after an initial euphoric period of grandiose expectations, manifested the same pattern. They have become, as Kanter calls them, "group households of convenience . . . with the life cycle of an affair rather than a marriage."[13] Many of them have succeeded in redistributing the responsibilities of men and women in the household and substituting negotiation and consent for adult-male authority. Since members of communal houses continue to work in regular jobs, they are not necessarily plagued by the continual economic difficulties of rural communes. For many people, they provide a familylike environment, without encumbering them with family obligations. A communal household then becomes, not something more than a family, but something less—a home that can be left without guilt or grief.

If the history of nineteenth-and twentieth-century communes is a study in contrasts, the history of cooperatives is a study in continuity. The most recent cooperative enterprises have met the same problems as their forerunners, and the ones that have survived show the same tendency toward convergence with established institutions.

The basic features of cooperative organization are democratic participation on a one-member-one-vote basis and refunds to members of any profits. Without these, an organization cannot legitimately call itself a cooperative. Open membership and political neutrality are common among cooperatives, but not universal. Communes and cooperatives share a similar relation to capitalism (indeed, producers' cooperatives have sometimes been organized communally). Both are attempts to transcend capitalism without confronting it in an open conflict. Communes are more concerned with changing the relations of the household; cooperatives, with changing the relations of the market. Whereas communes are typically a retreat from the larger economy, cooperatives can survive only by competing successfully in it. For nineteenth-century communes, the enclaves to which they retreated became indefensible as they were overtaken and encompassed by American society. Cooperatives, on the other hand, have been drawn into capitalism by competing against it. The two forms of exemplary organization have followed different routes to collapse or convergence, but they have generally arrived there just the same.

In the United States, some early resistance to industrial capitalism in the nineteenth century took the form of cooperative enterprises among threatened skilled craftsmen. Their ventures proved noncompetitive and short-lived, but American farmers succeeded where urban workers had failed. Cooperative organization was a central part of the Populists' program in the late 1800s, and it became an enduring part of America's rural economy after Populism faded. Through marketing and purchasing cooperatives, American farmers today sell about one quarter of their products and buy much of their equipment, supplies, electricity, insurance, and other goods and services. Some agricultural cooperatives have grown into enormous enterprises—several appear on *Fortune*'s annual list of the five hundred largest American corporations. One such cooperative, Farmland Industries, owns oil fields, refineries, sulphur and phosphate mines, fertilizer plants, slaughtering houses, warehouses, a fleet of trucks—in short, it manages a vertically and horizontally integrated organization that supplies its 750,000 member-farmers with all manner of goods and services. Such cooperatives are not easily distinguished from capitalist firms in their structure and behavior, but they do generate savings for their members.

Essentially, cooperatives have become the functional equivalent of the oligopolistic corporation for family farmers, giving them some countervailing leverage and market power.[14]

Consumer cooperatives have been more faithful to the original spirit of the cooperative movement, but they too have moved toward convergence with capitalist firms. While the farmers' cooperatives emerged from the Populist movement, consumers' cooperatives came from two other sources—Jewish democratic socialists in eastern cities and Scandinavian, especially Finnish, socialists and communists in the northern Midwest. In 1916, these groups, plus assorted other cooperativists, formed the Cooperative League of the United States of America, still in existence today. In 1930, after an unsuccessful effort to take control, the communist faction walked out of the league, which thereafter continued to voice the lame and pious hope that cooperatives would peacefully supersede capitalism. But even rhetorical gestures to an alternative society diminished in the 1940s, as managerial influence rose in the cooperatives and increased emphasis was placed on business competence in the struggle for survival. "It is not so important," wrote the editor of the Cooperative League's journal in 1943,

> to explain the relationship of cooperative food store service to the parable of Jesus and the loaves and fishes as it is to describe the proper ways of buying and stocking and displaying loaves and fishes in the co-op store, and then get every possible Mrs. Consumer to buy and buy—and become an owner, too.[15]

The 1960s brought a revival of interest in cooperatives, but the new ones may well be following the same path. Radicals started cooperatives with the hope, as one proponent of food cooperatives wrote, of substituting community for private ownership, paying workers decent wages, holding open meetings and making decisions collectively, and abolishing all forms of discrimination.[16] The food cooperatives also wanted to encourage people to eat nutritious food, and they initially refused to stock "junk" foods and other products they regarded as unhealthy. At the same time, they expected to be able to offer cheaper prices by eliminating the profits made by food stores.

The reality proved somewhat different, as Daniel Zwerdling pointed out in a report on food cooperatives in Washington, D.C., in 1975. Most of the new cooperatives were too small to buy in sufficient quantity to get prices as low as those paid by supermarket chains. Inadequate floor space led them to employ additional manpower to restock shelves. Consequently, in spite of eliminating profits, their prices were in some cases actually higher than those of supermarkets, and their wages were uniformly lower. The cooperatives at that time (1975) could not afford to pay more than $2.50 an hour, while checkers at the regular supermarket began at $4.81.

Unable to attract as much business as they expected, the cooperatives were forced to make compromises. They began carrying "everything the community wants," including junk food. To build up sufficient volume to get lower prices, one co-op leader explained to Zwerdling, they would have to concentrate on building "supermarket-sized stores." But of course, with increases in size, they would lose their distinctive personal atmosphere and any chance of community participation in decision-making. In fact, the relationship of member-consumers to the cooperatives was not much different from their relationships to other stores. True, the co-ops would warn them of bad buys and unhealthy products, but most seemed to develop no special loyalty. They came to shop at the co-op only for those items they could buy at lower prices there. "The nonprofit food cooperatives, far from their vision of becoming community resources, have become specialty stores," Zwerdling wrote.[17]

The organizers of the cooperatives did not anticipate the managerial complexities or consumer resistance they would meet. Much the same difficulties were awaiting the alternative human-service institutions seeking to deprofessionalize education and medicine. Dispensing with professional authority meant acquiring some other means of achieving compliance. As Ann Swidler has shown, teachers in free schools who could not rely on authority were forced to draw on their own personal resources. Some "courted" students, hoping to win their loyalty and affection by being intimate with them. Emotionally exhausted, these teachers eventually "burned out" and quit.[18] And in the free clinics, as Rosemary Taylor reports, some patients believed in professionalism more than the professionals did. They wanted to be seen by doctors, not paramedics, no matter what they were told (in itself, ironically, an assertion of lay judgment).[19] By their nature, the clinics had a limited appeal; they could not be much more than outpatient departments for the counterculture and the underclass.

One of the ways in which exemplary organizations sought to be exemplary was in the representation of the community in their decision-making. By "the community" radicals often had in mind blacks, Hispanics, or low-income white ethnics—the groups they wanted their organizations to serve. But who actually represented "the community" and what were its true interests? Many of the people the radicals wanted to see represented had no communal consciousness or organization. Their representatives often had to be invented; their interests often had to be imputed. The community—so palpable in its misfortune— became elusive whenever its presence was sought.

Just as the food cooperatives became "specialty stores," so the free clinics and schools and counseling centers met the needs of special groups rather than whole communities. Supported by only a fragment of society, they had a tenuous grasp on survival. They were easily vulnerable to encroachment by more powerful, established institutions that had only to adopt enough of their ideas to cut the ground from under them. Some found a narrow niche to support their work, but even where in the late seventies they continue to function, they no longer embody the hopes of a movement.

Adversary Organization After the Movement

The radical movement of the sixties had no unified organizational structure, no central committee, not even a guiding or coordinating coalition. It was an agglomeration of small, independent movements that more or less felt some kinship with one another. But they were never joined together because they could attract more support separately than if they had been obliged to settle on a common ideology and program. The predominant feeling was also hostile to any central bureaucracy. Radicals built organizations, but then easily abandoned them. No one was more mistaken than those left-wing sectarians or right-wing police agents who thought they could capture the movement if they controlled or destroyed its organizations.

The new radicalism was also distinctive in the forms of adversary organization it created. Political parties and unions, usually prominent in left-wing movements, played almost no part in the left of the sixties. Many radicals longed to establish such organizations, but they had too little support to challenge the parties and unions in power.

Four other types of adversary organization, with substantially different structures, stand out in the period. These were movement organizations, community organizations, public-interest lobbies, and the "advocacy" or "alternative" media. The structural differences among them help explain which kinds of organization were best able to survive the end of the era that gave them life.

1. By *movement organizations* I mean those groups, like SDS, the Congress of Racial Equality (CORE), Environmental Action, and the National Organization for Women (NOW), that have sought to mobilize protest, often including forms of "direct action," as part of a broader struggle for change.[20] The typical movement organization is, or tries to be, national in scope, with a network of local chapters and periodic conventions to elect its leaders and resolve major questions of policy. It has a staff of organizers, and its leadership usually rotates annually. It does not put up candidates for political office, although it may lend some its backing and attempt to defeat others. It calls on members and supporters for funds and participation in protests. To adopt the vocabulary of Peter Clark and James Q. Wilson,[21] the incentives for membership tend to be more "purposive" than "material"—that is, members join primarily to achieve goals like ending racial discrimination or changing foreign policy, which may or may not benefit them directly.

2. *Community organizations,* like those that Saul Alinsky established in Chicago and Rochester, are local groups concerned with bread-and-butter issues. Typically, they have a strong staff of organizers, often middle-class in origin and more radical than the members, and an elected leadership drawn from the community. Members pay dues, which represent the main source of financing, and they are called on, as in movement organizations, to take part in protests. The incentives for membership, however, tend to be primarily "material" rather than "purposive": members are attracted explicitly by the promise of direct benefits. The Alinsky organizers like to distinguish this "organization" approach from that of a "movement":

> As Ed Chambers [an Alinsky organizer] explains it, a movement relies on charismatic leaders, other people's money, indiscriminate recruitment, amateur devotion, and "flash, image, consciousness-raising." An organization [i.e., a community organization] is built on dues, collective leadership, army-like regularity, systematic daily work, professionalism and playing to win. Movements are ideological. In the Alinsky model of an organization, people act democratically in their own self-interest, and ideology is irrelevant.[22]

In other words, community organization aims to be the "business unionism" of the radical movement.

3. *Public-interest lobbies,* like Ralph Nader's various organizations, have yet a third structure. The two largest, Nader's Public Citizen and Common Cause, have, at one time or another, attracted several hundred thousand "members," drawn —as in movement organizations—primarily by commitment to the group's objectives rather than any hope of direct gain. Membership, however, typically entails no more than financial support, in the form of a small annual contribution. Members are not asked to take part in any protests more demanding than letter-writing, and they have no role in electing or controlling the organization's leadership. The public-interest lobby typically consists of a staff of professionals, mainly lawyers, who have successfully established themselves as advocates of a public otherwise unrepresented. Usually they are based in a single

office in Washington or a state capital. Compared to movement and community organizations, whose leaders must be able to mobilize supporters for action, public-interest lobbies are relatively distant from the people they claim to represent.[23]

4. Finally, the *alternative media*—local weekly papers, national monthly magazines and quarterly journals, a few radio stations, and even news services—vary in structure. Some have exemplary features—they are run by "editorial collectives" with a minimum of hierarchy; others are profit-making enterprises not much different from regular businesses, except that they necessarily allow a looser style of work than most firms would tolerate. Like some of the public-interest lobbies, they have a constituency—their readers or listeners—who, in subscribing, provide financial support.[24]

Nearly all these adversary organizations are inherently unstable, for want of any reliable flow of income. Only the alternative media, of the four types, can regularly obtain most of their resources by sale of a product. The others acquire their means of support from a combination of "voluntary" sources—from their staff in the form of underpaid labor; from their membership in the form of dues or volunteer services; and from outside sources in the form of money from individual contributors, donated services from performers and others (as at benefit concerts), or grants for specific projects from private foundations and public agencies. Adversary organizations are often in competition with one another to obtain this support; each tries to stir up enthusiasm for its own particular cause (peace, civil rights, environmental safety, tax reform) and get "out front" on issues likely to win it recognition. In this process, charismatic leadership and media attention play a critical role. For it is through the media that movement, community, and public-interest organizations are able simultaneously to reach large numbers of people, gain leverage on government and private officials, and persuade their own supporters (and perhaps themselves) that the organization is accomplishing great things. Thus the dependence on irregular contributions puts them at the mercy of ebbs and flows in sentiment and changing perceptions of their newsworthiness.

The Vietnam War and the crisis that accompanied it set in motion countless adversary organizations, brought them support and resources, and helped them make the kind of "news" that the press and television were likely to report. But as the crisis died down, for historical reasons beyond their control, the organizations had to adapt to less propitious circumstances. The media paid less attention, and the spontaneous support and readiness for mobilization dwindled.

The change in political conditions did not affect adversary organizations equally: some stood up better than others. Of the four types, movement organizations were the hardest hit. Lacking any firm base of support, they declined the most rapidly as the sense of crisis abated. Some peaked early, some late; the antiwar organizations were already in decline as the environmental and women's groups emerged. But none of them had much capacity to sustain themselves as movement organizations over the long run. On the other hand, public-interest organizations seem to have held up rather well. Some have put themselves on a relatively firm foundation by mastering sophisticated direct-mail techniques that enable them to appeal to thousands of small contributors instead of depending on a few "financial angels."

Why did movement and public interest organizations fare differently? The people who had been active in the protests of the sixties did not turn conservative. They turned inward, becoming preoccupied with their private lives, and it became harder to mobilize them for protest. Whereas movement organizations require a high level of involvement from their supporters, public-interest lobbies require very little and are perhaps for that reason better suited to a quieter time. Furthermore, while radical activism has waned, Americans have also become, according to studies of public opinion, more "issue-oriented" and less "party-oriented" in their politics.[25] As a result, issue-oriented organizations have been able to raise large sums of money when the established political parties have found it difficult.[26] Furthermore, the public-interest organizations do not challenge any fundamental premises of the public, whereas some of the movement organizations did. So long as the public-interest groups work on issues that are concrete, specific, and "nonideo-logical" (i.e., not based on any ideology other than the prevail-ing one), their lease on public approval and support has been renewed.

Movement organizations were also particularly susceptible to escalating demands for "exemplary" conduct that under-mined their effectiveness. Radicals tended to oppose as "elitist" strong leadership and professionalism, and frequently insisted that privileged whites subordinate their concerns to those of blacks and other "third world" groups. Male dominance of organizational politics also came under attack. The result, espe-cially in the early seventies, was a competition in piety, a kind of radical perfectionism, that directed attention to the purifica-tion of organizational structure—a purification from which some movement organizations never recovered.

Like public-interest groups, community organizations also seem to have withstood the ebb of radical sentiment in the seventies more successfully than movement organizations. They too have avoided diffuse "ideological" issues. By concen-trating on problems like property taxes and utility rates, low-income community groups—such as ACORN in Arkansas and Fair Share in Massachusetts—have been able to grow stronger at a time when most poor people's organizations have grown weaker. ACORN, in fact, expanded in 1976 and 1977 into ten new states from its original base in Arkansas, opening up door-to-door organizing programs as far away as Philadelphia.[27]

The Black Panther party exemplifies this change in political direction. Although it emerged in the late sixties as a movement organization with revolutionary aims—and thereby brought down upon itself the wrath of the police and the FBI—it shifted in the seventies to a community organization concerned with local, bread-and-butter issues. In Oakland, California, its politi-cal base, the party became an acknowledged power in city affairs. Like an old-fashioned ethnic machine, it traded support for a highway project that would cut through the city in return for a guaranteed number of jobs for blacks. In 1977 the Pan-thers conducted a voter-registration drive in minority districts, helping to elect the city's first black mayor and sending one of their own members, Erika Huggins, to the county school board

—examples that Huey Newton, the party's founder, cited as evidence of its growing "maturity."[28]

The alternative media have been showing signs of "maturity" too. Most of the "underground" papers of the sixties have disappeared. Left in their wake are a number of what Andrew Kopkind calls "sea-level" publications, which have much of the style and some of the politics of radicalism but are run on a commercial basis and aimed at an audience of hip young professionals. Boston's *Real Paper* was for a time cooperatively owned, until its writers sold it to a group including David Rockefeller, Jr. The general tendency in the alternative press has been toward convergence and accommodation. In pursuit of respectability and wider audiences, publications like *Rolling Stone* and New York's *Village Voice* have toned down their language, diversified their reporting, and tried to bring moderate views into their pages.[29]

As such publications have grown older and more successful, the low pay and poor working conditions that their writers had been willing to endure at first have become increasingly anomalous. In the early 1970s, writers at the *Village Voice,* including people as well known as Nat Hentoff, were typically earning less than $100 a week, according to Ellen Frankfort, a former *Voice* columnist. Those who were not on the staff—and that included most of the columnists and regular contributors—had, besides low pay, no health insurance or other benefits commonly associated with employment. "The *Voice* was a place of integrity," Frankfort later wrote. "If writers were earning very little, I assumed it was because there was very little to give us." But in 1974, the two founders of the paper sold it for $3 million, and it became obvious that the paper was making more money than its writers had dreamed. They finally summoned the courage to ask for a raise of $25 a week. As he turned them down, their editor explained that hundreds of journalists would be eager to take their places if they were so unhappy that they wanted to leave.[30]

Such scenes were not uncommon. At a number of leading alternative publications, like San Francisco's *Bay Guardian* and the *Boston Phoenix,* meager pay and job insecurity led to prolonged, bitter struggles over unionization, which put the editors and publishers of supposedly left-wing publications in the position of union-busting employers. The papers insisted that they were at the edge of insolvency and could not afford to meet demands for wage increases, and some of them may have been. But the situation was, to say the least, awkward: here were organizations highly critical of the society being faced with precisely the kinds of protests that they themselves supported, when they occurred elsewhere. The fate of the alternative media has still further ironies. The *Voice,* which was the oldest of the adversary papers, eventually fell into the hands of Rupert Murdoch, an Australian press magnate and publisher of sensational tabloids. The *Los Angeles Free Press,* started in 1964 by Art Kunkin, who had been active in civil-rights protests and was on the national committee of the Socialist party, evolved into a pornography magazine and was eventually bought by Larry Flynt, who gained a certain notoriety as the publisher of *Hustler.* (Convicted in Georgia for violating local standards of decency, Flynt converted to born-again Christianity, and then turned *Hustler* over to one of the elder statesmen of the counterculture, Paul Krassner. Asked whether Flynt was using him to prove *Hustler* had "redeeming social value," Krassner replied, "It's mutual. I'm using him in the same sense he's using me."[31]) *Rolling Stone* thrived because it served the interests of the big record companies, which bailed it out in 1970 when it was in financial straits. "The underground papers that survived in the end," remarks the British journalist Godfrey Hodgson, "were those that found some way of making themselves useful to the rich, capitalist society they had failed to overthrow."[32]

The Incorporation of Alternatives: From Counterculture to Subculture

A sense of futility and disappointment has set in among the once ardent exponents of counterinstitutions. They have watched many of the exemplary organizations converge in structure with established institutions, and many of the adversary organizations gravitate toward accommodation. Some think the process of political and cultural incorporation inevitable. In an analysis of social movements of the poor, two theorists of the welfare-rights struggle, Frances Fox Piven and Richard Cloward, argue that poor people can improve their condition only by spontaneous mass defiance; any kind of organization will prove useless. It will, they say, "blunt" the momentum of protest in moments of insurgency and usually collapse in the aftermath.

> As for the few organizations which survive, it is because they become more useful to those who control the resources on which they depend than to the lower-class groups which the organizations claim to represent. Organizations endure, in short, by abandoning their oppositional politics.[33]

This argument rests on the proposition that the poor cannot sustain organization on their own. But even if this were true, the poor could still gain allies from other classes or win the support of institutions like the church, as revolutionary movements have often done. In any event, the counterorganizations of the sixties generally enjoyed support from the middle classes, which had the resources to build effective and lasting counterorganizations.[34]

The lesson of the sixties is not that counterorganizations of all kinds necessarily fail, but that in the absence of a general social transformation, they can survive only in certain limited forms. In the "political ecology" of American society, there are niches where counterinstitutions can sustain themselves. Community and public-interest organization are examples of relatively "defensible" niches, as are highly structured communal and cooperative organization. Some groups in the sixties started out in unstable positions; they either collapsed or, like the Panthers, moved into one of the more secure niches (in their case, community organization). Organizations do not have to survive by "abandoning their oppositional politics" (Piven and Cloward's iron law of accommodation); they can adjust their opposition to the structure of opportunities for furthering their interests that the society offers.

In at least some cities and regions of America, counterinstitutions of both kinds, exemplary and adversary, have grown sufficiently strong to reinforce each other and constitute a new cultural enclave. As Catholics have their own schools and hospitals, their churches and welfare organizations, so the radical culture has developed its own schools, its own press, its food cooperatives, even restaurants and shops. Some Americans now live almost entirely within these enclaves. They are not likely to spread over the whole middle class, much less the whole society. But in the long run, they may represent, if not a counterculture, then another "subculture," concentrated in particular neighborhoods of cities and in the rural areas of states like California, Oregon, Colorado, and Vermont.

Many more people pass through the counterorganizations that hover around these areas than remain. They come in search of community, but most stay for only a short time. Most of the counterinstitutions—the cooperatives, clinics and schools, the alternative media, the movement, community, and public-interest organizations—experience high turnover in staff for the simple reason they cannot offer much of a career. Since the organizations have few rungs in their hierarchy, a staff member "peaks" within a few years. Salaries that might be adequate for young professionals who are still used to student living become unacceptable as the staff members grow older and develop higher expectations and heavier commitments.

In a sense, these organizations resemble the urban communes in that both provide way stations for middle-class young people who are not yet established in regular families and professions. For many, the organizations offer a point of entry into careers. As a haven for the disenchanted, more acceptable than a conventional bureaucracy, they help people figure out what to do with their lives. Ironically, the counterinstitutions play a part in adjustment to adulthood, and thus have a function in the life cycle of their participants. The counterinstitutions tend to be high-intensity, low-commitment organizations: those who work for them or live within them often oscillate between moments of exhilaration and depression, before they burn out and go on to something else.

But radical organizations, like radicals themselves, are not immune to age, and as we have seen, many of them turn toward "maturity" and "respectability." They move from an almost religious enthusiasm to an almost bureaucratic routine. Some of the characteristics that radicals liked about counterinstitutions, such as flexibility and informality in the definition of roles and functions, may have been due as much to the youth of the organizations as to the radicalism of their ideology.

The routinization of community was hardly what radicals of the sixties expected. In politics, as in our private lives, we generally set out to do one thing, and end up doing another. It may be painful to look back at what illusions we once held, but the results, even if not up to expectations, are not necessarily so terrible. Such has been the fate of the counterinstitutions of the 1960s. That they failed in their grand design is no secret, nor should it have been a surprise. At no time have they been more than an epiphenomenon in American society. They have accounted for a negligible fraction of the gross national product, and they never attracted enough support to pose much of a threat to any of the core institutions of America. But however marginal to the larger world of money and power, they occupy a historical position of some importance for the experiments they conducted in the reform of human attachments. In their effort to restore the bonds of community that modern society has broken, they gave expression to a widely felt need. No one should take any satisfaction from their failure.

Notes

1. The two terms "accommodation" and "convergence" are complementary. By "accommodation" I mean compromise in an organization's adversarial stance; by "convergence" I mean a narrowing of the distance between exemplary features and the norm. An adversary organization loses its oppositional character through accommodation; an exemplary organization loses its oppositional character through convergence.

2. An adversary organization, however, cannot freely disregard its putative values; otherwise, it lays itself open to charges of betrayal. It can often realize some values more easily than others, and at least take symbolic measures to retain the semblance of consistency. For example, a union may retain the formal apparatus of consent when decisions are made hierarchically, and a radical political party may elevate some working-

class members into prominent positions to affirm its commitment to represent the oppressed.

3. A qualification needs to be entered here. The narrow IRS definition of impermissible political activity enables many nonprofit organizations to carry on what are in fact adversarial activities. Thus while there is a dual structure to counterorganizations, the dividing line is not drawn precisely on the exemplary/adversary distinction. Some legally acceptable adversary organizations are grouped with the exemplary. An analogous point can be made about the earlier example of movements under repressive regimes, where some legally acceptable adversary organizations may be "above" ground if tolerated by the state.

4. Albert Hirschman, *Exit, Voice and Loyalty: Responses to Decline in Firms, Organizations and States* (Cambridge: Harvard University Press, 1970).

5. I don't wish to suggest that affluence alone brought about the shift from a "classical" to a "romantic" style in the left. The new radicalism reflected more general changes in American culture: the declining confidence in science and reason, the pervasive preoccupation with personality and the self, the relaxation of traditional standards of conduct and restraint.

6. See, in this regard, Robert Nisbet, *The Quest for Community* (New York: Oxford University Press, 1953) and Wilson Carey McWilliams, *The Idea of Fraternity in America* (Berkeley: University of California Press, 1973).

7. Godfrey Hodgson, *America in Our Time* (New York: Doubleday and Co., 1976), p. 221.

8. Rosabeth Moss Kanter, *Commitment and Community: Communes and Utopias in Sociological Perspective* (Cambridge: Harvard University Press, 1972), pp. 3–8. By "psychosocial," Kanter means that the critique of society of these latest communes stresses "alienation and loneliness" and their utopian visions look toward "liberating situations that are conducive to intimacy and psychological health, enabling people to 'grow' or 'do their own thing.'"

9. Mark Holloway, *Heavens on Earth: Utopian Communities in America, 1680–1880* (New York: Dover Books, 1966), pp. 18–19; Charles Nordhoff, *The Communistic Societies of the United States* (New York: Harper and Brothers, 1875).

10. Kanter, *Commitment and Community,* pp. 75–125. Whether the "commitment mechanisms" were the causes of success, or merely correlated with it, is unclear. The communities that did not demand sacrifices may not have been able to because their members were too weakly committed to begin with for them to be sure such demands would not simply drive them away. The willingness to adopt the practices may be a result of commitment as well as a "mechanism" for reinforcing it. Since Kanter's analysis gives little sense of the historical development of communes, either singly or as a movement, we have no way of knowing whether adopting the mechanisms produced stronger commitment in communities where it was initially weak.

11. Personal communication to Kanter, *Commitment and Community,* p. 168.

12. See Kanter, *Commitment and Community;* Andrew Kopkind, "Up the Country: Five Communes in Vermont," *Working Papers for a New Society* 1 (Spring 1973): 44–49; and Sara Davidson, "Open Land: Getting Back to the Communal Garden," *Harper's,* June 1970, pp. 91–102.

13. Rosabeth Moss Kanter, "Communes in Cities," *Working Papers for a New Society* 2 (Summer 1974): 36–44; revised version in this volume.

14. On the history of cooperatives, see Lawrence Goodwyn, *Democratic Crusade: The Populist Movement in America* (New York: Oxford University Press, 1976); Joseph G. Knapp, *The Rise of American Cooperative Enterprise,* vol. 1: *1620–1920;* vol. 2: *1920–1945* (Danville, Ill.: Interstate Printers and Publishers, 1969, 1973); Richard J. Margolis, "Coming Together the Cooperative Way: Its Origins, Development and Prospects," *The New Leader* 55 (Apr. 17, 1972).

    In 1977, Farmland, with 500,000 farmer-members, merged with another large cooperative conglomerate, Far-mar-co, owned by about 250,000 families (James L. Nagle, "Merger of Far-mar-co and Farmland Industries Voted at Annual Meeting," *New York Times,* Feb. 12, 1977).

15. Clarke A. Chambers, "The Cooperative League of the United States of America, 1916–1961: A Study of Social Theory and Social Action," *Agricultural History* 36 (1962): 77.

16. Bruce Singer, "Food Co-ops and Politics," cited in Daniel Zwerdling, "Shopping Around: Nonprofit Food," *Working Papers for a New Society* 3 (Summer 1975), 24.

17. Zwerdling, "Shopping Around," pp. 21–31. Zwerdling makes most of the same points in this volume. I should emphasize that despite their problems, cooperatives remain a useful institutional form and could play a larger part in the American economy, as they do in northern Europe.

18. Ann Swidler, "Teaching in a Free School," *Working Papers for a New Society* 4 (Fall 1976).

19. Rosemary C. R. Taylor, "Free Medicine," *Working Papers for a New Society* 4 (Fall 1976); reprinted in this volume.

20. The term "movement organization" is used in a more general sense in Mayer N. Zald and Roberta Ash, "Social Movement Organizations: Growth, Decay and Change," *Social Forces* 44 (Mar. 1966): 327–41. For some histories of movement organizations in the sixties, see Kirkpatrick Sale, *SDS* (New York: Random House, 1973); August Meier and Elliot Rudwick, *CORE: A Study in the Civil Rights Movement, 1942–1968* (New York: Oxford University Press, 1973); Michael Useem, *Conscription, Protest and Social Conflict: The Life and Death of a Draft Resistance Movement* (New York: John Wiley,1973); Frances Fox Piven and Richard A. Cloward, *Poor People's Movements: Why They Succeed, How They Fail* (New York: Pantheon Books, 1977), 264–361 [National Welfare Rights Organization]; Ronda Kotelchuck and Howard Levy, "MCHR [The Medical Committee on Human Rights]: An Organization in Search of an Identity," *Health/PAC Bulletin* 63 (Mar.–Apr. 1975): 1–29.

21. Peter B. Clark and James Q. Wilson, "Incentive Systems: A Theory of Organizations," *Administrative Science Quarterly* 6 (1961), 129–166.

22. David Moberg, "Chicago's Organizers Learn the Lessons of CAP,"

Working Papers for a New Society 5 (Summer 1977): 18.

23. For a general survey, see Jeffrey M. Berry, *Lobbying for the People: The Political Behavior of Public Interest Groups* (Princeton: Princeton University Press, 1977).

24. As a group, the alternative media are not easily classified as exemplary or adversary. Some are as much one as the other, and some have passed through an exemplary phase on their way to becoming more hierarchical and bureaucratic. I put them here because, while they differ in the degree of exemplary structure, they share a style of "advocacy" reporting that rejects the ideal of objectivity and gives them an identifiably adversary character.

   The case of Liberation News Service (LNS) vividly illustrates how some counterinstitutions were split over the relationship between exemplary and adversary action. LNS was founded in Washington, D.C., in the fall of 1967 by two former college-newspaper editors, Marshall Bloom and Ray Mungo. It was a shoestring operation, run as an anarchic free-for-all, until it moved to New York the following year, when revolutionary Marxists began to assume greater influence. The original staff, as Mungo later wrote, wanted to live the "post-revolutionary" life immediately; they wanted LNS to exemplify their ideals of a "free" community. In a fairly typical statement of countercultural radicalism, Mungo wrote, "A free community does not have meetings, and your attendance is never required in a free community. You are welcome to do whatever comes to mind so long as it does not actively harm others, in a free community. Nothing is expected of you, nothing is delivered. Everything springs of natural and uncoerced energy." Needless to say, the Marxists found this style of organization unacceptable, and their influence increased. To keep control, Bloom and his followers early one Sunday morning loaded all the contents of their office, including a press, on trucks and in cars and moved by caravan to a farm in western Massachusetts. When the other side awoke to find the equipment gone, it dispatched a second caravan in much larger numbers. Brandishing knives and rods, the hard-liners beat up the anarchists, wrecked their new house, and took as much back as they could. The result was more devastating than any injuries to the body; the violent encounter was the end of innocence. Mungo wrote in his memoir of the struggle, "We took from them the machinery with which they planned to voice their politics, and their politics are their identities; they took from us our blood, our energy, and whatever vision we had left of a 'revolution.' " See Raymond Mungo, *Famous Long Ago: My Life and Hard Times with Liberation News Service* (Boston: Beacon Press, 1970), pp. 56–57, 153 ff.

25. See Norman H. Nie, Sidney Verba, and John Petrocik, *The Changing American Voter* (Cambridge: Harvard University Press, 1976), pp. 156–73, and studies cited therein.

26. John Herbers, "Interest Groups Gaining Influence at the Expense of National Parties," *New York Times,* Mar. 26, 1978.

27. Andrew Kopkind, "ACORN Calling," *Working Papers for a New Society* 3 (Summer 1975): 13–20; and "ACORN Update," ibid. 6 (Jan.–Feb. 1978): 4.

It might be argued that the fate of organizations is better explained by their politics than by their structure. The two are clearly related, but my argument would be that given an organization's politics, its chances of survival are better in the community or public-interest forms than as a movement organization, during a period when radical sentiment is ebbing. Indeed, some of the movement groups of the sixties, particularly in civil rights and environmental and women's issues, have shifted toward a structure more like that of public-interest groups by pulling back from direct action and concentrating their efforts on research, lobbying, and litigation.

28. Les Ledbetter, "Panthers Working Within the System in Oakland," *New York Times,* July 18, 1977.

29. Kopkind, "Sea-Level Media: Up From Underground," in this volume. On *Rolling Stone,* see Robert Sam Anson, "Citizen Wenner," *New Times,* Nov. 26, 1976, pp. 16 ff., and "The *Rolling Stone* Saga: Part Two," ibid., Dec. 10, 1976, pp. 22 ff.

30. Ellen Frankfort, *The Voice: Life at the Village Voice* (New York: William Morrow, 1976), pp. 48, 141. The staff subsequently formed a union that included freelance writers—probably a unique arrangement. See Barbara Garson, *"Village Voice* Workers Unionize," *In These Times* 1 (Nov. 23–29, 1977): 17.

31. Leslie and Michael Goldberg, "Paul Krassner on the Very Zen Art of Hustling a Porn King (and Vice Versa)," *In These Times* 2 (Apr. 5–11, 1978): 24.

32. Hodgson, *America in Our Time,* p. 348.

33. Piven and Cloward, *Poor People's Movements,* p. xi.

34. For a detailed critique of Piven and Cloward, see my review in *Working Papers for a New Society* 6 (Mar.–Apr. 1978): 70–73.

Experimenting with the Future: Alternative Institutions and American Socialism

by David Moberg

Eight years ago I joined with some friends to start a commune in Chicago. We had only a diffuse notion of communal living for "the house," but it seemed like a good antidote to "bourgeois individualism" and the isolation of couples. We hoped that it might also be part of a wave of new alternative institutions that hinted at the shape of a future socialist America.

Neither individualism nor coupling has disappeared in the interim, although each has been tempered. Socialism hasn't arrived yet either. Many of the alternative institutions that were supposed to be building the new world within the old have long gone, but within a few minutes of home there is still a great and changing variety. We shop at the Hyde Park Co-op, a remnant from the thirties that differs from other large, well-stocked supermarkets mainly in its support of the farm workers' boycott over the years. The three-year-old goes to a parent-run cooperative day-care center. A few blocks to the south, a veteran of antiwar activities has established a thriving recycling center that has expanded beyond collecting cans, bottles, and paper to work on occasional solar and wind projects, car repair and bread-baking. A local and a citywide free weekly provide news, features, and services, including some leftist writing, that would otherwise be unavailable. Farther south there's a community-development corporation bringing business and housing to Woodlawn—after the neighborhood group acceded to the University of Chicago's "urban removal" of thousands of poor blacks. In South Shore, the neighborhood beyond Woodlawn, people committed to preventing the flight of capital from the area as whites moved out and blacks moved in have taken over the bank. They have reversed the normal financial abandonment of racially changing communities and initiated planning for comprehensive economic redevelopment.

They are all worthy ventures—providing needed goods and services, lessening the fragmentation of city social life, giving a boost to the economy of local areas, offering meaningful paid and volunteer work. But the old Daley machine still runs the city, and the University dominates the neighborhood. Black unemployment in Woodlawn is staggering. There are persistent rumors that the steel mills to the south will shut down, adding to the hundreds of thousands of industrial jobs lost by the city in recent decades. Public transportation costs much more and provides much less service than when we moved in. And Jimmy Carter reminds us that, yes, life is unfair. The alternative institutions continue, less forcibly in some ways than at the beginning of the decade, more actively in other ways. Have they left their mark?

Movement and Counterculture: Living the Revolution

When the new left was at its high point, having passed from dissent and protest through declarations of resistance, rebellion, and revolution, certain propositions seemed almost common sense among young activists. Corporate capitalist institutions were corrupt and corrupting. The political values of the left—especially democracy, equality, nondiscrimination by race or sex, cultural liberation—should be lived and not just preached for "after the revolution." Alternative institutions could not only sustain new-left bases of strength but should also reach out to ordinary people concerned more with day-to-day survival than with seemingly remote issues of foreign affairs or federal legislation.

Not all of the alternative institutions have been self-consciously connected with the political left, by any means. Yet there were many themes common to the left and to people drawn toward the alternative institutions—a desire for community, a faith in spontaneous and direct action, a vision of total social and personal transformation, a belief in a combination of democracy and self-realization, a distaste for things big, impersonal, and bureaucratic, and a hostility to the America of the Corporate Fifties.

The new left overlapped broadly with the counterculture, which was itself a potentially powerful oppositional force. In consolidating its hold on American life in the period after World War II, corporate capitalism relied increasingly on sophisticated, pervasive shaping of images of the world and of values through mass media, advertising, commodity consumption, and prolonged (but constricted) education. More than ever, the left had to contest that culture if there was to be any chance of focusing discontent and organizing for a new society. The counterculture raised a critique of American society that went far beyond the bounds of the political left, even if it often missed essential leftist insights about power, economic exploitation, and class.

Looking not for "revolution in our lifetime" but for "revolution in our youth," the new left and the counterculture had a shortened historical perspective that encouraged a sense of urgency and immediacy. That was also sustained both by the rapid swelling of The Movement and, ironically, by the frustrating failure to budge Leviathan very much (although the impact of the new left was greater than participants realized at the time). The capacity to take the long view was blunted by the romantic hopes easily quickened in youth, by a disdain for established political channels, by the belief that reformism led to moral corruption and co-optation, and by images of worldwide political upheaval—from cultural revolution in China to near-revolution in France. A sense of immediacy was also linked to an old American penchant for untheoretical practicality: if the revolution is so great, why not start living it now? As Jerry Rubin, the Yippie, urged, "Do it!"

Cultural contradictions of American capitalism certainly fed the liberating impulses of the new left and shaped the alternative institutions, but the contradictions of socialism made a distinctive contribution as well. Although most of those touched by sixties movements had grown up with distorted cold-war images of socialism, there was plenty that was truthfully distasteful about the Soviet version of socialism: bureaucratic, grim, secretive, closed to dissent and variety, undemocratic. Cuba, then Vietnam and China, provided some inspiration for alternative socialisms by emphasizing conceptions of revolution that looked forward to construction of "new socialist men and women" guided by a genuine desire to serve the people.

Models for the new world were also generated from an eclectic improvization of scraps of America's past—Indian tribes, frontier settlers, even homesteaders and rebels, who for a few represented the traditions of communal and cooperative experiment. Added to that was a bricolage of the rich discards of a boom economy, drug experiences, the freedoms of a threadbare but relatively easy and invigorating life in the counterculture community, and later feminist claims for autonomy and equality.

The generation of new models was affected by the transitions in life that so many new leftists shared—an extended rite of passage into adulthood that consisted of a prolonged liminality (suspension outside the dominant structures of society) that supported a communal experience in much the same way as rites of passage in traditional societies. Beyond that, confrontation with the complacently monolithic, liberal-conservative establishment in universities, mass media, government, and big business provided another source for models: the inverse of anything that existed must be better (and was probably in itself revolutionary). From the Diggers of seventeenth century England to the Diggers of 1960s San Francisco, such radical inversions have been common in the history of social revolutions. And typically such movements share a sense of being outside historical time, often skirting the social dialectic with existing powers that is necessary in order to transform established institutions.

Increasingly, as the movement and the counterculture spread and deepened in intensity, more people developed a need to find a way to live life and make history at the same time.[1] Instead of working at one's trade and being a member of the party, many new leftists wanted to practice their vocations directly for social change[2] and to find ways to support an alternative, surrogate socialist style of living. Actually, a great many people drawn to various alternative institutions were only slightly concerned about making history or about politically acting to change relations of power, wealth and privilege in society. Although I will be judging the past decade of alternative institutions in large part in terms of how they may help to bring a humane, democratic socialism to the United States, not every practitioner applied such criteria and few thought of it as their only objective in starting an underground newspaper or radio station, forming a commune, working in a free clinic, encouraging urban gardens or community factories, or teaching in a free school. They were looking for a better way to live and to work.

Yet various alternative institutions have been integral to upsurges of populist, socialist, and other anticapitalist movements in the past. The Socialist party in its 1912 platform even elevated consumer cooperatives to the same level as trade unions and the party itself as the leading forces for socialism. Their model of a cooperative, however, was taken from Belgium, where the co-op not only provided low-cost food for members but also gave food to strikers, provided jobs for blacklisted organizers, and retained a portion of its earnings to spend on socialist propaganda. Marx supported consumer cooperatives, even though he argued that "restricted . . . to the dwarfish forms into which individual wage-slaves can elaborate it by their private efforts, the co-operative system will never transform capitalistic society." Cooperative production was more promising, he argued, but ultimately general changes in society required the "transfer of the organized forces of society, viz., the State power, from capitalists and landlords to the producers themselves."[3]

The progressive-school movement had a self-consciously socialist wing, especially associated with Alexander Meiklejohn, and both populists and socialists in the United States in the early twentieth century established municipal utilities and other public enterprises. At the start of the socialist movement, of course, the utopian socialists inspired communal efforts—especially in America, where it seemed they had a chance to compete with nascent capitalism. Those efforts were part of a wave of anticapitalist sentiment that took other forms as well. Despite their criticisms of the methods of the utopians, Marx and Engels, along with much of the early socialist movement, were deeply influenced by their models.

Contrary to their image of well-meaning ineffectiveness, alternative institutions have at times been powerful political forces. Consider the Highlander School established by Myles Horton in 1932. Inspired in part by socialist writings and the progressive-school movement, as well as by the tradition of "folk schools" that were established in Denmark in the nineteenth century to aid peasants and preserve their culture, Horton taught people in the hills around Monteagle, Tennessee, how to organize themselves for social change, including organizing unions. From that time on there has been hardly a movement in the South that has not been aided and influenced by Highlander's work. In 1954 Horton helped some poor blacks on the Georgia Sea Islands to set up schools to learn how to read and write and become active citizens. Students from each school became teachers and spread the system. Later the Southern freedom schools formed a crucial part of the civil rights movement. When Staughton Lynd returned north with accounts of the schools, it was one of the first times that young new leftists on the campuses began thinking about alternative institutions—places where people could "live the revolution," according to early SDS leader Paul Booth. Small as it was, Highlander not only kept alive an important radical tradition but spread its influence far beyond alternative institutions.

Contemporary alternative organizations continue the work

of sixties protest that broke through the complacency of powerful banality from the fifties. There has not been a clear sense of
an overall, systematic alternative to contemporary capitalism
on the political scene for at least the past three decades. The
alternative institutions and the movements associated with
them provide fragments of the needed choice. But they are a
peculiar mixture of the political and the personal. The goals
they pursued comprise a long list: transforming a dominant
institution (schools or the medical industry, for example),
demonstrating that participatory democracy works, experi-
menting with new social relationships, living in ecological har-
mony with the earth, pursuing a simpler, more rational life
style, serving "the people" (often a special constituency, such
as women helping other women), attracting and establishing a
deeper base for political action, building the community of the
counterculture or of a particular group (poor, working class,
black, Latino, Native American), prefiguring the new society in
microcosm (often with the hope that others would be inspired
and copy the example), producing goods (from whole-wheat
bread to solar collectors) or providing services (from holistic
therapy to nonauthoritarian education) that otherwise would
not be available. At the margins the alternatives blur off into
various hip-capitalist projects, yielding Red Zinger tea, hash
pipes, dynamite Colombian, or spiritual guides.

Some projects share many goals, but they are not all easily
compatible. Dropping out and building a political base don't
mesh nicely, for example. Also, an overriding obsession with
one goal—providing a service or improving human relationships within the group—might easily conflict with changing
surrounding social institutions. All too often some goals slipped
away as the initial euphoria turned to routine, a guru-leader
moved on, outside pressures wore down spirits, or simple survival demanded most of the time.

The virtues admired in most alternative institutions were
shared by the new left. But it is typical of recent social movements in this country that so many institutions could be labeled
alternative without it being clear what kind of alternative they
offered and to what they offered an alternative. Black capitalism

is one alternative to the exclusion of blacks from the economy, but it is clearly different from the Black Panther party's clinics, schools, or free-breakfast programs. *The Seed* was an alternative newspaper in Chicago that identified strongly with the new left and the counterculture. Its successor as an alternative, *Reader,* is open to leftists but scrupulously avoids a social or political stance. There is even a magazine called *Alternatives:* it pushes Edgar Cayce and herbal healing, hardly the original passions of the builders of free schools and food co-ops.

Alternative institutions, in short, can offer a *different* way of living, but they don't always represent an opposition to or an attempt to confront the powers of the state and capital directly. Raymond Williams writes:

> There is a simple theoretical distinction between alternative and oppositional, that is to say between someone who simply finds a different way to live and wishes to be left alone with it, and someone who finds a different way to live and wants to change the society in its light. This is usually the difference between individual and small-group solutions to social crisis and those solutions which properly belong to political and ultimately revolutionary practice. But it is often a very narrow line, in reality, between alternative and oppositional. . . . As the necessary area of effective dominance extends, the same meanings and practices can be seen by the dominant culture, not merely as disregarding or despising it, but as challenging it.[4]

The key is wanting to change society. Yet liberal America can tolerate a variety of attempts to reshape it. If the numbers get large, the aims threatening to the core of wealth and control in society, the strategies effective, and the ideas appealing, alternative institutions and ways of life become oppositions. However, instead of innumerable communes and co-ops gradually eating away the foundation of U.S. society, alternative institutions have often turned out to be juicy little morsels for consumption by prevailing powers.

A give-and-take between alternative and dominant institutions, as well as between alternative institutions and other potential parts of a left, is unavoidable. Consequently the pattern of alternatives has changed in the past decade. But their growth, change, and impact are hard to assess because of their peculiar organizational form. The motivating sentiments against bureaucracy and hierarchy often lead to suspicion of all structure. Lacking organization, many alternative institutions rely on "networks" of newsletters and personal contacts. One observer coined an acronym for such nonorganizations: SPIN —segmented, polycentric, integrated through a network.[5]

In judging the success of alternative institutions, it can't be forgotten that by comparison with the boom of the 1960s, the 1970s have been a long-term economic bust. That has added to the nearly universal plague of alternative institutions—money, not enough of it. As a result, alternatives often depend on low wages or volunteer work, which burns out the dedicated and winnows out those who need at least average wages. The quest for money continually shapes alternatives, often steering them away from original goals. The 1970s have also been a "down" period politically. As a result of the fragmentation of the left and the counterculture, there is no movement with which alternative institutions can associate to reinforce their political character. Not only do the alternative institutions outside the women's movement have less force for change without a coherent political movement, but also they are more likely to become routinized internally.

Business cycles and changing political climates sharply affect alternative institutions, but there doesn't seem to be a consistent pattern: they have formed in hard times (often as defensive organizations) and in good times (often as euphoric, utopian experiments). Nineteenth-century communal experiments were destroyed equally by business panics bringing collapse and by economic booms that seemed to turn the whole country into individualized utopias. Although some institutions have been hurt by the stagnant seventies, others have emerged as adaptations to the energy crisis, the decline of the central cities, and other challenges.

The Sixties: Alternative Means of Reproduction

In the sixties, the alternatives tended to focus their attention on the means of reproduction—renewing people, developing sensibility and education, maintaining body and spirit, biological reproduction, and consumption, for example. Although they persisted to varying degrees through the seventies, a new form of alternative began to develop that stressed production —energy, work, city-building, technology, investment and finances, alternative businesses, worker-community control. This was a response to the economic, urban, work, ecological, and energy crises of the seventies. The sixties had seen a confrontation with the corporate consensus forged in the mid-fifties over the proper kind of citizen society should encourage; during that time there was a struggle to create a new sensibility and morality that broke with the fifties. Each attempt followed slightly varied and complex twists of fate. Yet the experience in each case was sobering but not devastating, as a brief look at food co-ops, communes, free clinics, alternative media, and free schools indicates.[6]

Food Co-ops

A modest success as providers of good, low-cost food, the food co-ops failed to change the agribusiness and corporate processing and distribution businesses that sit atop America's food chain. After their renewal in various guises in the sixties, food co-ops continued to spread. During the late seventies they found a better reception in medium-sized, fairly typical cities than in the university bases that nourished the sixties co-ops. Some highly political co-ops were wracked by factionalism characteristic of the times: in Minneapolis there was a bitter battle between the fresh-produce people and the "proletarian-line" faction that favored canned goods, since that was "worker food." More typically, activists who wanted to reach the masses through food co-ops became discouraged that the demands of keeping the enterprise going overwhelmed other concerns. The organizing or radicalizing potential was not clear. Many customer-members were more interested in cheap eats than in tax reform or community organizing. Often middle-class people who want their artichokes fresh and get off on trips to bustling markets form buying clubs, but poor people lack time, self-confidence, or necessary experience to start their own co-op. To serve poor communities, several co-ops have taken over central-city grocery-store buildings abandoned by chains following the profit trail to the suburbs.

If food co-ops have not succeeded in mixing Marxism and mung beans for their members, they have become part of a growing "food movement." Concerned with nutrition, quality, additives, organic-production methods, and contamination of foods, the food movement activists occasionally forge ties between consumers and small farmers. These alliances take on a political edge, as they oppose policies of agribusiness and giant food corporations. Yet the giants may still have their day: with the disappearance of small grocery stores, wholesale markets that co-ops need may disappear from many cities as truckloads of supplies go directly to chain stores.

Food co-ops are the leading alternative institution, probably reaching more people than all but media alternatives. Despite their problems surviving in a market that gives strong price breaks to the big buyer, food co-ops have demonstrated both the viability of alternative institutions and the ease with which alternatives develop a narrow vision. Food co-ops are nonoppositional alternatives. "Food co-ops are not going to threaten any established institution," co-op veteran Dan McCurry concludes. "Anybody who thought it was going to was foolish. But it is a step."

Communes

Two different types of commune have persisted from the sixties: the rural and the urban household. The transitory drop-in commune has virtually disappeared. Although the farms have come on harder times, the city "houses" have proliferated in diverse forms. The two forms have become an established minority option, which, despite the small numbers involved, represent an important and active option to the typically privatized life of American capitalism. The number of rural communes peaked in 1970 at nearly 3,500. By 1978, about 30 percent of that number—or a total of 1,000—were still operating, a significant decline, but still more than had existed in earlier historical periods.[7] Today, with the movement waning, established country communes even report difficulties recruiting replacement members. One of the founders of Twin Oaks, a large and successful community, recently argued, "Please don't *start* a commune in 1977. The chance for success of such ventures is minimal; the cost of failure is high—and is not borne solely by the initiators of the doomed groups," she wrote.[8] Commune problems can be as endless as those families encounter and quite similar, but communes do not have the same proclivity to stick together. Illness, poverty, conflicting demands on limited resources, disputes between people earning money and those who aren't, and struggles for power over communal direction—all have contributed to the failures. Yet many of the survivors are ready for the long haul, and they are forming a tighter network of communication and support.

Communal living in cities takes a variety of forms, from groups sharing a house or even an old warehouse to more privatized families buying a group of houses or an apartment building together. For heirs of the new left and counterculture, such housing arrangements have become an unexotic option, although the style of living has also been adopted by quite different groups, such as old people who might otherwise be alone or in a nursing home. In a city it is hard to sustain for long a hope of creating a radically different world inside the four walls of the house. The people derive their material support from outside. Thus, one commune budges the dominant culture very little, even for its members. But most urban communes are not trying to become utopian islands. Instead, they resemble the "family commune," described by two British sociologists, Philip Abrams and Andrew McCulloch, as "attempts to institutionalize friendship on the basis of place-making.'"[9]

Despite some attempts, communes do not often replace the family, although the three-year-old in our house refers to us as her family. Rather the urban commune is usually a new, loose domestic institution that incorporates "families," individuals and couples, providing an intermediary between individuals and the larger social world. They vary immensely in their modifications of other intimate ties, but in trying to achieve both community and individuality, communes go against the grain of modern capitalist life. At odds if not always in conflict with capitalism, Abrams and McCulloch suggest, communes generally represent experiments in a new, less atomized, social life.

> The culture in which we find ourselves is one which in a pro-
> found way denies the possibilities of social life. Yet critics of that
> culture, from Marx onwards, have found it strangely difficult to
> give an account in any practical depth of what a more authentic
> existence would be like. By attempting to practice such an exis-
> tence, communes begin to give us that account.[10]

Not so strangely, communes at this point give an account mainly of how difficult it is to lead a social life when everything in the surrounding society militates against it.

Communes have not been failures, however, even when they have been unstable. They remain a powerful symbol of one ideological legacy of the new left, counterculture, and women's movement: our personal, private lives are not divorced from "public politics." Nonetheless, even if dramatic change must occur at all levels of people's lives, expectations of change in personal relationships through communal friendship have been tempered in recent years. Like the advocates of open marriage, modern communards have had a similar, sobering experience; they have modified their enthusiasms to recognize the difficul-ties in radically changing institutions of intimacy without sup-port from the general culture. Yet urban family communes remain an appealing adaptation of domestic life to changes in the division of labor, gender typecasting, and city residential patterns. The commune, even if it less frequently called that today, will be with many of us in some form for a long time.

Free Clinics

The free clinics were divided even at the outset between those designed primarily to provide a service for the needy—usually a poor minority or a hip, youthful community—and those conceived with a more political intent, as presaging a socialist health-care system of the future. Advocates of this second type, the more transformative clinics, saw the provision of neglected services as a way of organizing people into a political movement. If successful, the health-care movement would shift American medical practice from its elitist, "heroic" preoccupation with curing disease, and toward an emphasis on primary care and preventive medicine.

At times, clinic advocates saw providing something *free* as in itself insurrectionary, like Yippies throwing dollar bills into the Stock Exchange. Most of the more thoroughly political clinics are now gone, although many community clinics, free or charging according to ability to pay, continue to uphold some of the political ideals. In Chicago in the early seventies, a coalition of clinics associated with a variety of left-wing groups—including the Black Panther party, Rising Up Angry, and the Young Patriots—collided head-on with Mayor Richard Daley and the medical establishment. Daley exhumed old licensing laws to harass the "communist clinics," as hospital administrators called them, and established a new network of city clinics which, coincidentally, were placed near preexisting free clinics. (The city clinics continue but are badly underfunded and of limited effectiveness.) The political clinics were among many free clinics that shunned the government money that was soon available for drug-abuse programs, VD treatment and care of Medicaid patients. Most of the groups now surviving latched on to the money, cleaning up their act and premises sufficiently to appear professional and nonpolitical, thereby getting licenses and money.

The clinics had an impact. People excluded from the medical system received help, although clinic workers soon saw how the medical establishment used them as a safety valve. Young people found sympathetic aid for drug problems, VD, or contraceptive needs. The clinic movement helped to stimulate the growing interest in primary care among medical students or to shape their social consciences. A veteran California free-clinic doctor known for his super-freaky appearance recently turned up clean-shaven and working in a county medical office. Another tale of cynically abandoned idealism? No, he said, he was newly married and needed more money, but he was still pursuing the same goals in his new job. Now, partly thanks to the clinic pressures, more hospitals have patient advocates and stress patient rights. Free-clinic radicals spread in all directions, including private practice, public health, organizing medical staff at hospitals, and involvement in various currents of unorthodox care, such as holistic medicine, bioenergetics, acupuncture, yoga, and various systems aimed at keeping people healthy more than at curing illness. Another small fraction has turned to a more traditional left-wing political struggle in medicine, fighting for a national health service.

Out of the free clinics and the women's movement came a variety of women's health centers, including self-help and self-awareness programs (with such successful literature as *Our Bodies, Ourselves,* by a Boston group). In turn, these are related to more recent battered-women's centers or rape crisis lines. These women's alternative institutions call attention to neglected issues. They form social nuclei and recruiting bases for the women's movement. Supported by the more general political pressure of the movement, women's centers have helped change the way rape victims are treated by hospitals, police, and courts and have pressured local governments to provide services for women at public expense. The women's health movement has also spurred criticism of medical technology and pharmacology, of doctors' arrogance or inattentiveness toward patients, and of the "medicalization" of aspects of life that are not illnesses.

Alternative Media

The alternative media reached more people and were more broadly influential than other alternative institutions, but they were in one way the least original: the left has always had its press, and for many decades the avant-garde in the arts has relied on small, noncommercial presses, galleries, and performance centers. In the sixties, however, the alternative media benefited from the growing importance of the mass media in the decades after World War II. They were distinctive—especially the newspapers and magazines—in their broad countercultural embrace of politics and life style, their exuberant personalization of writing, their up-front partisan reporting, and their rapid spread through loosely linked, locally autonomous efforts.

The old underground press has largely vanished, reappearing above ground in more businesslike garb, with more restrained, disciplined writing and less political advocacy. Now most of the local weeklies even shun the description "alternative" as a barrier to lucrative advertising.[11] Yet there are many alternative publishing efforts, including academic, intellectual journals renewing Marxist studies, and newsletters or special-interest periodicals on topics reflecting the fragmented issues that emerged from the movement—women's interests, energy, environment, agriculture and food, homesteading, occupational health and safety, alternative technology, and local-level politics. At the national level, a few alternatives have folded (like *Ramparts*); others have become commercial successes and blunted their cutting edge (like *Rolling Stone*); and others have become more dull and sectarian (like *The Guardian*). New entries (including *Mother Jones, Working Papers, In These Times,* and *Seven Days*) have begun a precarious struggle toward solvency and a mass audience. Pacific News Service and Internews expand the diminished leftist syndicated publishing first initiated by Liberation News Service, which survives, and by the defunct Underground Press Syndicate. Several publications continue some of the new left and countercultural concerns with the addition of a more pronounced spiritual or mystical sentiment (*East-West Journal, New Age,* and to a lesser extent, *Co-Evolution Quarterly,* heir to the *Whole Earth Catalog* tradition). Several of these newer publications are trying to use more conventional publishing and promotional practices in order to reach a wide audience with a radical message, while at the same time investigating new financial bases, such as nonprofit foundations as publishers. Most, but not all, try to make their staff relations fit their democratic or radical ideals.

The record is mixed in other cultural enterprises. Progressive radio catered to left and counterculture ideas but mainly served artistic and adventurous musical tastes. It has suffered such commercial dilution in most cases that it is barely an alternative, although listener-sponsored and community-oriented, noncommercial FM stations have been expanding slowly despite repeated crises at the old stalwart stations. New publishers, record labels, and film networks distribute works that would otherwise be ignored by the entertainment monopolies—ranging from the Feminist Press and several mainly feminist record companies to new and established left-wing publishers and independent film distributors of *Union Maids, Lovejoy's Nuclear War,* and similar films. Professional values in production have superseded the deliberately free-form and exuberant amateurism typical of the sixties.

Since writers like Jack Kerouac, William Burroughs, and Allen Ginsberg were instrumental in fashioning the sensibilities that gave birth to countercultural institutions, it would be a mistake to ignore the minority and popular arts, critical of today's established society. The civil-rights and antiwar movements, as well as contradictions of commercialism and avant-garde sensibilities in the booming art market of the sixties, have pushed many artists to the left. Marxist criticism and journals have popped up, cooperative and feminist galleries or performance centers have opened, and a vast range of small magazine and book publishers have continued what is almost itself an alternative institution—the "bohemia" surrounding the cutting edges of the arts.

Free Schools

"Free schools," often toned down to "alternative schools" or lately conceived of as "community schools," seemed to offer great hopes. They tackled one of the most basic mechanisms for reproducing society. By abandoning hierarchy, discipline, and a curriculum designed to integrate obedient kids into twentieth century American capitalism, and replacing it with a program of equality, freedom, love, spontaneity, and the development of strong individuals, they could help students escape the dreary regimen of public schools and strengthen the forces of social change. Although anecdotes, observations, and some studies suggest that many alternative schools have been successful, especially with young people who are well motivated and have basic skills but can't stand the public-school structure, there are also reports of kids who never learned to read (and teachers who didn't think that was very important anyway, in the manner of Ivan Illich). There is a growing confusion among education critics about how education should be arranged, even if there is agreement that the current schools are disasters.

While the partisans of "deschooling" have little interest in reconstituting school of any type, other education activists think that pursuit of alternatives abandons the vast majority of students in the public schools. Within the alternative schools, there has been a partial retreat from the complete do-your-own-thing attitude of the late sixties in favor of some structure and deliberate teaching by teachers. Teachers shouldn't be afraid to teach, Herb Kohl admonished a group of alternative-school activists. Jonathan Kozol was even harsher on the free-school formlessness:

> I think that one of the reasons that we now face the frightening "back-to-basics" movement in this country is because many of us, and I include myself here, were very reckless and careless and stupid in our behavior in the late sixties and would just say, "kids are beautiful and neat and can learn at their own organic and spontaneous pace."[12]

The problems faced by alternative schools over the past decade are instructive about alternative institutions more generally. If supported by tuition, they have been underfunded and lacked pleasant surroundings or basic equipment, or else they become upper-class retreats with a few scholarship students. Although teachers are drawn to the schools by a desire to have better relationships with students and to enjoy their work more, the low pay and insecurity remain a serious problem. "I'm tired of getting seven thousand dollars a year," one long-time alternative teacher wearily said,

> but I really like what it does for the kids. I like the control I have. I can be Karen and not Ms. Morrill, the teacher. The parents are my friends. I can take the kids on my lap and kiss them. I can teach what I want. But with the turnover and constant changes it's almost like a new school year after year.

Schools soon become dependent on government funding for programs controlling drug addiction, truancy, and juvenile crime. In the later seventies, three-fourths of the alternative schools in Chicago were in poor neighborhoods, but they are admitted into the education system as a low-cost way of controlling students who would otherwise roam the streets. Along the way many of the schools succeed, nonetheless, in teaching basic skills, promoting knowledge and pride in ethnic heritages, and conveying a left-wing perspective on politics. When set up as an alternative by the public school system, the school usually loses its connection with goals of changing society, of providing models of nonauthoritarian relationships, or of giving students a sense of personal mastery of knowledge. Such schools "use the rhetoric of alternatives and options, but what they're talking about is a more liberated tracking system," says Lynn Miller, director of the National Alternative Schools Program.

The notion of alternative school becomes even more perverted in other instances. There are, of course, the segregationist academies in the South and elsewhere. In recent years, strongly authoritarian, reactionary schools stressing "basics" and inculcating traditional sex roles have called themselves alternative and received both tax support and popular backing from parents. Probably the fastest growing "alternative" is the magnet school, theoretically a specialized, high-quality school that draws students of all backgrounds from across a city, but in practice a subterfuge to avoid desegregation.

Although some educational activists, such as Don Moore of Designs for Change, see hope in turning parents into advocates within the public system and in expanding the provision under federal special-education law requiring parental approval of programs for handicapped kids, many fear that teachers' unions will continue to show antagonism toward most radical reform of education. Activists are also discouraged that the alternative-education movement has had virtually no effect on mainstream schools or teaching colleges. Although the alternative schools seemed to have held their own in a few places, like Minneapolis and Cambridge, they seem largely on the defensive. A survey by Miller turned up only 1,300 alternative schools of all types in the United States that were receiving public funds in 1977. At best the alternative-school assault on mainstream education has resulted in a stalemate: the alternatives holding out on their own tiny turf and the established schools proceeding in their lumbering, destructive, and ineffective fashion, acknowledging the alternatives only to adopt and distort them for traditional ends of social control.

The Seventies: Alternative Means of Production

As the alternative institutions that exploded in the late sixties attempted to cope with difficulties that were exacerbated by the hard times of the seventies, new alternatives emerged that were more specifically addressed to issues of reorganizing the productive life of society. Primarily, these include movements for comprehensive local political action and economic development under community control (part of what has been dubbed "the new localism"[13]), for alternative technology, and for workplace democracy. These alternatives generally involve a deeper engagement in the political and economic life of communities and less withdrawal than the earlier alternative institutions. For example, people talk of "seizing the city" in order to use its power to create alternative economic institutions, such as producer cooperatives for building solar technology. Activists often try harder to reach blue-collar workers, who were largely ignored in the earlier wave of alternative institutions, and to employ established political institutions for alternative ends.

The New Localism

There are several strands to the new localism. First, there has been a resurgence of leftist interest in city and state politics, a phenomenon reflected in and encouraged by the Conference on Alternative State and Local Public Policies. Beyond using municipal or state power to do more predictable legislative or administrative good—affirmative-action hiring, better welfare administration, equalization of public services—local activists want government to redirect economic development. They want their city councils to favor cooperatives, solar technology, urban gardening, recycling centers, energy-conservation projects, and municipal enterprises. They propose that public economic development aid poorer neighborhoods and old central-city areas, rather than trying to bribe or beg banks and businesses to invest. Of course, there are also efforts to control private investment (with laws against redlining by financial institutions, for example) or to take over private companies such as utilities. "Alternatives" in such a context take on a completely different meaning. With governmental power and finances behind these initiatives, the chances of success increase —as long as lefties have power.

In 1978 there were two dramatic examples of this strategy. In California a plan for a statewide public agency (SolarCal) to develop and finance solar water- and space-heating in homes and businesses was introduced in the legislature and promoted by the Campaign for Economic Democracy, a group that formed out of the remnants of Tom Hayden's bid for the Democratic nomination to the U.S. Senate. In its original form Solar-Cal would provide half a billion dollars for low-interest loans to homeowners to install solar equipment, and, in the process, encourage small businesses to employ the hard-core unemployed. Most controversial of all, the SolarCal legislation would enable the state to enter into production of solar equipment if private companies did not meet state needs.

On the other side of the country, community leaders, union officials, and clergy in Youngstown, Ohio, were investigating worker-community purchase of the Youngstown Sheet and Tube steel mill that had closed in 1977, throwing five thousand people out of work. There are probably over two hundred worker-owned enterprises of at least modest size in the United States. Although only a tiny proportion of enterprises in America, they have been quite successful and, when combined with community investment, offer a strategy for the redevelopment of cities abandoned by capitalists. They are also a step, as Marx recommended, toward the introduction of producer cooperatives.

Some of the local-development strategies continue to extol the potential of Community Development Corporations, even though the Carter administration budget proposal for fiscal year 1979 slashed money for CDCs by nearly half, possibly as a prelude to phasing out the program. CDCs were originally an odd child born of Republican hopes for black capitalism and the desires of some left-wing Democrats and independent radicals for community-controlled economic development of poor neighborhoods. Roughly forty CDCs were operating in the late 1970s with a wide variety of structures: in some instances, outside private capital underwrote the project and controlled much of it; in some, nearly all the money was public. Typically, community representatives must be on the board, but the CDC can use its money to encourage private, profit-making businesses, cooperatives, or profit and nonprofit enterprises owned by community groups.

Economic development has proven to be much slower than expected. CDCs attempt to start small businesses—which have a high failure rate in any case—under the most economically disadvantageous conditions. Originally their goals were as much social as economic: if a new business didn't make money but did employ ten people who would otherwise be jobless, the business was regarded as a success. But such social accounting has largely disappeared; now CDCs are judged on strict profit criteria.

Community Development Corporations are exceedingly fragile and easily frustrated or even crushed by hostile forces in government and business; that accounts for their drift toward business ends. Although some proponents of solar power and other small-scale "appropriate" technology hope that CDCs can hitch their work to such forward-looking products, a former consultant to a major Chicago CDC has argued that, because of their shakiness and the difficulty that they have obtaining financing, CDC businesses can't take risks with something that isn't tried and true. Beyond the drift toward profit-oriented concerns and conservative ventures, there is also a strong tendency for CDCs to become entrenched during the long, slow period of initial development. Under all of these pressures—and with little in the culture to support the development of cooperative ventures guided by social rationality rather than by simple profit—CDCs gradually become less of an alternative institution.

Some people, recognizing the limitations of CDCs (and similar problems with both workers' and consumers' cooperatives), now see the economic alternatives in a different light. "The alternative institutions serve at best as experimental models," said Mark Looney, co-director of Strongforce, which advocates co-ops and worker-community ownership of factories.

> In the sixties some people had visions that they would proliferate in large numbers and overtake existing institutions, whereas now I think people are more realistic about their value and more aware of their limitations. People realize that the whole economic system has to change for these to be a success, and people in the alternatives are more involved in other kinds of political work.

Another strain to the "new localism" is concerned with both neighborhood government and neighborhood economies but tends to emphasize direct, voluntary citizen action. Here, the object is comprehensive creation of "urban alternatives" that foster "self-reliance" (key terms in the names of two groups in this camp). The most prominent community organizations are still the Saul Alinsky–style direct-action groups that use confrontation and embarrassment to pressure public officials. They have spread rapidly in the 1970s, forming defense groups of stable working-class, white-collar, and small-business people feeling the recession and inflation crunch. They have also combined into statewide federations in some instances, and frequently turn their attention to neighborhood preservation and rehabilitation (occasionally with unfortunate undertones of whites wanting to keep out blacks). The advocates of urban self-reliance stress much more direct action to prevent the export of a neighborhood's capital and to supply as many of the basic needs as possible from within the community. That could involve neighborhood financial institutions, such as credit unions or even a bank, like the local development-oriented South Shore Bank in Chicago. Other elements in this strategy for "alternative neighborhoods" might include food co-ops, recycling centers, a community soap factory or bakery, composting privies, rooftop gardens, windmills, solar heating and cooling of houses, and local cultural centers. Urban homesteaders taking over decrepit buildings and rehabilitating them through "sweat equity," gaining ownership through work, are pioneers in such a strategy.

In these visions of "neighborhood power,"[14] tight-knit, self-sufficient communities embracing means of consumption, production and social reproduction would be linked with other such autonomous units through a minimal state apparatus. Some architects and engineers have drawn up plans of such communities, combining compactness (so that everyone can walk or bicycle wherever necessary) with trees and open space to provide privacy and the relief of natural beauty. It is the city equivalent of attempts to establish land trusts and homesteads in the country. But one of the enduring weaknesses of the perspective is its failure to confront the issue of how existing institutions of wealth and state power would be dismantled or how the benefits that can derive from large-scale or even complex trade would be coordinated.

Appropriate Technology

The theory of the new-localist movements draws heavily on the arguments for "appropriate technology" and on the celebration of smallness inspired by E. F. Schumacher's work and taken in dozens of directions by a burgeoning horde of activists trying to wed a social vision to a technology—or the other way around.[15] In the long run, when all costs and benefits are considered, they argue, small-scale operations that "tread lightly" on the planet can often match the effectiveness of much large-scale technology, at the same time causing less environmental damage and providing more satisfying ways of living.

Actually, like "alternative," the concept "appropriate" in itself provides no guide. But it does raise critical issues: appropriate for what? For stability, equality, autonomy, individuality, justice, security, community, craft and skill, imagination? For profit, power, growth in the abstract, domination, inequality, plunder? The most appropriate technology for producing steel is probably large blast furnaces with continuous casting machines and highly automated strip mills (although small electric furnaces work well for some tasks). However, for producing electric power, photovoltaics—arrangement of wafers of materials like silicon that yield electric current when exposed to sunlight—will soon be more appropriate in many ways than giant, centralized power stations, especially those powered by nuclear reactors. Technology is not the only consideration. If we want to provide jobs for everyone, we could—to make a crude comparison—choose small backyard blast furnaces yielding much more work than a modern steel mill. The small furnaces were probably quite appropriate for China as it was trying to develop industry in recent years but would not be for the United States. On the other hand, most solar technologies yield energy as efficiently as nuclear power plants or better, yet also offer a bonus of far more useful work. In order to judge what technology is appropriate, we must first define our goals and then judge what best satisfies them. That is essentially a political process, but one which now is carried on undemocratically in corporate offices and for capitalist goals.

Smallness has had its appeal to many people not only as response to environmental destruction and the large-scale energy price and supply crises but also because of the frustration experienced in attempts to change or control the large corporations and government agencies. A new circle of people has been drawn into the orbit of the left—engineers and tinkerers, architects and craft hobbyists, small farmers and independent manufacturers. Yet alternative technology also appeals to ultra-individualistic, right-wing anarchists, the sort of folks who imagine perfect self-contained fortress-homes where they can observe and escape the collapse of civilization. Other individualists, sharing a dislike of government, imagine alternative technology reviving a yeomanry within the city.

Some appropriate technologists assume that their more efficient, more elegant and less energy-intensive ways will also lead to revolutionized social institutions. Most share an ideology that sees the crucial dichotomy of our time as centralists vs. decentralists. Decentralism in itself, however, is only slightly more useful as an ideology than appropriateness. Decentralism and injustice have hardly been incompatible. The garment industry is still small-scale and decentralized, for example. Is it beautiful for the people working there?

Appropriate technologists tend to ignore the dynamics of capitalism that lead to concentration. Those are social and economic conditions rather than technological determinants that lead toward centralization, as capitalist firms skew technology in favor of large, centralized, capital-intensive operations. Although the energy empires are still pushing for coal, oil, and nuclear power at the expense of solar energy, some appropriate technologists are rightfully worried that big corporations do not seem terribly threatened by the new alternative technology. They will take advantage of the best ideas worked out by the small inventors and then mass-market them for profit, compromising the potential that the appropriate technologists see in their tools.[16] Families in the future may be more secure knowing that their household energy supply does not depend on Consolidated Gas, Electric, and Everything Else, but the huge concentrations of capital will not disappear as a result. Self-reliance and local or household production can erode their dominance and reduce dependence on the market, reversing some of the past century's tendencies for capital to penetrate into every facet of life, but ultimately the society must confront what is done with the immense accumulations of capital that now exist as private corporations.

To its credit the movement has helped to politicize the issues of what is produced and with what technology, unmasking the ideology of scientific neutrality and progress that has been an effective cover for capitalist decisions on the direction of society. Under the influence of interest in technological alternatives, people have come to ask new questions about the ways human labor is used and for what ends. The movement does, of course, have its weaknesses and contradictions. For example, both Barry Commoner and Amory Lovins[17] advocate solar energy for both the immediate and long-term future. Yet Lovins vigorously argues that solar energy is compatible with capitalism and advocates rising prices for oil and natural gas as a way of speeding the transition. Commoner, on the other hand, condemns the rising energy prices as eroding the real earnings and employment possibilities of the working class through rapid inflation and economic disruption. He advocates not a capitalist market guided only by profit but rather "social governance of production" as the means for making the transition to solar energy in an equitable fashion.

Although many appropriate technologists ignore traditional leftist issues of income redistribution, many old leftists fail to understand that the struggle over forms of technology can be a classic confrontation over who gets how much of society's wealth. For example, should capital be redistributed in the form of many people individually or cooperatively owning solar heating devices and photovoltaic cells, or should it be concentrated in the hands of electric utilities building nuclear power plants that require more capital per unit of energy and provide fewer jobs per dollar invested? In Chicago in 1978 a skirmish developed over the city's plans to control pollution of Lake Michigan by digging tunnels and reservoirs under the city at a price of at least $2.6 billion and possibly many billions more. Rather than quickly flushing all the water away during a storm and holding it in the deep tunnels to prevent flooding of sewage into the lake, critics advocate using simple, cheap, intermediate technologies to catch the raindrop where it falls with resurfaced, porous parking lots, local ponds, rooftop retainers and more open, grassy space. If their plan were adopted, they argue, the job could be done at a lower cost, provide more jobs, yield new amenities for neighborhoods and leave hundreds of thousands of dollars per neighborhood for anything from housing rehabilitation to local economic development. A question of appropriate technology can become a question of who controls the city's wealth.

Workplace Democracy

The movements of the sixties and the counterculture helped to legitimize protest, demands for rights and respect, participatory democracy, and personal fulfillment, which—particularly after the widely reported strike by workers at the Lordstown, Ohio, General Motors plant in 1972—bolstered expectations of workplace democracy and satisfaction in work. There is a rising chorus of working-class ire at the power of companies to shut down operations and abandon diligent workers and dependent communities. Likewise there is resentment that democracy, the Bill of Rights, and personal freedoms disappear for workers as soon as they walk on the job.

There is no question that increased democracy at work brings greater worker satisfaction and higher morale.[18] Also, workplace democracy need not mean higher production costs, although that would be acceptable in balance against the cost to individual workers and to society of existing work patterns and authoritarianism. In many instances, productivity increases dramatically. The "myth of the assembly line" has been destroyed in a few years at the Volvo and Saab plants in Sweden, even though workplace democracy has barely begun there.

Elsewhere, democratization has brought greater labor stability, more flexibility and adaptability in production, higher quality goods and services, and many other benefits, including increased safety.[19]

Advocates of workplace democracy—perhaps a bit surprisingly—often show a hostility toward American labor unions that is common throughout the little world of alternative institutions. It is true that few unions want to take up the challenge of worker control on the job.[20] Some have not-so-honorable reasons, such as wanting to maintain their union bureaucracy or to preserve the historic trade-off of mangement dictatorship in the factory for wage and benefit gains every few years.

Unions have some reasonable fears as well, however. Activists in alternative institutions see themselves as engaged in creative work with a mission of providing a valuable good or service, changing society, and enhancing their own talents and character. Most people, however, only incidentally have work; above all they have a job; they must first of all hold on to and defend that meal ticket. Unions as now organized respond to that concern with the job, a condition created by capitalism and not by unions of blue-collar workers. Even if unions still had their former goals of abolishing wage slavery and creating a cooperative commonwealth, they would still quite rightly want to improve the income and security of their members. Now union leaders fear, for example, that some forms of work reorganization are used by management to weaken or prevent the collective worker defense that unions at their best offer. They fear that employers will take advantage of the increased productivity that nearly always comes with even partial democratization to lay off some of the workforce. Some are reluctant to be drawn into participation for fear that it will restrict their antagonist's role.

The fears are not entirely unfounded, but democratization of work can strengthen a democratic union. Although management may favor some limited plan, such as job enrichment, democracy is seductive and workers tend to want more, eventually leading to conflict at first with lower-level supervisors who feel threatened, eventually with the top management over major corporate decisions. One very successful experiment in a modicum of worker control at the Topeka, Kansas, General Foods plant was scuttled because management felt its power threatened.[21] Worker participation can be used as a means of control, but in the long run it is more likely to push firms, and if organized politically, push the country toward a democratic socialism. It is reminiscent in some ways of the contradictions in Robert Owen's philanthropic socialism. Workers were attracted to Owenism as an alternative to capitalism, but there were also some enlightened capitalists who saw such organization of work and community as the best means of motivating workers.[22] The outcome in such instances depends on the political struggle that goes on over the character of the alternative institution. That is true for all of them.

The Eighties and Beyond: The Democratic Commonwealth

Contrary to the brightest hopes, alternative institutions have not developed rapidly into an incipient alternative society nor have they had a marked effect on the mainstream. Yet they have not been a failure. Alternative experiences have enriched the heritage of the left and contributed towards visions of the future —the classic and neglected task of shaping a distinctly American socialism.

The alternative movements suffer not just because the future is inadequately prefigured by the fledgling efforts of the sixties and seventies, but because most Americans still pursue another utopia. They still dream of individual success and of "getting ahead" (meaning nearly anything other than falling behind). They dream less of a nourishing community than of a cozy family, long one of the most vivid American utopias.[23] Their visions of a bigger color television or a new stereo or a suburban ranch house are still more concrete than those of a cooperative, creative workplace dedicated to socially beneficial work. Certainly the dreams that were part of the myth of the fifties have been deeply tarnished. Most Americans now have other dreams that coincide more with the visions of the alternative institutions. Yet to say that capitalist culture is still hegemonic is to say that those alternative dreams are not as persuasive, do not seem as realistic or attainable, and are relegated to a distant hazy future.

Try though they might, the alternative institutions could not be islands unto themselves, nor could they influence society without reciprocal buffeting from the dominant culture. People involved in the alternatives carried with them the results of years of socialization. They were regularly exposed to the propaganda of values contrary to their own. More important, the alternatives had to contend with the larger structures and cycles of American society, difficulties in obtaining capital, business cycles, massive military spending, laws written for the support of dominant institutions, direct and indirect subsidies to corporate capitalist needs, advertising, and other means of shaping the culture. The existence of a thriving counterculture and new-left movement provided markets, clients, contributors, and new recruits. They supported the sense of mission of the alternative institutions, just as the institutions deepened the meaning of the social movements. They made more plausible the claim that the alternative institutions were subversive of the corrupt mainstream.

But, oddly enough, the alternative institutions did not take their own statements of opposition to American capitalist ways of doing business and living life very seriously, for they did not prepare for conflict. Many participants, from the counterculture or emerging spiritualist camp, disdained conflict. The movement provided the alternative institutions with a sense of conflict that also supported many of the goals of the alternatives. Lacking that creative antagonism and succumbing unprepared to forces from the dominant culture, many alternative institutions were rendered relatively harmless as another market choice.

Nearly all of them also faced organizational problems. Often people didn't know what they were doing in their experiments. City kids flocked to rural communes without knowing hoes from hogs. Free-school teachers worked on an antitheory that was based on simple opposition to the mainstream. "They ring a bell, so we won't ring a bell; they take attendance, so we won't take attendance," Don Moore said.

> But you can't run an alternative school just not doing what the system does. There was the idea that if we just get rid of all the old restrictions, cooperation will develop. But then kids just did whatever they would have done otherwise. "Doing your own thing" was like an extension of what everyone grew up with.

The distaste for hierarchy and bureaucracy often led to disorganization rather than reorganization on more democratic principles. Now a New School for Democratic Management has started in San Francisco, a sign that the task of democratization is taken more seriously.

Activists in alternative institutions failed to recognize that class shapes consciousness. They badly misunderstood the blue-collar working class, and this limited their impact. The alternatives were more successful with people who were outside the mainstream, such as the very poor or very hip. But for those with one uncertain foot up on the ladder, the alternative institutions seemed to offer little, and sometimes they appeared threatening. The more recent emphasis on local economic development and alternative technology addresses working-class issues more directly, stressing how such alternative technology and means of production can offer more, better, and more stable jobs.

Alternative-institution activists often seem to have assumed that significant change could come from piecemeal, cumulative construction of their projects. They even cite Mao's parable about the foolish old man who dumbfounded his neighbors by moving a mountain rock by rock. But societies are not mountains. They can be seen as composed of a hierarchy of principles or structures. Changes at a lower level will be encompassed and constrained by higher-level structures, such as the allocation of privately owned capital according to where it returns the greatest profit. A total transformation of society must tackle all levels. Change in many basic principles comes abruptly even if the piecemeal work helps to prepare the break.

Despite all these reservations, I believe that alternative institutions are likely to remain a valuable part of a movement for radical social change, particularly if such work is linked to a broader political movement for a socialism compatible with the alternative-institutional ideals. The alternatives have already been important in giving people a chance to live their beliefs while working to bring about more widespread change. Many people—including the activists who gained experience in democracy and learned to form solid proposals for transforming mainstream institutions—have been helped and educated by the work of the alternatives.

Even if alternative institutions by themselves will not radically change the world, they can contribute to the development of a civic culture that is vital for any mass socialist movement. The most important contributions to making a more activist, democratic political culture are likely to come from those alternative institutions that bring greater worker control over the work process and the economy. Decision-making at work increases a sense of political efficacy and involvement. Over the years democracy has come to mean representation by elites accountable by some means to the people who choose among competing rulers. Yet there is a tradition of democracy that emphasizes direct participation by people in governing their affairs.[24] It was largely based on a society of independent property holders, artisans, farmers, small businessmen and professionals, who had some security of subsistence and mastery of their work. In early America, by one argument, the democratic ideal was linked to superiority of the society over the state.[25] That time has long passed, but the experience of security and mastery of work in contemporary collective workplaces can become the basis of a new democracy of socialism. Such changes at work, along with a redistribution of income, are essential for the success of radical reforms in education and for other ideals of the alternative institutions. In a way the new localism is a return to the desire to see society supreme and to create active citizens who can manage their own affairs. As Richard Kazis of the Institute for Self-Reliance said,

People have to understand how to become citizens again, that they can do things for themselves. From there you hope that once they become citizens, they will become involved in the political process, will know who has power and that once they're involved in something that means a lot to them, they'll get angry if it's threatened.

Much as the alternative institutions are associated with the political resurgence of the sixties, they also resurrect buried values of the broader American political tradition—popular democracy, the self-determination linked with liberty and individualism, local autonomy. The alternative institutions provide, too, a safe expression of the suppressed "secondary yearnings" that Philip Slater saw as linked to antiradicalism in American culture—yearnings for community, engagement, and dependence.[26] They present a left-wing alternative both to the increasingly disliked bureaucracy in American life and to the typical right-wing exploitation of those sentiments. In their effort to link living life and making history, the alternative institutions provide a way of harnessing desires for self-realization to more altruistic, socially constructive ends than the arrogant self-aggrandizement of the "me decade."[27]

There is also a contradictory way in which the alternative institutions capitalize on the deep American distrust of the state as an instrument for change and justice. They demonstrate that socialism is not the same as statism. They offer direct action and appeal to a native streak of anarchistic radicalism. That is one of their failings, too. Many poor people and blue-collar workers have come to look more to the state for redress of wrongs, and with good reason. Beyond that, failure to contend for control of the proverbial "commanding heights" of the economy by ignoring the state would stymie the goals of the alternative-institution activists.

The alternatives have not only reclaimed some American political ideas but also have enriched the growing leftist movement with critiques of nearly all aspects of daily life in capitalist America. Unlike capitalism, which accomplishes its rational calculations because all relationships can ultimately be translated into monetary terms and judged on a single criterion—

profitability—the alternative institutions point the way toward a more complex social organization balances many goals through conscious, democratic decision-making.

In their fragmented, indirect way the alternative institutions, along with other heirs of the new left and the counterculture, have posed for the "wealthiest" nation on earth the subversive question: What is wealth? Marx asks the same question after commenting on how the "ancients," meaning the classical Greeks and Romans, did not ask what kind of property produced the most wealth but rather, "What mode of property creates the best citizens?"

> Thus the old view, in which the human being appears as the aim of production, regardless of his limited national, religious, political character, seems to be very lofty when contrasted to the modern world, where production appears as the aim of mankind and wealth as the aim of production. In fact, however, when the limited bourgeois form is stripped away, what is wealth other than the universality of individual needs, capacities, pleasures, productive forces, etc., created through universal exchange? The full development of human mastery over the forces of nature, those of so-called nature as well as of humanity's own nature? The absolute working-out of his creative potentialities, with no presupposition other than the previous historic development which makes this totality of development, i.e. the development of all human powers as such the end in itself, not as measured on a *predetermined* yardstick? Where he does not reproduce himself in one specificity, but produces his totality? Strives not to remain something he has become, but is in the absolute movement of becoming?[28]

In this sense, the alternative movement has sought to put on the agenda of society the central issue of the control of wealth. It is ironic that so many of the alternative institutions have nevertheless sidestepped the fundamental issue posed over the years by socialists: the control of capital (and with that the redistribution of income). Since the state embodies the commitment of the society as a whole to the preservation of existing property rights, there is no alternative to the simultaneous pursuit of a strategy to win control of and to radically alter the state (most happily of course through various peaceful means, including formal elections). Thus, in recent years people involved in alternative institutions have given greater attention to winning political office, formulating legislation, gaining access to capital for cooperative public enterprises. They have sought to control the prerogatives of private capital through legislation, and to use alternative institutions, technology, and organizational models to redistribute power and income as much as possible.

No doubt in another ten years many of the same kind of alternative institutions will be found in my neighborhood, if not exactly the same ones. Although issues of reproduction of society —families, education, consumption, communication—will continue to occupy the energy of many alternatives, the shift toward alternatives in work and production makes it more plausible to think of various alternatives linking together and supporting each other in an "alternative society." If those alternatives are in turn connected with a mass political movement, then they can strengthen the "siege" of capitalist institutions that is necessary in preparation for the radical breaks in capitalist hegemony—which may occur in boom times and not necessarily in economic crises.[29] Some of the alternatives will undoubtedly be copied in distorted form by dominant institutions and they will be stripped of their social vision. Some may be made public projects, thus eroding dependence on private enterprise and strengthening municipalities. So far the alternative institutions have made more of a mark on the imagination of Americans than on their day-to-day existence, but the impulses behind their continued development are too solidly rooted for them to disappear.

Their growth and impact will depend on the development of a mass socialist movement that can implement the models and programs of alternative institutions as part of overall democratic control of investment, redistribution of income, and the democratization of work and all institutional life. That will require a national redirection of government policy and public control of what is now private corporate power. Only at that point will the alternatives disappear. They will be part of mainstream socialist America.

Notes

1. Richard Flacks, "Making History vs. Making Life: Dilemmas of an American Left," *Working Papers for a New Society* 2 (Summer 1974): 56–68.
2. *Vocations for Social Change* has published job listings and articles to help people find work with political significance.
3. Karl Marx, *Documents of the First International 1864–6* (Moscow: Foreign Languages Publishing House, 1964), 1:346–47, cited in Ken Coates, ed., *The New Worker Cooperatives* (London: Spokesman Books, 1976), pp. 20–22.
4. Raymond Williams, "Base and Superstructure in Marxist Cultural Theory," *New Left Review* 82: 11
5. Luther Gerlach, quoted in *Politicks and Other Human Interests,* Jan. 3, 1978, p.7.
6. I will ignore dozens of other alternatives, some of which have succeeded well on a small scale—communication centers, hot lines, youth hangouts, learning and teaching exchanges; various alternative psychotherapies, community clinics, group practices and halfway houses; day-care co-ops; socialist schools and free universities; leftist and counterculture bars, cafés, restaurants, and cultural centers; new religious and spiritual alternatives; leftist, environmental, consumerist, and other progressive research institutes; cooperative housing; film collectives; and many more.
7. Hugh Gardner, "When Utopia Was a Commune," *Chicago Tribune,* Mar. 12, 1978, reprinted from *Human Behavior.*
8. Kat Kinkade, "Please Don't Start a Commune in 1977," *Communities* 25 (Mar.–Apr. 1977): 3.
9. Philip Abrams and Andrew McCulloch, *Communes, Sociology and Society* (Cambridge: Cambridge University Press, 1976), p. 31.
10. Ibid., p. 219.
11. Calvin Trillin, "Alternatives," *The New Yorker,* Apr. 10, 1978, p. 118.
12. Jonathan Kozol, *New Schools Exchange Newsletter* 134 (June 30, 1976): 9.
13. David Ruth, "The New Localism—An Ideology for Our Age?" *Communities* 25 (Mar.–Apr. 1977): 40.
14. David Morris and Karl Hess, *Neighborhood Power* (Boston: Beacon Press, 1975).
15. E. F. Schumacher, *Small Is Beautiful* (New York: Harper and Row, 1975).
16. Tom Bender, "Why Big Business Loves A.T.," *Rain,* Jan. 1978, pp. 4–6.
17. Barry Commoner, *The Poverty of Power* (New York: Bantam Books,

1977); Amory Lovins, *Soft Energy Paths* (Cambridge, Mass.: Ballinger Publishing Company, 1977).

18. Paul Blumberg, *Industrial Democracy* (New York: Schocken Books, 1973).

19. David Moberg, "Workplace Democracy Aboard Ship," *In These Times,* Dec. 21–27, 1977.

20. The United Auto Workers is a partial exception. They support a few experiments in work reorganization, back food co-ops in Detroit, use solar power at the Black Lake educational retreat, and support a community-development corporation in East Los Angeles.

21. *Business Week,* Mar. 28, 1977.

22. John F. C. Harrison, "The Owenite Socialist Movement in Britain and the United States: A Comparative Study," in Herbert Gutman and Gregory S. Kealey, eds., *Many Pasts,* vol.1 (Englewood Cliffs, N.J.: Prentice-Hall, 1973).

23. Kirk Jeffrey, "The Family as Utopian Retreat from the City: The Nineteenth Century Contribution," in Sallie TeSelle, ed., *The Family, Communes and Utopian Societies* (New York: Harper and Row, 1972).

24. Carole Pateman, *Participation and Democratic Theory* (Cambridge: Cambridge University Press, 1970).

25. Martin J. Sklar, "The Socialist Transition to Democracy in America," *Communications,* Transnational Institute, Dec. 1977/Jan. 1978, pp. 17–19.

26. Philip Slater, *The Pursuit of Loneliness* (Boston: Beacon Press, 1970).

27. Tom Wolfe, *Mauve Gloves and Madmen, Clutter and Vine* (New York: Farrar, Straus and Giroux, 1976).

28. Karl Marx, *Grundrisse* (New York: Random House, 1973), pp. 487–88.

29. Paul Sweezy and Harry Magdoff, "Review of the Month," *Monthly Review,* Nov. 1976, pp. 11–12.

Index

About the Contributors

John Case is the managing editor of *Working Papers for a New Society.* He was co-editor (with Gerry Hunnius and David G. Garson) of *Workers' Control: A Reader on Labor and Social Change.*

Rosemary C. R. Taylor is an assistant professor of sociology and director of the Community Health Program at Tufts University. She is also a research associate of the Center for European Studies at Harvard University. Her fields of interest include formal organizations and social change, political sociology, and medical sociology. She is an editor of *Socialist Review.*

Allen Graubard is a writer and teacher now living in Berkeley. He has participated in alternative education activities over the past decade and is the author of *Free the Children: Radical Reform and the Free School Movement.* He is a senior editor of *Working Papers for a New Society* and is currently working on a study of the idea and actuality of competition, to be published by New Republic Books.

Larry Hirschhorn teaches social policy planning in the Department of City and Regional Planning, University of Pennsylvania. He is also a research analyst with the Management and Behavioral Science Center at the university. He is particularly interested in the problems social agencies face today in satisfying both their clients and their employees.

Rosabeth Moss Kanter is a professor of sociology at Yale University. She is the author of *Men and Women of the Corporation, Work and Family in the United States,* and *Commitment and Community,* as well as editor of *Life in Organizations, Another Voice,* and *Communes: Creating and Managing the Collective Life.* She has also taught at Brandeis University and

Harvard University and has been a fellow in law and sociology and visiting scholar at Harvard Law School. She is a distinguished fellow of the Public Agenda Foundation, as well as a consultant in organizational planning and change and the quality of work life for major corporations and government agencies in America.

Andrew Kopkind is a journalist who writes about political and cultural affairs. He has been a staff member of the *Real Paper,* the *Phoenix*, and WBCN radio in Boston. He is currently a senior editor of *Working Papers for a New Society*.

Jane J. Mansbridge is an assistant professor of political science at the University of Chicago and the University of California at Santa Barbara. The essay in this volume is adapted from a section of her forthcoming book, *Radical Democracy*.

David Moberg is an anthropologist, journalist, and political activist. A staff writer for *In These Times*, a national news weekly, he has contributed to many alternative publications and is a contributing editor of Chicago's *Reader*. He is completing a book on blue-collar workers based on his dissertation study of the strike by auto workers at Lordstown, Ohio, in 1972.

Joyce Rothschild-Whitt is a senior research associate with the New Systems of Work and Participation Program, New York State School of Industrial and Labor Relations, Cornell University. Through this research program she is investigating cooperatively owned workplaces in the production sector of the economy. She has recently completed a dissertation study of democratically managed alternative organizations in the social service sector, on which the essay was based in this volume. She is currently engaged in a study of the structural barriers to worker ownership in the United States.

Anthony P. Sager is an assistant attorney general in the Civil Rights Division of the Massachusetts attorney general's office. He was a member of the original Cambridge law commune from 1971 to 1976.

Paul Starr, an assistant professor of sociology at Harvard University, is a contributing editor of *Working Papers for a New Society* and a frequent contributor to the *New York Times Book Review* and the *New Republic*. He is the author of *The Discarded Army: Veterans After Vietnam*, co-author of *Up Against the Ivy Wall*, and co-editor (with Immanuel Wallerstein) of *The University Crisis Reader*. His most recent work is a study of the social and economic history of American medicine.

Daniel Zwerdling, a Washington-based free-lance writer, writes frequently on the food industry and on workplace democracy for a variety of publications.

INVENTORY 1983

Co-ops, Communes
& Collectives

Co-ops, Communes & Collectives

Experiments in
Social Change
in the
1960s and 1970s

Edited by
John Case and Rosemary C. R. Taylor

Pantheon Books
New York

Copyright © 1979 by John Case and Rosemary C. R. Taylor

Library of Congress Cataloging in Publication Data

Co-ops, Communes & Collectives.

  Includes index.
  1. United States—Social conditions—1960–
2. Social change—Case studies.   3. Collective settlements—United States—Case studies.   I. Case, John,
1944–   II. Taylor, Rosemary C.R., 1946–
HN65.C627   301.24   78–51798
ISBN 0–394–42007–1
ISBN 0–394–73621–4 pbk.

Grateful acknowledgment is made to the following for permission to reprint previously published material:

An earlier version of "Communes in Cities" by Rosabeth Moss Kanter appeared in *Working Papers for a New Society* 2 (Summer 1974). Copyright © 1974 by Center for the Study of Public Policy. Reprinted by permission. Additional material previously appeared in Max Rosenbaum and Alvin Snadowsky, *The Intensive Group Experience* (New York: The Free Press, 1976).

An earlier version of "Hip Deep in Capitalism" by Andrew Kopkind appeared in *Working Papers for a New Society* 2 (Spring 1974). Copyright © 1974 by Center for the Study of Public Policy. Reprinted by permission.

"Free Medicine" by Rosemary C. R. Taylor reprinted by permission from *Working Papers for a New Society* 2 (Fall 1976). Copyright © 1976 by Center for the Study of Public Policy.

Certain sentences in "The Agony of Inequality" by Jane J. Mansbridge also appeared in her article "Acceptable Inequalities," *British Journal of Political Science* 7 (1977).

An earlier version of "Conditions for Democracy" by Joyce Rothschild-Whitt, entitled "Conditions Facilitating Participatory Democratic Organizations," appeared in *Sociological Inquiry* 46 (Spring 1976).

Manufactured in the United States of America

    ʾdition